# TAKING THE STRUGGLE OUT OF MINISTRY

Understanding The Dynamics And Covenant Keys To Effective, Sustainable, Ever-Growing And Ever-Producing Ministry

**MICHAEL HUTTON-WOOD**

**HWP**

Unless otherwise indicated, all scriptural references are taken from the King James Version of the Bible.

**TAKING THE STRUGGLE OUT OF MINISTRY**

ISBN 978-0-9562541-2-2

Copyright © JUNE 2011 by Michael Hutton-Wood
Hutton-Wood publications

In the UK write to:
Michael Hutton-Wood Ministries
P. O. Box 1226
Croydon.
CR9 6DG.

Or in the UK
Call: Tel. 020 8689 6010; 07956 815 714
Outside the UK call: +44 20 8689 6010; +44 7956 815 714

Or contact:
WEBSITE: www.houseofjudah.org.uk
Email: michaelhutton-wood@fsmail.net
houseofjudah@ymail.com
leadersfactoryinternational@yahoo.com

Published & distributed by: Michael Hutton-Wood Ministries (Incorporating Hutton-Wood World Outreach Ministries)

All rights reserved under international copyright law. Written permission must be secured from the publisher to use or reproduce any part of this book.

Printed in the United Kingdom

# THE MANDATE:

'...SET IN ORDER THE THINGS THAT ARE OUT OF ORDER AND RAISE AND APPOINT LEADERS IN EVERY CITY.' - Titus 1:5

**MICHAEL HUTTON-WOOD MINISTRIES**
RELEASING POTENTIAL
- MAXIMIZING DESTINY

**HOUSE OF JUDAH (PRAISE) MINISTRIES**
&
**LEADERS FACTORY INTERNATIONAL**
RAISING GENERATIONAL LEADERS
- IMPACTING NATIONS

## SIMPA:
**SCEPTRE INTERNATIONAL MINISTERS & PASTORS ASSOCIATION**
EQUIPPING, EMPOWERING, COACHING, MENTORING AND PROVIDING COVERING FOR PASTORS, MINISTERS AND LEADERS ACROSS THE NATIONS!

# CONTENTS

DEDICATION 6

INTRODUCTION 8

1. SETTLE THIS BEFORE YOU STEP OUT! 13

2. DEVELOPING INTIMACY WITH GOD 19
   The four levels of intimacy with God

3. UNDERSTANDING MINISTRY 49

4. MINISTRY ORACLES FOR DISCERNING YOUR SEASON 107
   AND STAYING IN THE MOVE

5. 5 WAYS OF SECURING BLESSINGS ON YOUR MINISTRY 119

6. 21 MAJOR DETERMINANTS OF LASTING SUCCESS AND 127
   LONGEVITY IN MINISTRY

7. 17 FUNDAMENTAL LAWS FOR FULFILLING YOUR 167
   MINISTRY, *Including Financing the Ministry without sweating*

8. HOW TO BE PRESERVED FOR YOUR ASSIGNMENT 239

9. RIDING ON THE WINGS OF SPIRITUAL FATHERS AND 253
   MENTORS TO TERMINATE ALL STRUGGLES IN MINISTRY
   - *The Crucial Role of MENTORS and SPIRITUAL FATHERS*
   - *Our Responsibilities To Our Spiritual Fathers and Mentors*
   - *The Law of Mentorship*

10. THE MINISTER AND HIS FAMILY 321

11. KNOWING & ENGAGING YOUR MINISTRY COVENANTS 325
    *[General, Personal, Specific and Ministry Covenants]*

# DEDICATION

I give thanks to God, for the teachers and mentors in my life and for this book, the third in the series of books on Ministry and out of a grateful heart, I wholeheartedly dedicate this book to my father in the Lord: Bishop David Oyedepo whose fatherhood, mentorship, covering and teachings which I have been eating and practising have literally taken the struggle out of ministry for me and many others.

TRULY: "The lines are fallen unto me in pleasant places; yea, I have a goodly heritage." - Psalm 16:6

WHERE THE ELEPHANT EATS IS WHERE IT GENERATES ITS STRENGTH!

ELEPHANTS DON'T NEED ADVERTISEMENT: THEIR VERY NAME CONNOTES SIZE!

AND SOURCE DETERMINES SIZE! OUR 'GIANCY' IS EMERGING FROM YOU A GIANT AND GENERAL WHO HAS BEEN DRAWING FROM GIANTS!

NO ONE CAN BECOME A GIANT BY WALKING AMONG DWARFS!

IT TAKES FATHERS TO FATHER YOU TO GROW

FEATHERS TO FLY AND GO FURTHER THAN THEY HAVE GONE!

Your teachings which I eat daily has transformed my life, my family and the ministry am privileged to lead. My life and ministry has never recovered positively from your scriptural, emulative, exemplary influence through your teachings since I met you merely five years ago.

I heard you say once at a ministers' conference: 'NO ONE HAS NONSENSE TIME TO SIT WITH YOU FOR HOURS ON END TEACHING YOU – GET THEIR RESOURCE MATERIALS MADE AVAILABLE AND EAT THEM, USE THEM, LIVE THEM, BECOME THEM AND FULFIL YOUR COLORFUL MINSTRY.'

That's what I have been doing ever since. This book is a product of what I have learnt from your teachings and your sons directly and indirectly. All I want to say is 'Thank God for your life and your selfless love and devotion to God and service to the kingdom.' Thank you for not holding back and God bless you with your minimum 120. I love you, Sir!

# INTRODUCTION

EMBARKING ON ANY CHURCH OR MINISTRY-RELATED ENTERPRISE WITHOUT UNDERSTANDING ITS DYNAMICS, REQUIREMENTS AND WHAT MAKES THINGS HAPPEN WITHOUT TOILING, SWEATING NEEDLESSLY OR STRUGGLE IS EQUIVALENT TO MADNESS.

IN ALL YOUR GETTING, GET UNDERSTANDING: WHY?

**At The root of everything outstanding is understanding! IF YOU WANT TO BECOME OUTSTANDING IN MINISTRY OR IN YOUR FIELD OF CALLING THEN FIRST GO FOR UNDERSTANDING.**

UNDERSTANDING, KNOWLEDGE, REVELATION AND WISDOM TAKES EVERY TOIL AND STRUGGLE OUT OF LIFE AND MINISTRY AND MAKES YOU STAND OUT.

Ministry is not a relegation to a life of struggles and suffering but a fulfilled life. (John 10:10) So, get your instructions from Source before stepping out. Ministry is not a business or industry, but about people's destinies so do not treat it like one. Ministry is not a journey of trial and error. It's not guess work. Ministry begins with a definite calling because ministry requires a definite and particular call. With this definite call comes grace, abilities, provision, endowments, confidence, boldness, manpower, resources, accuracy and precision in activating spiritual gifts, guidance, protection, financial provision, God's presence, weight, power and authority backing the words you speak and utter, confirmed with signs and wonders, angelic ministry, effectiveness, success and undeniable results/proofs.

All you need to do is learn of Him (Joshua 1:8) and from the fathers and credible mentors who have obtained what you desire to obtain. IT TAKES FATHERS TO FATHER YOU TO GROW FEATHERS TO FLY AND GO FURTHER BOTH IN LIFE AND MINISTRY THAN THEY HAVE GONE!

APPLYING AND LIVING THE CONTENTS OF THIS BOOK WILL TAKE THE SWEAT, TOILING AND STRUGGLE OUT OF YOUR MINISTRY PERMANENTLY!

WELCOME TO YOUR SEASON AND YEARS OF SWEATLESS, RESULT-ORIENTED AND RESULT-PRODUCING MINISTRY.

**MINISTRY IS NOT A VOCATION, A CAREER, A HOBBY OR A 9-5 JOB - IT IS A LIFELONG SCHOOL AND A MISSION FOR LIFE!**

# TRUTHS YOU MUST KNOW:

1. Ministry begins with discovering your Source and is sustained by continuous communication with your Source - God. - Jeremiah 1; 29:11

2. Ministry begins with self-discovery - a discovery of your self - who and what you really are and adequate and relevant preparation. - Jeremiah 1

3. Ministry begins with a purposeful discovery of your purpose in life – why you are here and what you are called to do. Since you are not called to do everything and into every ministry (the 5-fold ministry) it must begin with a knowing, an assurance and a full persuasion of your definite calling - Ephesians 4:11, 'And he gave some, apostles; and some, prophets; and some, evangelists; and some, pastors and teachers;'

Are you called to be an apostle, a prophet, an evangelist, a pastor or a teacher? You must know this.

4. Ministry begins with a discovery, clear understanding and appreciation of your passion, gifts and talents - knowing what you are passionate about and your wiring i.e. why you're wired the way you are – potential.

5. Ministry begins with a discovery, recognition and clear understanding of your strengths, weaknesses and operating

the law of compensation.

6. Ministry begins with a CERTIFIED / DEFINITE SENDING. (Eph. 4:11) Every time a sent man speaks, THE SENDER [the one who sent him] SHOWS UP.

7. **So,** ministry must first of all begin with a certified sending and with that sending comes definite heavenly backing. Are you called to be a Pastor, Teacher, Prophet, Evangelist or Apostle? Paul said he was not disobedient to the heavenly vision. Acts 26:19, 'Whereupon, O king Agrippa, I was not disobedient unto the heavenly vision:'

# WHY YOU MUST KNOW THIS:

A need is not equal to a calling on your life. That there is a need is not equal to a calling on your life. There are needs every day. An open door is not equal to an open vision.

CHAPTER ONE

# SETTLE THIS BEFORE YOU STEP OUT!

WHAT ARE YOU CALLED TO DO SPECIFICALLY – WHAT MINISTRY?

ONE OF THE MAJOR WAYS YOU TAKE THE STRUGGLE OUT OF MINISTRY IS WHEN YOU KNOW, UNDERSTAND AND SETTLE IN YOUR MIND AND SPIRIT FROM THE ONSET THE DIFFERENCE BETWEEN:

1. THE 5-FOLD MINISTRY
2. THE MINISTRY OF HELPS AND
3. THE MARKETPLACE MINISTRY

Which One are you called into? Finding out and staying there faithfully will take the struggle out of ministry. Some are called into the five-fold ministry [Full time or Part Time] either as Pastors, Evangelists, Apostles, Prophets or Teachers and others are called into the Ministry of Helps, [assisting the fivefold ministry] or Marketplace Ministry, like Leisure, Administration, Secretarial, IT, Health, Politics, Industry, Business, Social, Education, Entertainment, Economic,

Technology, Sports, Recreational, etc.

## MINISTRY OF HELPS:
Romans 12:3-8, " For I say, through the grace given unto me, to every man that is among you, not to think of himself more highly than he ought to think; but to think soberly, according as God hath dealt to every man the measure of faith. For as we have many members in one body, and all members have not the same office: So we, being many, are one body in Christ, and every one members one of another. **Having then gifts differing according to the grace that is given to us**, whether **prophecy**, let us prophesy according to the proportion of faith; Or **ministry**, let us wait on our ministering: or he that **teacheth**, on teaching; Or he that **exhorteth**, on exhortation: he that **giveth**, let him do it with simplicity; he that **ruleth**, with diligence; he that **showeth mercy**, with cheerfulness."

## MARKETPLACE MINISTRY:
The emboldened words are all various ministries. Daniel and the three Hebrew boys, Abraham, Isaac, Jacob, Joseph, Dr. Luke, King David, Joseph of Arimathaea, Nehemiah, Gideon, Joshua, Cornelius, Mary Magdalene, were not preachers but they all fulfilled their ministry just like the apostles who were called into full time ministry did.

## GRACE FOR GIVING OR MINISTRY OF GENEROSITY TO PARTNER WITH MINISTRIES/MINISTERS:

The ministry or grace of generosity or giving is revealed in 2 Corinthians 8:1-7, "Moreover, brethren, we do you to wit of the grace of God bestowed on the churches of Macedonia; How that in a great trial of affliction the abundance of their joy and their deep poverty abounded unto the riches of their liberality. For to their power, I bear record, yea, and beyond their power they were willing of themselves; Praying us with much entreaty that we would receive the gift, and take upon us the fellowship of the ministering to the saints. And this they did, not as we hoped, but first gave their own selves to the Lord, and unto us by the will of God. Insomuch that we desired Titus, that as he had begun, so he would also finish in you the same grace also. Therefore, as ye abound in every thing, in faith, and utterance, and knowledge, and in all diligence, and in your love to us, see that ye abound in this grace also."

Luke 8:1-3, 'And it came to pass afterward, that he went throughout every city and village, preaching and showing the glad tidings of the kingdom of God: and the twelve were with him, And certain women, which had been healed of evil spirits and infirmities, Mary called Magdalene, out of whom went seven devils, And Joanna the wife of Chuza Herod's steward, and Susanna, and many others, which ministered unto him of their substance.'

Philippians 4:15-19, 'Now ye Philippians know also, that in the beginning of the gospel, when I departed from Macedonia, no church communicated with me as concerning giving and receiving, but ye only. For even in Thessalonica ye sent once and again unto my necessity. Not because I desire a gift: but I desire fruit that may abound to your account. But I have all, and abound: I am full, having received of Epaphroditus the things which were sent from you, an odour of a sweet smell, a sacrifice acceptable, wellpleasing to God. But my God shall supply all your need according to his riches in glory by Christ Jesus.'

EVERYONE IS GIVEN GRACE TO FUNCTION WHERE THEY HAVE BEEN CALLED AND PLACED AND AS EVERYONE STAYS IN THEIR ASSIGNMENT AND PLACE, IT CAUSES INCREASE TO COME TO THE ENTIRE BODY: Ephesians 4:7-16, 'But unto every one of us is given grace according to the measure of the gift of Christ. Wherefore he saith, When he ascended up on high, he led captivity captive, and gave gifts unto men. (Now that he ascended, what is it but that he also descended first into the lower parts of the earth? He that descended is the same also that ascended up far above all heavens, that he might fill all things.)'

**THE PRIESTHOOD [FIVEFOLD] MINISTRY:**
'And he gave some, apostles; and some, prophets; and some, evangelists; and some, pastors and teachers; For the perfecting of the saints, for the work of the ministry, for the edifying of the body of Christ Till we all come in the unity of the faith, and of the knowledge of the Son of God, unto a perfect man, unto the measure of the stature of the fulness of Christ: That we henceforth be no more children, tossed to and fro, and carried about with every wind of doctrine, by the sleight of men, and cunning craftiness, whereby they lie in wait to deceive; But

speaking the truth in love, may grow up into him in all things, which is the head, even Christ: From whom the whole body fitly joined together and compacted by that which every joint supplieth, according to the effectual working in the measure of every part, maketh increase of the body unto the edifying of itself in love.'

SO: HOW DO WE KNOW WHICH SPECIFIC MINISTRY, VOCATION, CAREER OR PROFESSION WE ARE CALLED INTO SO WE DON'T MAKE A SHIPWRECK OF OUR FAITH IN THE PURSUIT OF DESTINY?

It comes through developing intimacy with the One who made you and put you here. The purpose of every product is found in the mind of the maker or manufacturer. So in the next chapter, we will introduce you to your Source so you can be well-placed to receive instructions to fulfil your ministry as instructed by Paul in Colossians 4:17, 'And say to Archippus, Take heed to the ministry which thou hast received in the Lord, that thou fulfil it.'

Hebrews 10:7, 'Then said I, Lo, I come (in the volume of the book it is written of me,) to do thy will, O God.'

Jeremiah 1:5, 'Before I formed thee in the belly I knew thee; and before thou camest forth out of the womb I sanctified thee, and I ordained thee a prophet unto the nations.'

# CHAPTER TWO

# DEVELOPING INTIMACY WITH GOD

Job 22:21, 'Acquaint now thyself with him, and be at peace: thereby good shall come unto thee.'

The amplified version reads, "Acquaint now yourself with him, [agree with God and show yourself to be conformed to his will - where you and his will are one and the same] and be at peace: by that you shall prosper and great good shall come to you."

Joshua 1:8, 'This book of the law shall not depart out of thy mouth; but thou shalt meditate therein day and night, that thou mayest observe to do according to all that is written therein: for then thou shalt make thy way prosperous, and then thou shalt have good success.'

When Solomon was about to take on the kingship, he was admonished in 1 Chronicles 28:9-10, 'And thou, Solomon my son, know thou the God of thy father, and serve him with a perfect heart and with a willing mind: for the LORD searcheth all hearts, and understandeth all the imaginations of the thoughts: if thou seek him, he will be found of thee; but if thou forsake him, he will cast thee off for ever. Take heed now; for the LORD hath chosen thee to build an house for the sanctuary: be strong, and do it.'

You can't know Him without seeking Him. I spend more time with God through the Word, praise, worship, prayer, fellowship, fasting, tapes, books, DVDs, CDs, materials, resources, and in order to know all or most of the rich secrets of my spiritual father, I seek what he knows through his resources, eat them and do them and sow into his life and ministry and that of my mentors. To know God you must seek after Him. The psalmist said, 'As the deer panteth for the waters so my soul (my heart) longeth after thee, you alone art my heart's desire and I long to worship you; you alone art my strength my shield, to you alone may my spirit yield, you alone art my heart's desire and I long to worship you.'

Seek God with all your heart, not just your mind; all your heart.

Because God searches the hearts of men and knows the imaginations that people think toward us good or bad, it is imperative that we don't walk through life blind with our eyes closed. We must know people for who they really are, not what they are portraying outside; dig into the spirit, weigh them in the spirit so they don't end up breaking our hearts or hurting us over and over again when we know for sure they have the tendency to do so. **JUST AS, NOT EVERYONE AT THE**

## AIRPORT IS TRAVELLING, IN THE SAME WAY NOT EVERYONE IN MINISTRY IS GOING SOMEWHERE!

My spiritual father made this statement: "THE HEARTS OF MEN ARE TOO DEEP TO UNCOVER, THE MINDS OF MEN ARE TOO UNSTABLE TO DEPEND ON AND THE WORDS OF MEN ARE TOO SWEET TO DOUBT."

Life is too short for us to play games with our destiny by entrusting our hearts to people who will break it or invest in projects that are not within our assignment. That is why we must become intimate with God who searches people's hearts and knows us through and through and stay in the Word because as Hebrews 4:12 says, '.......it is a discerner of the thoughts and intentions of the heart.' You can't afford the luxury of sailing through life deaf, dumb and blind. That is a risky way of living.

2 Corinthians 5:16 says, 'Wherefore henceforth know we no man after the flesh: yea, though we have known Christ after the flesh, yet now henceforth know we him no more.'

You must love everyone, win souls, disciple them and everything but not everyone can be your friend. Don't walk through life blind and don't just give anyone at all access to your inner circle - that is where your heart is and you have only one heart. You can't go to any shop and buy a new heart; so guard your heart with all diligence. Know people after the spirit not after the flesh. Walk in the spirit. Know God for

yourself, spend time in the Word and get to know Him so you stop doubting Him.
- Anyone who doubts God doesn't know God.
- Anyone who doubts this God doesn't know this God.
- It is impossible to know Him really and doubt him.

Daniel 11:32, '......... but the people that do know their God shall be strong, and do exploits.'

It is impossible. Study, find out what God has done in the past, let it get into your heart, be fully persuaded and see if you can doubt Him - that is where you and I must get to. Has He said it and will He not do it. He is not a man that He should lie. You may doubt in your mind if it will happen or not but if you trust Him with your heart (there is a difference) - trust Him with your heart not just your mind - start from the heart and it will influence and convince your mind so you don't doubt Him - you can't believe Him and doubt HIM at the same time. Paul so believed and trusted in God that he said in Romans 8:38-39, 'For I am persuaded, that neither death, nor life, nor angels, nor principalities, nor powers, nor things present, nor things to come, Nor height, nor depth, nor any other creature, shall be able to separate us from the love of God, which is in Christ Jesus our Lord.'

Put your trust in Him - not stuff - in Him - trust in the Lord.

Proverbs 3:5-8, 'Trust in the LORD with all thine heart; and lean not unto thine own understanding. [mind alone] In all thy ways acknowledge him, and he shall direct thy paths. Be not wise in thine own eyes: fear the LORD, and depart from evil. It shall be health to thy navel, and marrow to thy bones.'

Many people don't have a healthy heart because they doubt God.

Mark 11:23-24, 'For verily I say unto you, That whosoever shall say unto this mountain, Be thou removed, and be thou cast into the sea; and shall not doubt in his heart, but shall believe that those things which he saith shall come to pass; he shall have whatsoever he saith. Therefore I say unto you, What things soever ye desire, when ye pray, believe (in your heart, not your mind) that ye receive them, and ye shall have them.'

Being convinced and fully persuaded about what God has said He will do begins from the heart. That is why you must get the word in your heart first hence what Paul said in Romans 12:2, 'And be not conformed to this world: but be ye transformed by the renewing of your mind, that ye may prove what is that good, and acceptable, and perfect, will of God.'

YOU CAN'T BE TRANSFORMED WITHOUT RENEWING YOUR MIND - THE WAY YOU THINK. YOU ARE ONLY TRANSFORMED, METAMORPHOSIZED - CHANGED IN THE WAY YOU THINK BY RENEWING YOUR MIND WITH HIS WORD WHICH YOU HAVE FIRST OF ALL DEPOSITED IN YOUR HEART - YOUR HEART - YOUR HEART!

That is why I said you can't believe and doubt at the same time. Proverbs 1:7, 'The fear of the LORD is the beginning of knowledge: but fools despise wisdom and instruction.'

Knowing God intimately only begins with fear/reverence, deep respect for God. If you don't fear or reverence God, you can never know Him intimately. There are some things that you must be afraid to do - such us eating or spending your tithe or touching what belongs to God or someone else or lying to God or your Pastor like Gehazi did or despising spiritual authority or parental authority or delegated authority or trying to correct a man of God or your senior pastor or gossip or invent lies about him or saying God said something he did not say which is just something you want to say; or plotting to dethrone, overthrow or planning with others to destroy or kill a man of God or troubling God's house. There are just some things that I am afraid to do. Scripture says fools despise wisdom and instruction so if God knows when He advises you or gives you access you will continually abuse it, you won't be given that access often or even again. When David's wife, Michal despised David for praising God in a dance, God closed her womb permanently. How many people's dreams in their wombs have been shattered and wombs closed permanently for despising wisdom and instruction both from God, spiritual authority and parental authority?

Proverbs 9:10, 'The fear of the LORD is the beginning of wisdom: and the knowledge of the holy one is understanding.'

So: Knowing Him brings understanding and as you are aware, everything outstanding in life is rooted in understanding - so know Him first. That's why the apostle Paul after many years of knowing and walking with God still prayed and desired in Philippians 3:10, 'That I may know him, and the power of his resurrection, and the fellowship of his sufferings, being made conformable unto his death;'

The highest and most meaningful form of intimacy you can ever have both on earth and in eternity is with God. He knows both your present and future and so don't just get to know about Him - know Him intimately - that is where no matter what happens in your life you say with the three Hebrew boys, 'Even if he does not deliver us we will still not bow down and serve your idol'; and with Esther, 'if I perish, I perish' and with Paul 'I am not ashamed of the gospel of Christ for it is the power of God unto salvation; am fully persuaded that, what He has promised, He is able also to perform.'

When you become intimate with God, He can interrupt your plans at anytime knowing that you will abandon your plans and submit to His like Abraham did with his son Isaac.

If God cannot interrupt your already made plans without your throwing a temper tantrum you are not intimate with Him yet. You must be ready to subject YOUR CREATIVITY TO DIVINITY FOR CORRECTION, ADJUSTMENT, CHANGES, APPROVAL AND EMPOWERMENT. In this chapter you will discover the four levels of intimacy with God.

We must all aim at and work at coming to a place where when we speak, it is as if God is speaking; we must look like, sound like and behave like people who slept in and woke up from the same bed with Him. That is intimacy - and it is possible as we will soon discover from the book of Job.

The word intimacy is defined as:
1. close relationship: a close personal relationship
2. quiet atmosphere: a quiet and private atmosphere
3. detailed knowledge: a detailed knowledge resulting from a close or long association or study
4. private utterance or action: a private and personal utterance or action

The greatest honour that can be accorded any person on this earth is to be called a friend of God. What greater honour could be given any man than that of the Almighty calling him His friend? In the scriptures only a few people had the privilege of being accorded that honour and title if I can call it that as listed in the following passages of scripture:

Exodus 33:11, 'And the LORD spake unto Moses face to face, as a man speaketh unto his friend. And he turned again into the camp: but his servant Joshua, the son of Nun, a young man, departed not out of the tabernacle.'

James 2:23, 'And the scripture was fulfilled which saith, Abraham believed God, and it was imputed unto him for righteousness: and he was called the Friend of God.'

2 Chronicles 20:7, 'Art not thou our God, who didst drive out the inhabitants of this land before thy people Israel, and gavest it to the seed of Abraham thy friend for ever?'

Isaiah 41:8-9, 'But thou, Israel, art my servant, Jacob whom I have chosen, the seed of Abraham my friend. Thou whom I have taken from the ends of the earth, and called thee from the chief men thereof, and said unto thee, Thou art my servant; I have chosen thee, and not cast thee away.'

James 2:23, 'And the scripture was fulfilled which saith, Abraham believed God, and it was imputed unto him for righteousness: and he was called the Friend of God.'

Genesis 18:17-19, 'And the LORD said, Shall I hide from Abraham that thing which I do; Seeing that Abraham shall surely become a great and mighty nation, and all the nations of the earth shall be blessed in him? For I know him, that he will command his children and his household after him, and they shall keep the way of the LORD, to do justice and judgment; that the LORD may bring upon Abraham that which he hath spoken of him.'

Of DAVID: Scripture says in 1 Samuel 13:14, 'But now thy kingdom shall not continue: the LORD hath sought him a man after his own heart, and the LORD hath commanded him to be captain over his people, because thou hast not kept that which the LORD commanded thee.'

Acts 13:22, 'And when he had removed him, he raised up unto them David to be their king; to whom also he gave testimony, and said, I have found David the son of Jesse, a man after mine own heart, which shall fulfil all my will.'

We must all aim at being called the friend of God. Someone may ask is that possible? Well let's hear what Job the most upright man in his day and Jesus our Saviour had to say about this.

Job said in Job 19:25, 'For I know [not I think] I know that my redeemer liveth, and that he shall stand at the latter day upon the earth:'

The word know has been so often used, it has lost its real meaning so when you say I know someone or know God, many don't actually fathom what they are saying. The word 'know' is defined as:

1. hold information in the mind: to have information firmly in the mind or committed to memory

2. be certain about something: to believe firmly in the truth or certainty of something

3. realize something: to be or become aware of something

4. comprehend something: to have a thorough understanding of something through experience or study

5. recognize differences: to be able to perceive the differences or distinctions between things or people; old enough to know right from wrong

6. Identify somebody or something by a characteristic: to recognize somebody or something by a distinguishing characteristic or attribute (I'd know him anywhere by his peculiar laugh.)

7. have sex with somebody: to engage in sexual intercourse with somebody (archaic)

8. - in the know - possessing information that is secret or known only to a small group of people

9. - know something back to front - to be completely familiar with all the details of or facts about something

10. - know something backwards - to be completely familiar with all the details of or facts about something

- All this was what Job meant when he said, 'I know my redeemer liveth' i.e. - I am fully convinced. NOTE: Knowing someone and saying with confidence what Job said about God only comes from spending quality time with them. Job's relationship with God begun with acquaintance and progressed into intimate knowledge. Because acquaint means slight knowledge. The more time you spend with someone the better you get to know them and draw your own conclusions despite what others may say about them - it's the same with God. There is nothing you can offer me that will make me give up on my God - nothing - I am addicted to God. I would rather miss or lose any man's friendship than miss God. My spiritual father said you can buy and read all my books and listen to all my tapes and CD's or watch all my videos and DVDs but until you catch my secret, none of the materials will benefit you - my secret he said is 'I love God with all my heart.'

You see, many people don't love God - they love what He has to offer. Many people don't come to churches because they love God, no, they come to church because of what they can get from God, the Pastor or the church. That is risky. Why else will you give up on church because your answer did not come within the time frame you expected or it came one minute after ten instead of ten sharp? You can't tell me you love God - you don't love God. Because if you truly love God whether you get the stuff or not you still stay hooked. If you really love someone whether they have or give you what you want or not, you still love them. There are a few things my family and I have been expecting for years that has not materialized yet; but I am more dedicated with my assignment of preaching, teaching, training, research and serving the people I am called to serve now more than ever. I am more passionate about God, my assignment than I have ever been throughout my entire life, investing more in people and it is going to get more passionate and fiery. **So stop serving God on contract and start loving Him all over again.** Return to your first love; acquaint now thyself with Him that great good will come unto you.

**Always REMEMBER THE FOLLOWING: INTIMATE PEOPLE KNOW GOD'S WAYS! NON-INTIMATE PEOPLE JUST KNOW GOD'S HANDS - what He provides - what He does - His acts - His deeds - there is a vast difference.**

Psalm 103:7, 'He made known his ways unto Moses, his acts [or deeds] unto the children of Israel.'

I repeat: INTIMATE PEOPLE KNOW GOD'S WAYS! NON-INTIMATE PEOPLE JUST KNOW GOD'S HANDS - what he provides - what he does - his acts - his deeds - there is a vast difference. Intimate people say with Job in Job 13:15, 'Though he slay me, yet will I trust in him: but I will maintain mine own ways before him.'

……..whether he blesses me or not, I will still serve him. God said, '……… shall I hide from Abraham my intentions concerning Sodom and Gomorrah.' In other words I can't do anything in this city - Sodom and Gomorrah without consulting Abraham my friend - that shall be your story. He makes known or reveals his ways - secrets to those who know him but his doings - acts to those who just want the crumbs. (Deuteronomy 29:29; Daniel 11:32)

Same with people - when you walk with me intensely you will not only know what I can provide but my ways too, mannerisms, behaviour, my intentions, my heart, my passion, you can tell by one look what I am saying or the shaking of my leg if I am in thought or not and when I go silent what I mean, etc. You only know the genuine secrets of people you are intimate with - I am not talking about KGB, MOSSAD, FBI, CIA OR British intelligence spy stuff. People whom you genuinely love and are intimate with open up their heart and share their heart, their innermost thoughts and feelings with you. They are willing to be unashamedly vulnerable with you without fear of you judging them - they feel comfortable in your presence to share intimate things with you - it's the same with God - you can't fake it in his presence.

Paul said in 2 Timothy 2:19 'Nevertheless the foundation of God standeth sure, having this seal, The Lord knoweth them that are his. And, Let everyone that nameth the name of Christ depart from iniquity.'

When I go before God, I am naked. I don't hide anything. I am a real genuine article. Why? He knows everything anyway, how I feel and all that.

The secret behind Job's confidence in saying he knows God is revealed in Job 22:21-30, 'Acquaint now thyself with him, and be at peace: thereby good shall come unto thee. Receive, I pray thee, the law from his mouth, and lay up his words in thine heart. If thou return to the Almighty, thou shalt be built up, thou shalt put away iniquity far from thy tabernacles. Then shalt thou lay up gold as dust, and the gold of Ophir as the stones of the brooks. Yea, the Almighty shall be thy defence, and thou shalt have plenty of silver. For then shalt thou have thy delight in the Almighty, and shalt lift up thy face unto God. Thou shalt make thy prayer unto him, and he shall hear thee, and [WHEN] thou shalt pay thy vows. Thou shalt also decree a thing, and it shall be established unto thee: and the light shall shine upon thy ways. When men are cast down, then thou shalt say, There is lifting up; and he shall save the humble person. He shall deliver the island of the innocent: and it is delivered by the pureness of thine hands.'

**Jesus also said in John 15:12-17,**
'This is my commandment, That ye love one another, as I have loved you. Greater love hath no man than this, that a man lay down his life for his friends. Ye are my friends, if ye do whatsoever I command you. Henceforth I call you not servants; for the servant knoweth not what his lord doeth: but I have called you friends; for all things that I have heard of my Father I have made known unto you. Ye have not chosen me, but I have chosen you, and ordained you, that ye should go and bring forth fruit, and that your fruit should remain: that whatsoever ye shall ask of the Father in my name, he may give it you. These things I command you, that ye love one another.'
A friend is someone you:
- have affection for
- A lover - someone you love dearly
- One you lay your life down for
- A true friend is there for you both in hard times and good times;
- It's only friends who know where their real friends are, what they are doing or do, where they are going, can tell just by one

look if they are alright or not; and what they mean by the looks they give; it's only close friends who exchange their personal unlisted phone numbers - why? They have access - the kind of access that others don't have. Close covenant friends more often than not speak to each other each day or in any two given days. They can't stand one day without speaking or communicating to each other. That is what God wants for us all. God desires to have friends not neighbours. God desires true friendship not just neighbourliness. How can you say you know God and not speak to him for a day or a week? How can you schedule time to eat when you have not scheduled time to pray?

Throughout Christendom today, many Christians are neighbours of God and not friends - they don't know who He is, where He is, what He is doing, what He is saying now, what He is capable of doing, what He has done before, what He is going to do next, whether He is reliable or not, they call Him a friend but they don't know which flight He is boarded or what frequency He is on now because they don't spend time with Him but I prophesy that through the instructions in this book, we shall all be known as the friends of God. You will never get to know someone very well if you don't spend time, quality time with them. Making a conscious decision to invest quality time in them and quality involves sacrifices. We can't develop quality relationships in our churches or out there without some sacrifices which is defined as: **Giving up something of immense value to us for the express benefit of others**. Our huge vision cannot be realized without a whole lot of sacrifices on our part. You only know the secrets of your friends by intentionally working at that friendship. It is the same with God and even more. You can only hear God's heartbeat if you spend time with Him.

Deuteronomy 29:29, 'The secret things belong unto the LORD our God: but those things which are revealed belong unto us and to our children for ever, that we may do all the words of this law.'

I remember years ago when I used to work in the post office, I was on the afternoon shift and my wife on the morning shift so one of us can take our children to school and the other pick them up. I arrived at work one day and was climbing the stairs from the ground floor; unknown to me, my wife was on the 3rd or 4th floor on her way to the canteen on the top floor and I either sneezed or coughed downstairs; the next thing I heard was my wife calling out my name in recognition of that sneeze; she didn't have to see my face to recognize that cough or sneeze; she didn't even have to hear my voice, why? Because she had spent some years with me and had heard that many times enough to recognize that sound anywhere.

It is the same with God - Jesus said, 'my sheep know my voice' - when you spend time with Him you discover and know without a shadow of doubt that He cannot fail, because He doesn't fail. He cannot lie because He is not a man that He should lie. Psalm 121 says, 'He neither slumbers nor sleeps', so He is ever awake to direct you. He is not learning how to love you - GOD IS LOVE. He loves you because He is love.

He will do what He says He will do because He only does what He says He will do. He says what He means and means what He says. After my wife's ectopic operation in 1991, when one of her fallopian tubes was removed and the doctors said all they said, we never doubted God once because in a dream long before we got married we had seen two children a boy and a girl sitting on the platform with us preaching the gospel so we knew no matter what happens, that our daughter would arrive sooner than later - she is here in her teens 'giving me instructions' now. God specializes in hastening His word to perform because He and His word are the same - that is what He does.

The only way David had courage to face GOLIATH WAS because he remembered that the GOD HE SERVED in the past had ENABLED HIM TO KILL THE BEAR AND LION SO HE KNEW THAT SAME GOD HE HAD SPENT TIME IN FELLOWSHIP WITH IN the WILDERNESS WILL DELIVER HIM FROM THIS UNCIRCUMCISED PHILISTINE. Hasn't it been said that a mother knows and can tell the cry of her child in a crowd of many other children without her seeing the child with her physical eye. How? She has spent time with the child. When you spend time with God through His word you get to know Him because He and His word are inseparable. (John 1:1) The general initial things you need to know about God is in the BIBLE and as you obey the rules in this general book then you can hear Him accurately on specific matters about your life but obey the contents of this book first.

Love is not just a feeling, it is a decision - you make it a thing you decide to do not only say but do irrespective. We use that word so loosely that in some circles it has lost its real meaning. You don't just say I love you, you demonstrate it for the person you are saying it to, to see and feel it and benefit from it. And you do that both in good times and bad times. You don't pick and choose. You don't love God just because of the things He does for you or because He answers your prayer; you love Him because it's a command - you must. Thou shall love the Lord thy God not....thou may love the Lord, if He does this and that.

**STOP SERVING GOD ON CONTRACT:** GOD IS NOT YOUR HEAVENLY BANKER; HE IS YOUR HEAVENLY FATHER! GOD IS NOT A CASINO – you put ten in, you get 100 back! Some people serve God on contract - If you do this for me then I will do that and then I will come to church to make you happy or if you do this for me then I will pay my tithe so you can have some food to eat. Listen to what God has to say about this kind of careless attitude. Psalm 50:7-15, 'Hear, O my people, and I will speak; O Israel, and I will testify against thee: I am God, even thy God. I will not reprove thee for thy sacrifices or thy burnt offerings, to have been continually before me. I will take no bullock out of thy house, nor he goats out of thy folds. For every beast of the forest is mine, and the cattle upon a thousand hills. I know all the fowls of the mountains: and the wild beasts of the field are mine. If I were hungry, I would not tell thee: for the world is mine, and the fulness thereof. Will I eat the flesh of bulls, or drink the blood of goats? Offer unto God thanksgiving; and pay thy vows unto the most High: And call upon me in the day of trouble: I will deliver thee, and thou shalt glorify me.'

From John 15, Jesus said, you can't say you love Him if you don't obey His commandments; you can never become intimate with someone you don't love; you can't become intimate with Him if you don't love Him and obey His commandments. You must come to a place in your life where you decide without any reservations that whether He does anything again for you or not for the rest of your life that you will serve Him wholeheartedly. **He is either Lord of all or not Lord at all of your life.** You must love Him with all your heart, all your soul and all your might and love your neighbour as yourself. That is how the world will know we are His disciples.

1 Kings 5:1, 'And Hiram king of Tyre sent his servants unto Solomon; for he had heard that they had anointed him king in the room of his father: for Hiram was ever a lover of David.'

Abraham was known as the friend or lover of God. What greater honour could be given any man than that of the Almighty calling him His friend? Many times the descendants of God's friends were blessed for the sake of their relationship with such men. Israel is blessed for Abraham's sake.

Genesis 26:24, 'And the LORD appeared unto him the same night, and said, I am the God of Abraham thy father: fear not, for I am with thee, and will bless thee, and multiply thy seed for my servant Abraham's sake.'

David's sake: 1 Kings 11:12-13, 'Notwithstanding in thy days I will not do it for David thy father's sake: but I will rend it out of the hand of thy son. Howbeit I will not rend away all the kingdom; but will give one tribe to thy son for David my servant's sake, and for Jerusalem's sake which I have chosen.'

Isaiah 37:35, 'For I will defend this city to save it for mine own sake, and for my servant David's sake.'

God has blessed other men for the sake of other friends of His.

Genesis 39:5, 'And it came to pass from the time that he had made him overseer in his house, and over all that he had, that the LORD blessed the Egyptian's house for Joseph's sake; and the blessing of the LORD was upon all that he had in the house, and in the field.'

Exodus 18:8, 'And Moses told his father in law all that the LORD had done unto Pharaoh and to the Egyptians for Israel's sake, and all the travail that had come upon them by the way, and how the LORD delivered them.'

2 Samuel 5:12, 'And David perceived that the LORD had established him king over Israel, and that he had exalted his kingdom for his people Israel's sake.'

Matthew 24:22, 'And except those days should be shortened, there should no flesh be saved: but for the elect's sake those days shall be shortened.'

2 Corinthians 4:5, 'For we preach not ourselves, but Christ Jesus the Lord; and ourselves your servants for Jesus' sake.'

2 Corinthians 4:11, 'For we which live are alway delivered unto death for Jesus' sake, that the life also of Jesus might be made manifest in our mortal flesh.'

2 Corinthians 12:10, 'Therefore I take pleasure in infirmities, in reproaches, in necessities, in persecutions, in distresses for Christ's sake: for when I am weak, then am I strong.'

It is a well-known fact that some Christians seem to enjoy a much closer intimacy with God than others.

**The question is:**
Is this familiarity a matter of favouritism on God's part or do such individuals or such people qualify in some way for that desirable intimacy?
1. Is it something that they did that we have not done or what?
2. Are there secrets we may discover that would admit us to a similar intimacy?

Both scripture and experience teach us that IT IS WE, NOT GOD WHO DETERMINE THE DEGREE OF INTIMACY WITH GOD THAT WE ENJOY AND NOT GOD.

## WE ARE AT THIS MOMENT AS CLOSE TO GOD AS WE CHOOSE TO BE!

James 4:8 says, 'Draw nigh to God, and he will draw nigh to you. Cleanse your hands, ye sinners; and purify your hearts, ye double minded.'

Hebrews 10:22 says, 'Let us draw near with a true heart in full assurance of faith, having our hearts sprinkled from an evil conscience, and our bodies washed with pure water.'

Hebrews 10:38-39, 'Now the just shall live by faith: but if any man draw back, my soul shall have no pleasure in him. But we are not of them who draw back unto perdition; but of them that believe to the saving of the soul.'

Jesus said in John 12:32, 'And I, if I be lifted up from the earth, will draw all men unto me.'

And Isaiah said in Isaiah 12:3, 'Therefore with joy shall ye draw water out of the wells of salvation.'

The question then is: are we willing to pay the price for such intimacy?

- You can only get out of a relationship what you are willing to put in.
- You can only get out of a relationship what you put in, nothing more, nothing less. It is the same with God.

- If you know more about soap stars, films and pop stars or soaps, that is the only soap you can use to bath and refresh yourself. But if you know more about the word then you can use the water of the word to refresh and cleanse yourself from every form of filthiness and have clear answers to life's many problems because the bible says we are cleansed by the washing of the water by the word. You are as close to your pastor as you choose to be - It's not entirely up to him. Some choose to come closer than others - it's as simple as that. The woman with the issue of blood made a decision long before she met Jesus – she chose and aimed at getting to and reached Jesus and went back home with her healing while others stood by and watched. It's all a choice!

Joshua said in Joshua 24:15, 'Choose you this day who or whom you will serve BUT AS FOR ME AND MY HOUSE WE WILL SERVE THE LORD.'

>YOU ARE AS CLOSE TO GOD AS YOU CHOOSE TO BE!

## FOUR CIRCLES OF INTIMACY WITH GOD
[In the Old Testament:]

### THE OUTER CIRCLE (Exodus 19:10-11; 24:2)

Exodus 19:10-11, 'And the LORD said unto Moses, Go unto the people, and sanctify them today and tomorrow, and let them wash their clothes, And be ready against the third day: for the third day the LORD will come down in the sight of all the people upon mount Sinai.'

Exodus 24:2, 'And Moses alone shall come near the LORD: but they shall not come nigh; neither shall the people go up with him.'

As the Law was about to be given, God told Moses to prepare the nation of Israel for his manifestation on Mt. Sinai. The OUTER CIRCLE was made up of the crowd i.e. people who when they saw the glory of God reacted in a way as if they had seen a devouring fire. Their perception of fear was what kept them in the outer circle, whereas Moses saw it as the glory of God.

## THE SECOND CIRCLE (Exodus 24:9-11)

Exodus 24:9-11, 'Then went up Moses, and Aaron, Nadab, and Abihu, and seventy of the elders of Israel: And they saw the God of Israel: and there was under his feet as it were a paved work of a sapphire stone, and as it were the body of heaven in his clearness. And upon the nobles of the children of Israel he laid not his hand: also they saw God, and did eat and drink.'

The group out of the whole of Israel made up of 74 pressed past the barriers and saw the glory of God, enjoyed intimacy, however it effected no permanent change in them because only a short time later in Exodus 32, they were found worshipping the golden calf. They did not qualify to ascend to the top of the mountain for a deeper fellowship with God.

## THE THIRD CIRCLE (Exodus 24:13-14; 33:10-11)

Exodus 24:13-14, 'And Moses rose up, and his minister Joshua: and Moses went up into the mount of God. And he said unto the elders, Tarry ye here for us, until we come again unto you: and, behold, Aaron and Hur are with you: if any man have any matters to do, let him come unto them.'

Exodus 33:10-11, 'And all the people saw the cloudy pillar stand at the tabernacle door: and all the people rose up and worshipped, every man in his tent door. And the LORD spake unto Moses face to face, as a man speaketh unto his friend. And he turned again into the camp: but his servant Joshua, the son of Nun, a young man, departed not out of the tabernacle.'

Of all Israel, only two qualified to be in the third circle i.e. Moses and Joshua. Joshua, Moses' servant the Bible says after Moses left the tent, would not leave the tent; he stayed on. He ascended higher on the glory-covered mountain above the others.

## THE INNER CIRCLE (Exodus 24:15-17; 32:32; 33:11,13,18-23; 34:6-7; Numbers 12:8)

Exodus 24:15,-17 'And Moses went up into the mount, and a cloud covered the mount. And the glory of the LORD abode upon mount Sinai, and the cloud covered it six days: and the seventh day he called unto Moses out of the midst of the cloud. And the sight of the glory of the LORD was like devouring fire on the top of the mount in the eyes of the children of Israel.'

Exodus 33:11, 'And the LORD spake unto Moses face to face, as a man speaketh unto his friend. And he turned again into the camp: but his servant Joshua, the son of Nun, a young man, departed not out of the tabernacle.'

Exodus 33:13, 'Now therefore, I pray thee, if I have found grace in thy sight, show me now thy way, that I may know thee, that I may find grace in thy sight: and consider that this nation is thy people.'

Exodus 33:18-23, 'And he said, I beseech thee, show me thy glory. And he said, I will make all my goodness pass before thee, and I will proclaim the name of the LORD before thee; and will be gracious to whom I will be gracious, and will show mercy on whom I will show mercy. And he said, Thou canst not see my face: for there shall no man see me, and live. And the LORD said, Behold, there is a place by me, and thou shalt stand upon a rock: And it shall come to pass, while my glory passeth by, that I will put thee in a clift of the rock, and will cover thee with my hand while I pass by: And I will take away mine hand, and thou shalt see my back parts: but my face shall not be seen.'

Numbers 12:8, 'With him will I speak mouth to mouth, even apparently, and not in dark speeches; and the similitude of the LORD shall he behold: wherefore then were ye not afraid to speak against my servant Moses?'

Moses only had the full experience to the extent of desiring to see God's face. He desired to know God more intimately. He became a friend of God who ministered in turn to Him face to face, mouth to mouth. He became so intimate with God that God was willing to unfold the mysteries behind creation, all the secrets about how the world was recreated in the Genesis account and the first books of the bible were revealed and entrusted to him to write even though he was not there when it all happened. Let's yearn for such intimacy.

QUESTION: Had we lived in the Old Testament times in which group would we have been found?
- THE CROWD?
- THE 70?
- THE 2?
- Or THE 1?

Now let's examine FOUR CIRCLES OF INTIMACY WITH GOD in the New Testament.

## FOUR CIRCLES OF INTIMACY WITH GOD
[In the New Testament:]

Jesus after a night of prayer chose an initial 12 for training. Then he chose 70 also. From among the twelve emerged a circle of 3 whom Jesus became especially acquainted with who were present on special occasions such as:
a. The raising of Jairus' daughter - Luke 8:51
b. The Mount if Transfiguration - Matthew 17:1; Luke 18:34; 2 Peter 1:16

c. On the Mount of Olives - Mark 13:3
d. In the Garden of Gethsemane - Matthew 26:37

NOTE:
- Their relationship with Him was a matter of their own choice.
- They were willing to go further.
- But out of them all was one (1) whom the Bible describes as 'the disciple whom Jesus loved' (John 21:20; John 13:25) His name was John. Even to the extent that on the cross just before Jesus died, John was the only disciple by him on the cross and Jesus placed his mother in John's care, charging him to take Mary as his mother and the mother to take him [John] as her son. (John 19:25-30)

- Q: Why did John have the primacy in the group?
- A: Because he drew closer in intimacy with Jesus than all the others. If Jesus loved John more, it was simply because John loved Jesus more. GUESS WHAT! The place on Jesus' breast is still vacant and you can fill it.

QUESTION: Had we been living in Jesus' day, in which category would we have been found?
- The 70
- The 12
- The 3
- Or The 1

REMEMBER:
YOU BECOME ACQUAINTED:
1. WITH THE ONE YOU PRAY TO
2. WITH THE ONE YOU PRAY WITH and
3. WITH THE ONE YOU PRAY FOR.

So, the question is who are you praying to, who are you praying with and who are you praying for? If the answer to all three questions is you, then you become acquainted with just you.

# CHAPTER THREE

# UNDERSTANDING MINISTRY

**MINISTRY - What it is and what it isn't.**

EMBARKING ON ANY CHURCH OR MINISTRY-RELATED ENTERPRISE WITHOUT UNDERSTANDING ITS DYNAMICS, REQUIREMENTS AND WHAT MAKES THINGS HAPPEN WITHOUT TOILING, BEGGING, SWEATING OR STRUGGLE IS EQUIVALENT TO MADNESS.

Scripture says: IN ALL YOUR GETTING, GET UNDERSTANDING: Proverbs 4:7, 'Wisdom is the principal thing; therefore get wisdom: and with all thy getting get understanding.'

BEHIND EVERYTHING OUTSTANDING IS UNDER-STANDING!

**At The root of everything outstanding is understanding!**

## So: EVERYTHING OUTSTANDING BEGINS WITH UNDERSTANDING!

IF YOU WANT TO BECOME OUTSTANDING IN MINISTRY OR IN YOUR FIELD OF CALLING OR ENDEAVOUR, THEN FIRST OF ALL GO FOR UNDERSTANDING. As in the life of Peter in the following passage of scripture, UNDERSTANDING TAKES EVERY TOIL AND STRUGGLE OUT OF LIFE AND MINISTRY AND MAKES YOU STAND OUT, SET THE STANDARD, BECOME OUTSTANDING MAKES YOU STAND OUT IN THE CROWD OF PEOPLE OR EXPERTS IN YOUR FIELD TO THE POINT OF BECOMING THE STANDARD [The Reference point, the bar or height or standard people desire to attain or the record people desire to break to set new ones].

Luke 5:5-11, illustrates his vividly:
'And Simon answering said unto him, Master, we have toiled all the night, and have taken nothing: nevertheless at thy word I will let down the net. And when they had this done, they enclosed a great multitude of fishes: and their net brake. And they beckoned unto their partners, which were in the other ship, that they should come and help them. And they came, and filled both the ships, so that they began to sink. When Simon Peter saw it, he fell down at Jesus' knees, saying, Depart from me; for I am a sinful man, O Lord. For he was astonished, and all that were with him, at the draught of the fishes which they had taken: And so was also James, and John, the sons of Zebedee, which were partners with Simon. And

Jesus said unto Simon, Fear not; from henceforth thou shalt catch men. And when they had brought their ships to land, they forsook all, and followed him.'

Ministry is not a relegation to a life of struggles and suffering but a fulfilled life. (John 10:10) So, get your instructions before stepping out. Ministry is not a business or industry, but about people's destinies so do not treat it like one. The money changers were trying to help make the temple worship easier but displeased God; they were kicked out, because they made kingdom business a trade. (2 Timothy 4:2)

Ministry is not a journey of trial and error. It's not guess work. Ministry begins with a definite calling because ministry requires a definite and particular call. With this definite call comes grace, abilities, provision, endowments, confidence, boldness, manpower, resources, accuracy and precision in activating spiritual gifts, guidance, protection, financial provision, God's presence, weight, power and authority backing the words you speak and utter, confirmed with signs and wonders, angelic ministry, effectiveness, success and undeniable authentic results/proofs.

With these in mind: It is a <u>self-inflicted curse</u> to embark on ministry out of circumstances, money needs, pride, strife, what you see others doing or the compliments or recommendations of people, etc. (Hebrews 5:4) Embarking on Ministry without a clear call is equivalent to a self-inflicted curse. I repeat: It is a <u>self-inflicted curse</u> to embark on any ministry enterprise that

God did not call you to embark on. God will only finance what He commands you to embark on. In the kingdom, common sense is nonsense. Examples of those who only embarked on God's clear instructions and assignment which culminated in their provision being guaranteed are: Elijah (1 Kings 17); Elisha (2 Kings 4); Abraham (Genesis 12&22); Isaac (Genesis 26); Job (Job 22:17-28; 42); Noah (Gen. 6-8)

Ministry is: Knowing and being persuaded of if you are called, why you are called, who you are called to, where you are called, to whom you are called, when to step out, what you are called to do and say, staying where you are called and knowing how to accomplish your calling.

BE AND GO WHERE HE TOLD YOU TO BE/GO, DO ONLY WHAT HE TOLD YOU TO DO AND STAY WHERE HE TOLD YOU TO STAY. Ministry is what you are within you not what is on the outside. It is the transaction of covenant. Ministry is not a popularity contest. Therefore, an initial understanding of what ministry is and isn't will give you a better approach and take the struggle out of every ministry venture you are called into.

## HOW TO EXPERIENCE EASE IN MINISTRY

Jesus said in Matthew 11:27, 'All things are delivered unto me of my Father: and no man knoweth the Son, but the Father; neither knoweth any man the Father, save the Son, and he to whomsoever the Son will reveal him. Come unto me, all ye that labour and are heavy laden, and I will give you rest. Take my yoke upon you, and learn of me; for I am meek and lowly in heart: and ye shall find rest unto your souls. For my yoke is easy, and my burden is light.'

The day a pilot is tired of checking his manual and stops reading or referring to his manual is the day he begins to dig his grave. Every pilot is married to his manual; it is impossible to embark on a flight without the manual in your bag. Every pilot is a bag carrier - he does not put biscuit or cake in his bag; he puts his manual in his bag. If he wakes up at night and is confused or not sure about something he refers to his manual before going back to bed, because you cannot fly on your opinions, you can only fly on valid instructions. That's why those who train pilots are called instructors not just teachers. You can't fly on your feelings; you can only fly on valid instructions. His uniform is not as important to him as his manuals so, he lays it on his lap because he can't risk guessing, depending on guess work as to which button to press, so he keeps checking it. **It is only those who want to crash who stop doing what makes them fly.**

Every time you see a man who is tired of checking the manual he is heading for disaster that will culminate in destruction to both his life and that of his passengers. That manual is the guarantee, the security of your destiny. How familiar you are with the manual will determine how smooth your flight will be. The manual! That is why God told Joshua at the onset of his ministry in Joshua 1:8, 'This book of the law shall not depart out of thy mouth; but thou shalt meditate therein day and night, that thou mayest observe to do according to all that is written therein: for then thou shalt make thy way prosperous, and then thou shalt have good success.'

It is the only way to make your way prosperous - by observing to do, not observing to quote or observing to preach but you observe to do. Observe to do! **So, you don't prosper on what you preach; you prosper on what you practice.** You don't get tired of reading this manual; when one is getting tired, worn out or old you renew it because you can't afford to miss one letter. You don't buy a new suit when your bible is torn or worn out; your suit is so they can have access to and listen to you. THIS IS YOUR Number one wife in ministry so, you have to get married to it; you and your wife can crash without it, but with it you can't crash. Take this manual in your hand; Take this manual in your hand; the pilot does not decorate his library with it; he decorates his mind with it.

This is how it is with the pilot; he puts the manual on his lap and looks out there. He looks at the sky and sees what is coming at him or what is approaching - the weather, rain, cloud, snow, turbulence, etc. at that time his focus is not on his home; he does not think of his wife or children but rather how he can fly and get the plane back on land so he can go and see his wife and family. That's why scripture says, 'Who are these that fly?' (Isaiah 60:8) i.e. who are these that are married to the manual who are not just preachers of the manual but are practitioners of its content? So it's not just reading or quoting. Concentrate your energies on what matters. If you are determined to remain on this flight then be married to this manual; keep checking it, keep checking it. Know why everything happens, know why you are prospering; know why you are growing as a church so you keep doing it. IF YOU LIVE YOUR LIFE ON CHANCE YOU DON'T HAVE A CHANCE. YOU HAVE TO LIVE IT ON FACTS!

The manual [The Bible] is the security of your destiny; you cannot afford to decorate your shelf with it, you cannot afford to be quoting it and sweating on quotations; you have to begin sweating on the practice. The scriptures say in Psalm 11:3, 'If the foundation be destroyed, what can the righteous do?'

We also know that Christ is the Cornerstone of our destiny in the kingdom. The church is built on the foundation of the apostles and prophets and Christ himself being the cornerstone and Christ is the anointed one or the anointed word.

**IN THE KINGDOM: IGNORANCE IS NO EXCUSE!**

In Luke 12:47-48, the fact that you don't know does not excuse you from what you have to suffer - stripes ... ... it may be reduced but you still have to pay for it. If someone said, 'I did know that Christ is the Son of God', that does not excuse him from going to hell - that does not exempt him from the punishment. As we look at these fundamental instructions which are major determinants of our lasting success and longevity both in life and especially ministry it will help to mould our behaviour towards practical accomplishment of His purpose for our lives because ignorance is no excuse in the kingdom.

We are told that the moon has no light of its own; rather all it does is to align itself at a particular angle to the sun and this glorious moonlight which is celebrated worldwide is nothing but a reflection of the light that comes from the sun. It does not generate its own heat but aligns itself to the heat of the sun and so reflects its light. In the same way the Sun of Righteousness generates the heat and the moon simply reflects the glory; so we are not created for heat generation - it's the glory. We are not programmed to go through a tough and tense life. Things are tough, rough and tense because of wrong alignment. He is the Sun of righteousness with healing in his wings so align and reflect His glory. He generates the heat that produces the light and when we are properly aligned we simply reflect the light.

The first day I heard my father in the Lord say, 'MINISTRY IS EASY!' I nearly passed out. I wondered what on earth had I been doing up until that time? I lined up and started practising the teachings and the covenant and I can tell you it is working.

AFTER HEARING HIM OUT, AND DOING, I CONCLUDED WITH HIM:
- THERE ARE NO HARD PLACES - THERE ARE ONLY HARD PEOPLE!
- THERE IS NO MOUNTAIN ANYWHERE, EVERYBODY'S IGNORANCE IS THEIR MOUNTAIN!
- YOU DON'T HAVE A SPECIAL CASE OR SPECIAL PROBLEM - YOU ONLY HAVE SPECIAL

IGNORANCE!
- ONLY THOSE WHO WANT TO CRASH ARE THOSE WHO STOP DOING WHAT MAKES THEM FLY!
- GOD IS NOT A RESPECTER OF PERSONS BUT OF COVENANT PRACTICE AND COVENANT PRACTITIONERS!

**THE REALITY OF EASE IN MINISTRY**

Jesus said: 'Come unto me all who are weak and are heavy laden and I will give you rest for my yoke is easy and my burden is light... come and learn of me...'

I.e. Come and find out how to be correctly positioned and you'll find rest for your life for my yoke is easy and my burden is light - all you need to do is learn of me (Joshua 1:8).

So, ministry is intended for ease not for struggle, not for tension, not for perspiration, not for sweating, not for frustration or suicidal tendencies, but rest. Ministry is designed for ease, for my yoke is easy and my burden is light if you are ready to learn of me. If it's not easy then there are things you should have learnt and until you learn them you'll keep suffering the tensions. In Matthew 11:28-29, Jesus is saying, I am not going to add to the load; rather I will give you rest, I will remove the load from you, I will give you rest, just follow me, follow my instructions by learning of me and I will remove the load from you, for the yoke is easy - the assignment is easy, so don't pose as if the assignment is an insurmountable mountain. My yoke is easy and my burden is light! My yoke is easy and my burden is light!

It is time to let the ease mentality of ministry enter your spirit. If I know what to do and put them to work, I will experience the ease that ministry is designed to offer - my yoke is easy and my burden is light. MY ONLY YOKE I need to carry is to learn - learn of Him.

**ALL YOU AND I NEED TO DO IS: Carry the yoke of a learner - come and learn of me and I will give you rest for your soul for my yoke is easy and my burden is light.**

There is one glory of the sun and another glory of the moon and one star and one exceeds the other in glory; we are never called the sun; no, we are only identified with stars; and stars reflect the light from the sun just like the moon does so we reflect the light of the sun just as the moon does. So we are to be reflectors not generators of heat and sweating all around and when you don't have a problem they wonder how do you not have a problem; everybody has a problem. But Jesus said, '... ... my yoke is easy and my burden is light.' In John 10 He said, 'I have come that ye might have life and have it more abundantly' and the path of a just man [the one that is doing it right] is as the shining light shining more and more, brighter and brighter unto the perfect day.

John 10:10, 'The thief cometh not, but for to steal, and to kill, and to destroy: I am come that they might have life, and that they might have it more abundantly.'

Proverbs 4:18, 'But the path of the just is as the shining light, that shineth more and more unto the perfect day.'

THEREFORE:
2 Timothy 2:15, 'Study to show thyself approved unto God, a workman that needeth not to be ashamed, rightly dividing the word of truth.'

SO LET'S BEGIN AT THE BEGINNING!

**WHAT IS MINISTRY? (EXPANDED VERSION of the first chapter of my book: WHAT IS MINISTRY?)**

To understand what Ministry is and isn't, let's begin by defining the different CLASSIFICATION OF MANAGEMENT SYSTEMS:

**THREE CLASSES:**
i. Managing people or people-management is Organization
ii. Resource management is Administration
iii. Destiny Management is Ministry

**So: Ministry unlike organisation and administration is about people's destinies.**

It is imperative therefore that we have a clear understanding of what ministry is before stepping out so we don't end up destroying our lives, families and destinies entrusted to us or those not entrusted to us.

[For more insight on this subject, you can order my books and leadership training manuals: **What Is Ministry, Generating Finances for Ministry** [Without Sweating, Begging, Toiling, Gimmicks, or Resorting to Tricks], **Pastoral Leadership 101, Ministry 101, Academy 101 and Leadership 101** from our bookshop or website www.houseofjudah.org.uk]

1. Ministry begins with discovering your Source and is sustained by continuous communication with your Source - God. - Jeremiah 1; 29:11

2. Ministry begins with self-discovery - a discovery of your self - who and what you really are and adequate and relevant preparation. - Jeremiah 1

3. Ministry begins with a purposeful discovery of your purpose in life – why you are here and what you are called to do specifically. Since we are not all called INTO THE SAME OFFICE (Romans 12:3-8) to do the same thing or everything i.e. into every ministry (the 5-fold ministry), it must begin with a knowing, an assurance and a full persuasion of your definite calling - Ephesians 4:11, 'And he gave some, apostles; and some, prophets; and some, evangelists; and some, pastors and teachers;'

Are you called to be an apostle, a prophet, an evangelist, a pastor, a teacher or into the ministry of helps or marketplace ministry? (Romans 12:3-8) YOU MUST KNOW THIS!

4. Ministry begins with a discovery, clear understanding and appreciation of your passion, gifts and talents - knowing what you are passionate about and your wiring i.e. why you're wired the way you are – potential.

5. Ministry begins with a discovery, recognition and clear understanding of your strengths, weaknesses and operating the law of compensation.

6. Ministry therefore is about people's destinies and fulfilling vision which comes through a discovery of your Source, your purpose, yourself, your gifts, talents, strengths and maximizing opportunities made possible by:

a. Fellowship in prayer with the Holy Spirit to introduce you to you, for an understanding of you - yourself - why you are 'wired' the way you are, to discover your assignment in life [purpose], your potential – your capabilities – gifting [gifts/talents], strengths / weaknesses.

b. Asking God for wisdom and engaging in spiritual warfare.

c. Having clarity of vision and pursuing it vigorously/diligently.

d. Addiction to The Word – This book of the Law should never depart out of your mouth; it should be your meditation all day long and be the final arbiter of your life/destiny. (Joshua 1:8; Psalm 119:97-100)

e. Knowing the following six crucial points: The 'who', the 'what', the 'way', [the how] the 'why', the 'when', and the 'where'. Rudyard Kipling said: "I keep six honest serving men (They taught me all I knew); Their names are What and Why and When And How and Where and Who."

**SO MINISTRY BEGINS WITH KNOWING THE WHO, THE WHAT, THE WAY, [the how] THE WHY, THE WHEN AND THE WHERE!**

**a. THE WHO:** Who is the target? Who are you called to? Who is to be involved? Genesis 11:6, '....and the people is one; nothing will be restrained from them which they have imagined to do' & 2 Samuel 6. Also, with whom are you to fulfil destiny since you are not called to serve with everyone. Paul to the Gentiles (Acts 26:14-19) recommended and supported by Barnabas, Luke, Timothy, Titus; Peter to the Jews.

**b. THE WHAT:** What is the assignment? What is the target? And all this must reflect His image and bring Him glory. That of Nimrod and those in Babel was nullified because it was for self - self-aggrandisement; it was aimed at bringing them the glory and not God. That is why God came down and interrupted their program.

**c. THE WAY:** [how to achieve it] In 2 Samuel 6, King David initially employed the wrong way to carry or bring the ark back to Jerusalem; there was a prescribed way as stated in 1 Samuel 5-7 which should have been studied by David the king before employing natural, physical, trial and error means using a cart to transport the ark resulting in Uzzah in trying to stop the ark from falling by touching it – helping God, being killed. King David eventually repented, wised up, found and followed the right way to bring the ark back. Find the divinely prescribed way or you'll end up using a blunt axe, exerting human effort and energy to accomplish little [Ecclesiastes 10:10] wearing everyone out or even killing yourself or others. Hebrews 8:5 says, '.....See, saith he, that thou make all things according to the pattern showed to thee in the mount.'

**d. THE WHY:** Why did God give you the vision you have? Why are you doing what you are doing? Why did He give you that assignment? Moses was told to tell Pharaoh, 'Let my people go [why?] That they may serve me, worship me and sacrifice to me in the wilderness.' (Exodus 4, 8, 9,)

1 Kings 3:5-9, 'Give me an understanding heart' – Why? Not for me but that I may be able to judge thy so great a people.

There is always a 'why' to everything God asks you to do - find it. It helps make the journey great and significant producing maximally with ease and keeps you focussed when others doubt and criticise you.

Hebrews 12:2 says, '… Jesus, who for the joy that was set before him, endured the cross, despised the shame and is now set at the right hand of majesty.'

**Why are we here?** Genesis 2:5, 'And every plant of the field before it was in the earth, and every herb of the field before it grew: for the LORD God had not caused it to rain upon the earth, and there was not a man to till the ground. But there went up a mist from the earth, and watered the whole face of the ground.'

There was no rain because there was no man to till the ground. There is always a reason for everything that God does. If certain things are not in place God doesn't do certain things because there is time for everything as stated in Ecclesiastes 3.

In Genesis 2:5-6, because, there was no man to till the ground God sent a mist out of the ground to water the ground.

**e. THE WHEN:** There is a when to every vision that God gives to every man. [Habakkuk 2 – though the vision tarries, wait for it, for it shall surely come to pass]. E.g. Esther in the palace; Moses in the wilderness with Jethro – the Midianites; David in the wilderness; Joseph sold into slavery ending up in prison for the preservation of life [posterity] - Ecclesiastes 3:1-3. The timing and environment must be right for the manifestation of the vision. Finding the when makes all the difference and takes the sweat out of life. In the fullness of time, God sent his Son.

**f. THE WHERE:** Where is God going to bring the promise to pass? In the accomplishment of every vision, all these six points or characteristics must be seen or satisfied just as it was in the scenario in Genesis 11.
- The who: Come let us – all of them of one language [vss.3&4]
- The what: let us build a city [vs. 4]
- The way & how: they had brick for stone and slime for mortar [vs. 3]
- The why: for a reason - we will not be scattered abroad [vs. 4]
- The when: let us build now [vs. 4]
- The where: a plain in the land of Shinar where they dwelt [vs. 2]

7. Ministry begins with an assurance of your general, specific, personal and ministry covenant with God. When you understand the covenant you have, you have confidence and boldness to summon your covenant to deal with demons and hindrances that stand in the way of the fulfilment of your divine assignment. If you are sent, you must know the covenant that comes with your sending. Moses knew 'I am that I am' was with him to back up his words. So did David in 1 Samuel 17 – that's why he called Goliath an uncircumcised philistine. The apostles knew He would confirm the words they preached with signs and wonders. Jesus knowing He was sent by God was bold enough to say, 'the works I see him do is what I do also', etc.

8. Ministry requires addiction to hearing and obeying God's voice daily. Get into God's agenda daily.

9. Ministry originates with the spiritual before the physical. Ministry markets, products and customers are all spiritual. As a result, every approach to ministry must first be spiritual before anything else. Failure to understand and act accordingly will lead to unending frustration culminating in failure. - 1 Thessalonians 2:4-8

Church growth is first spiritual, ministry is first spiritual. When a bill arises, the first thing you do must be to discern spiritually as to whether this bill has arisen because of something I wanted or it was divinely authorized. (Lamentations 3:37) If it was of the flesh then I must find a way of paying for it or repent but if it was sanctioned from heaven, then I can call on heavenly supply – 'God I have done this at your instruction so I am expecting divine provision to meet this need; thank you for it in Jesus' name. Amen!' (Luke 22:35) In Acts 13, they preached the word of God, and God emptied the cities into the church. SO YOUR PRAYER MUST BE: **LORD, EMPTY OUR CITIES INTO OUR CHURCHES IN JESUS' NAME!**

10. Ministry is only effective and sustainable when the rule of focus is consistently applied. If the enemy can steal your focus, he has your victory and testimony. You need to ask yourself, 'Why am I called and for what purpose?' - Matthew 6:22
   a. SEE! Your cutting edge is your ability to be precise in what God has called you to do.
   b. Leadership is lonely because of focus and people do not

see the position as you (e.g. Elijah on Mount Carmel).
c. The enemy will do anything and everything to break your focus on the assignment God has committed to your hands.
d. The battle for exploits is won when you refuse to break your focus. ADVICE: Do not be diverted by running around solving diversion problems. Your prayer must be: 'Lord, keep my eyes single.'
e. Focus is the discipline and ability to concentrate and produce results when the circumstances are not right. Despite no friends, no money, no comfort, in ridicule, you are focussed like Paul in Romans 8:35-39.
f. If you are not focused in the ministry, you cannot last. For example:-
   **i.** SAMSON: When the Philistines caught Samson, even though his strength was in his hair, they removed his eyes (vision). Without your eyes (sight/vision) you will be led to do what others want you to do. If your eyes are intact, if your eyes are full of light, then your whole body will be full of light. The person he was close to whose soul was knit to him caused him to lose focus. That's why Samson asked for vengeance for his eyes - his last prayer was, 'revenge my eyes.' (Judges 16:28) Disassociate from distracters! (1 Corinthians 15:33)
   **ii.** DAVID: David's greatest error was committed when his focus was lost. (2 Samuel 11:1-4)
   - It was at the time of least focus.
   - The advice is: Don't lose your focus. Seek God's face first on everything.
g. If you sit in your office and you cannot see or hear, you are bound.

11. Ministry is not a relegation to a life of struggles and suffering but a fulfilled life. (John 10:10) So, get your instructions before stepping out.

12. Ministry is not a business or industry, but about people's destinies so do not treat it like one. The money changers were trying to help make the temple worship easier but displeased God; they were kicked out, because they made kingdom business a trade. (2 Timothy 4:2)

13. Ministry is not a journey of trial and error. It's not guess work.

14. Ministry begins with a definite calling because ministry requires a definite and particular call. With this definite call comes grace, abilities, provision, endowments, confidence, boldness, manpower, resources, accuracy and precision in activating spiritual gifts, guidance, protection, financial provision, God's presence, weight, power and authority backing the words you speak and utter, confirmed with signs and wonders, angelic ministry, effectiveness, success and undeniable results / proofs.

a. With this in mind: It is a <u>self-inflicted curse</u> to embark on ministry out of circumstances, money needs, pride, strife, what you see others doing or the compliments or recommendations of people, etc. (Hebrews 5:4)

b. Embarking on Ministry without a clear call is equivalent

to a self-inflicted curse. I repeat: It is a self-inflicted curse to embark on any ministry enterprise that God did not call you to embark on. God will only finance what He commands you to embark on. In the kingdom, common sense is nonsense. Examples of those who only embarked on God's clear instructions and assignment which culminated in their provision being guaranteed are: Elijah (1 Kings 17); Elisha (2 Kings 4); Abraham (Genesis 12&22); Isaac (Genesis 26); Job (Job 22:17-28; 42); Noah (Genesis 6-8)

15. Ministry is: Knowing and being persuaded of if you are called, why you are called, who you are called to, where you are called, to whom you are called, when to step out, what you are called to do and say, staying where you are called and knowing how to accomplish your calling. BE AND GO WHERE HE TOLD YOU TO BE/GO, DO ONLY WHAT HE TOLD YOU TO DO AND STAY WHERE HE TOLD YOU TO STAY.

16. Ministry is what you are within you not what is on the outside. It is the transaction of covenant.

17. Ministry is not a popularity contest.

18. Ministry is not initially about you being famous but making Him known and famous and in the process of you exalting, lifting, glorifying Him and making Him known, you also become known because of Him. As confirmed in the following passage: John 12:32, 'And I, if I be lifted up from the earth, will

draw all men unto me.'

19. The foundation for a successful ministry is not your eloquence – it is emphatically your divine calling.

20. Ministry begins with and is sustained by a heavenly calling. **In ministry there is no such thing as luck. FOOLS BELIEVE IN LUCK - THE WISE BELIEVE IN THE LAW OF CAUSE AND EFFECT i.e. Your Input Determines Your Output. If you are not heavenly-called, you have no heavenly backing and if you don't have heavenly backing, you are an easy prey/target exposed to the gates of hell prevailing against you - even angels can't help you.**

21. Ministry requires daily consultation with your Caller for clear, divine instructions that secure undisputed, maximum and lasting supernatural results. Your creativeness/creativity and innovation in ministry must be accompanied by and subjected to daily consultation with the Holy Spirit [the owner of the Church] for approval and divine direction.
- **In every endeavour of ministry, learn to submit your creativity to Divinity for instruction, correction, adjustment, approval, or empowerment. SUBMIT AND SUBJECT YOUR CREATIVITY TO DIVINITY BEFORE PROCEEDING!**
- **REASON: WHEN DIVINITY COMES UPON HUMANITY OR MORTALITY, IT PRODUCES AN UNCOMMON PERSONALITY!**
- If there is no call, there is no grace. (Ephesians 4:7)

- IT IS GRACE THAT MAKES GREAT! (1 Corinthians 15:10)
- With this call comes a principle: Ministry begins with and is sustained by receiving four major instructions. You must of necessity receive these instructions from God before you embark on your journey/enterprise in ministry: This is what makes your journey colourful, impactful and lasting. They are namely:
a. Description
b. Inscription
c. Prescription and
d. Subscription.

- The statement: WRITE THE VISION DOWN in Habakkuk 2 means:
- **Describe it**
- **Inscribe it**
- **Prescribe For it and**
- **Subscribe To it.**

- 1st of all **describe it – define clearly what the vision is.**

- 2nd, **inscribe it – write it down so you don't keep changing it because of circumstances/people's opinion** so it cannot be erased.

- 3rd, you must **take a prescription from God as to the How!** God said you will pastor a church of 10,000 - you have the target. Now, **wait on Him to tell you how. This is what you**

**need to do so what I said will come to pass.** For you to be what you should be, take this prescription twice or thrice daily, hold this or that specialised or general relevant event daily, weekly, monthly or yearly. (1 Kings 3:7)

- 4th, **subscribe to it** - after you've received the steps and prescription, **act upon it; do it; subscribe to the prescription. This ensures you don't sway from the original path.**

22. Ministry is not for personal gain but essentially and initially for the benefit of those you are assigned to serve, add value to, impact and influence positively to also serve, add value to, impact and influence others positively.

23. Ministry is about serving the people and not yourself. 'Serving self makes a slave, serving others makes a leader and commitment to serving others makes a great leader.' – Bishop Oyedepo

24. Ministry is a yoke that is easy, not burdensome. If you are not called, ministry will be full of constant struggles and even suicidal tendencies. Matthew 11:28-30, 'Come unto me, all ye that labour and are heavy laden, and I will give you rest. Take my yoke upon you, and learn of me; for I am meek and lowly in heart: and ye shall find rest unto your souls. For my yoke is easy, and my burden is light.'

1 Thessalonians 5:24, 'Faithful is he that calleth you, who also will do it.' SO: If He called you, **He will do it, but if He did**

not call you then you will do it.

25. Ministry is a tongue baptized with fire [not noise]. - Isaiah 6:6-8

26. Ministry is about being a news-maker not a noise-maker.

27. Ministry begins with a certified sending. People who are sent by God triumph divinely. 2 Corinthians 2:14, 'Now thanks be unto God, which always causeth us to triumph in Christ, and maketh manifest the savour of his knowledge by us in every place.'

28. Ministry is not a career you decide upon; it is a <u>divine calling</u>: this knowledge will preserve you from pride and prevent you from leaping into endeavours which God did not commission. (1 Timothy 1:12)

a. Divine appointments avert severe disappointments. (Lamentations. 3:37)

b. Divinely-sent people triumph by God's hand. (2 Corinthians 2:14) Some say, 'Someone else has done it so I can also do it.' (Ephesians 4:7, 11) That kind of approach can floor you. Do you have the grace to do the same? NOTE: Venturing into someone's assignment can kill you.

29. Ministry is not fame, wealth, popularity, respect, position, radio or TV, Real Estate, your bank balance or the number of

people in your church or ministry or being seen or heard of or known. (Acts 2:22-37; 2 Samuel 18:22-30)

30. Ministry requires diligence. Laziness is a guarantee for failure or stagnation in ministry. God does not put his seal of approval on lazy people. Laziness is not permitted in ministry.

a. Diligence and enterprising work pleases God. (2 Timothy 2:15; Hebrews 11:6; Proverbs 22:29; Ecclesiastes 5:3, 18-20; 3:13,22 )

b. Laziness is not excessive sleep; it is missing opportunities such as failing to exercise yourself in your calling; am I productive with my time?

c. You will know if you are productive with your time if you are doing the following: Reading, studying and praying more, engaged in more creative thinking, writing more books, manuals, training and raising leaders, etc.

d. Spiritual labour commands material blessings. (1 Timothy 5:17)

e. Labour to be filled with knowledge and increase your success potential.

f. Also engage yourself in self-development and personal development involving home-acquired knowledge to make you a more productive and better person.

g. Study and pray consistently during the week long before Sunday services or meetings.

h. Duplicate yourself in your protégés; mentoring does not have to be from the pulpit always – it can be on a one-on-one basis or in small groups.

i. Be Diligent in ministry because God sees our labour in secret and rewards us openly. God is not a debtor to anyone; if you spend faith, He will pay you back. When you sow a seed, He will pay you back before you ask for pay.

j. Engage in Spiritual Labours – Labours of insight, word and prayer, because our investment determines what God does for us; i.e. your input determines your output – what you sow determines what you reap. (Genesis 8:22; Galatians 6:6-10)
- **REMEMBER: MAKING the most of your time is making the most of your life, career and ministry and WASTING the most of your time is wasting the most of your life, career and ministry. (1 Thessalonians 4:11)**

31. Ministry is not just confession of faith but profession of your faith.

32. Ministry is your ability to know and understand the mind of God and to communicate it effectively to people - saved or unsaved. If you don't know what God is saying [the heart of God] you are not in ministry - period! I need to know, 'What is the mind of God in different ways for our ministry - House

of Judah? REASON BEING: I must communicate the heart of God.' We must be an oracle of God – the mouth-piece of God.

- **True ministers are oracles of the mind of God.** (2 Samuel 18)

33. Ministry is digging into the heart of God to reach men. It's downloading God's mind and heart to people. (Jeremiah 3:15)

34. Ministry is preaching and teaching His message, [not yours or a good sermon]. (Ezekiel 2:4) Anywhere you go to minister, place a demand on the Godhead, i.e. expect God to confirm what HE IS SAYING. Tremble at the concept of saying what He did not say or is not saying and putting a burden on people He did not put on them. THE VOICE OF GOD IS MIGHTY, VALUABLE AND PRECIOUS.

35. Ministry is OPERATING BY THE SENT WORD - go preach saying the kingdom of God is at hand…

**EVERY TIME A SENT MAN SPEAKS, THE SENDER SHOWS UP to confirm what He has sent him to speak.**

- John the Baptist came with a message of repentance. Jesus came initially with a message to the household of Israel.

36. Ministry is running and preaching His message, not your message.

37. Ministry is not cheap talk - it is hard, smart, creative work, backed by prayer, studying God's word, warfare, power, training and raising leaders but you should not struggle, toil or sweat. If ministry is a struggle, then revisit your calling because God promises us in Proverbs 4:18, that the path of the just is as the shining light that shineth more and more unto a perfect day. If you are fighting the same fight always, check it.

38. Ministry is not about the glory we see but settling down to investigate and understand the story behind what brings the glory and paying the required price to see the same or more.

39. Ministry is secured by heavenly backing. It is your calling into ministry that secures and guarantees heavenly backing. Is your church on God's agenda? Then He will supply every need. If God did not send you on TV then don't go there. Be in God's agenda or you will struggle.

40. Ministry is: Knowing and down-loading the mind of God [a specific message] to humanity - saved or unsaved. This implies that we musn't run without getting the message or else we'll be asked to stand aside like Ahimaaz.

When you are asked, 'What message do you have for us?' like Ahimaaz, whilst others like the Cushite who waited for the message will be asked to speak because they carried a message and had the mandate, you may be asked to stand aside.

2 Samuel 18:28-33, 'And Ahimaaz called, and said unto the king, All is well. And he fell down to the earth upon his face before the king, and said, Blessed be the LORD thy God, which hath delivered up the men that lifted up their hand against my lord the king. And the king said, Is the young man Absalom safe? And Ahimaaz answered, When Joab sent the king's servant, and me thy servant, I saw a great tumult, but I knew not what it was. And the king said unto him, Turn aside, and stand here. And he turned aside, and stood still. And, behold, Cushi came; and Cushi said, Tidings, my lord the king: for the LORD hath avenged thee this day of all them that rose up against thee. And the king said unto Cushi, Is the young man Absalom safe? And Cushi answered, The enemies of my lord the king, and all that rise against thee to do thee hurt, be as that young man is. And the king was much moved, and went up to the chamber over the gate, and wept: and as he went, thus he said, O my son Absalom, my son, my son Absalom! would God I had died for thee, O Absalom, my son, my son!'

**So, wait for the message before moving.**

41. Ministry is vision and mission – Joel 2. Your life must be driven by a God-ordained vision and mission. Don't mistake ambition for vision. Vision is what God wants whilst ambition is what you want.

42. Ministry - Church growth is a downloaded answer – it is downloaded from heaven. It is about what you heard.

43. Ministry is the things you do that are productive with value-

adding traits [VAT]. It's about influencing your world positively by adding value to people, places, societies, communities and nations.

44. Ministry is hearing God and doing what God says. Before you do or say anything, make sure it is God you heard and are hearing.

45. Ministry is doing your job (and it will show) and doing your job is knowing the mind of God. - John 5:39

46. Ministry is hearing, doing and delivering what is on God's heart, not what's on your mind. David was described as a man after God's own heart – a man that carried God's heart, a man that knew His heart. **WHAT WE SHOULD PURSUE IS THE MIND [heart] OF GOD AND THE THINGS WILL PURSUE US (Matthew 6:33). Knowing the mind of God is the biggest challenge and asset of a minister.**

Scripture says in Proverbs 3:5-8 that we should trust in the Lord and lean not on our own understanding. (Don't go into that pulpit with your own mind but His mind and say what HE IS SAYING, SO HE CAN BACK IT UP!) In all our ways we should acknowledge Him that He would direct our paths.

Mark 16:15-20 says He went with them confirming the words they preached with signs following. If it's His word, He is obligated to and will confirm it with transformation of lives and signs and wonders but if it is your word then you will have to back it up with carnal strategies. The value and quality of your individual calling [material supply and provision] resides in the quality and value of your hearing God. DESIRE DRIVES YOUR ABILITY TO HEAR. Your wages for bearing the mind of God is paid by the One who sent you. (1 Kings 17; Luke 22:35) The people you are sent to are not your employers or employees. He said to the disciples, 'When I sent you did you lack anything? They said nothing.' (Luke 22:35) REMEMBER: YOU ARE SENT TO THE PEOPLE NOT BY THE PEOPLE.

47. Ministry is a long distance haul not a hundred meter dash. Do not be frustrated with limited growth; rather enjoy the journey / process. - Exodus 23:28-30

48. Ministry is about accomplishments not entitlements for there is no entitlement in titles but in achievements.

49. Ministry begins with a CERTIFIED / DEFINITE SENDING. What are you called to do specifically? (Ephesians 4:11)
a. **EVERY TIME A SENT MAN SPEAKS, THE SENDER [the one who sent him] SHOWS UP. So,** ministry must first of all begin with a certified sending and with that sending comes definite heavenly backing. Are you called to be a Pastor, Teacher, Prophet, Evangelist, Apostle or into the helps ministry or marketplace ministry? (Refer to Chapter one) Paul said he was not disobedient to the heavenly vision. Acts 26:19, 'Whereupon, O king Agrippa, I was not disobedient unto the

heavenly vision:'
b. If heaven sent you then expect heavenly funding – funding from above through human vessels and angelic activations – heaven will speak to men and men will respond as they did for Elijah, Elisha, Jesus, Paul, etc.

50. Ministry has ranking and ranking is not the same thing as titles. Ranking is placement and sequence for collective good.
a. This army did not break its ranks: Joel 2:7, 'They shall run like mighty men; they shall climb the wall like men of war; and they shall march everyone on his ways, and they shall not break their ranks:'
b. Mark 6:40, 'And they sat down in ranks, by hundreds, and by fifties.'
c. **The Holy Spirit moves mightily where there is purpose, order, honour, keeping of ranks, oneness, unity, love and one accord.**
d. Joshua 9:2, 'That they gathered themselves together, to fight with Joshua and with Israel, with one accord.'
e. Acts 2:46, 'And they, continuing daily with one accord in the temple, and breaking bread from house to house, did eat their meat with gladness and singleness of heart,'
f. Titus 1:5, 'For this cause left I thee in Crete, that thou shouldest set in order the things that are wanting, and ordain elders in every city, as I had appointed thee:'

51. Ministry is about accomplishments, not titles.

52. Ministry is about serving and adding value to others.

53. Ministry is initially and essentially about transforming, translating and transfiguring destinies.

54. Ministry involves an understanding of and eradication of certain diseases in churches. (Refer to page 98 of PASTORAL LEADERSHIP 101)

55. Ministry is a journey not a brief trip.

56. Ministry involves challenges and solving problems - it is not void of problems. With greatness in ministry comes a perpetuation of tests, trials, challenges and problems to solve. It comes with the terrain – new heights, new levels and new devils to deal with. So have and show mercy (by applying oil and wine) for the sheep; but 'a rod and fight' for the wolf when it shows up in the house. Psalm 34:19 says, 'Many are the afflictions of the righteous: but the LORD delivereth him out of them all.' (John 16:33; 2 Corinthians 4:17-18)

57. Ministry is full of all kinds of opposition. There are two kinds of opposition in ministry [Spiritual and physical]. Expect to have to deal with both kinds from time to time (and remember that it is a normal process of ministry).

58. Ministry is about impact. Until your ministry has an impact on the outside world you've not started ministry.

59. Ministry is sustained by an understanding of and operating in both your personal and ministry covenants [General,

Specific, Personal and Ministry Covenants]. (Refer to the last chapter of this book)

60. Ministry involves an understanding of and activation of Angelic Ministry [How to deploy angels to work for you, those you are called to and your entire ministry]. (Hebrews 1:14; Psalm 103:20)

61. Ministry is about pouring into, empowering, developing and raising men; not raising offerings or money. After you raise men, empower them and develop them to fulfil destiny, there will be more than enough money to do what you are called to do. REMEMBER: **Money does not make ministry - it is ministry that makes money.**

62. Ministry involves preaching (pandering and responding) to what's in your spirit, not what you see. Provide depth for your spirit and message. If you tailor your message for the people, they are leading you (and the ministry). Jeremiah 1 - What you see in your spirit is what is performed.

63. Lasting ministry requires solid sustainable structures both for now and the future. Church growth is sustainable. To achieve sustainability of continuous acceleration and impact we must put structures in place for our destination and also what we preach must be structured. Preaching must not be done just anyhow - one subject must be taught at a time and dealt with in detail for clear understanding and application of the subject matter resulting in daily proofs in the lives of the

flock i.e. What is taught must be clearly understood, practised and become lifestyle, for e.g. faith, finance, praise, outreach, dominion, faithfulness, loyalty, etc.

64. Disappointment in ministry is eradicated with divine appointment. You cannot be <u>disappointed in ministry if you are appointed by God.</u> I was appointed by God to do what I am doing. It is He who is working in me both to will and to do of His own good pleasure. There is no room for pride when I know He is the One working in me. – Lamentations 3:37, 'Who is he that saith, and it cometh to pass, when the Lord commandeth it not?'

65. Ministry involves being on the lookout for opportunities to maximize your potential and opportunities.

66. Ministry must begin with an understanding of the know-how - it takes wisdom to sustain a divine move. Principles backed by power will guarantee the future outcome of any church or ministry. A minister shouldn't embark upon a journey that will cost him/her everything (burning the bridges behind them - like Elisha did with his family) if they do not know the sure route to the destination – the how. (Proverbs 4:7)

67. Sustained Ministry requires all that you are and all that you own. It takes everything you are and have to do something significant for God. Jesus said get a **CROSS,** not a **CROWN**. The Cross produces the Crown.

68. Every marvellous, mighty experience or achievement in ministry is definitely an act of God. Psalm 118:23 says, 'This is the LORD'S doing; it is marvellous in our eyes.' And Psalm 78:12 reads: 'Marvellous things did he in the sight of their fathers, in the land of Egypt, in the field of Zoan.'

69. Sustained ministry requires adequate relevant ongoing preparation. When God is going to do something, <u>prepare in the draught</u> (and not when the rain comes pouring down.) Because, the blessing [rain] will drown the unprepared. (1 Kings 18:41-45; Hebrews 10:36-38) Noah could not build the ark in the flood and Ahab could not run in the storm (that's why fore-warning was given in each instance).

70. Ministry requires and involves being delivered from the people. Acts 26:17, 'Delivering thee from the people, and from the Gentiles, unto whom now I send thee,'

71. Ministry requires excellence not mediocrity. If you are not prepared to set your sights on 'awesome' (unction and glory) then quit ministry. **Mediocrity is not the language of the ministry. EXCELLENCE IS!**

72. **Impactful and life-transforming ministry is initiated, not waited for. The next move of God in your life is entirely up to you. Discard the doctrine of waiting for God; God is waiting for you to 'pay the price – the required price.'**

73. Productive ministry requires cognisance of the promises more than the challenges. Know and be acquainted with the PROMISES of God to you and your ministry. Otherwise you will not know what to expect or how to prepare for it (or recognise it when it comes.) The PROMISE must be more real to you than the PROBLEM. Starve the problems by paying them no attention; feed the promises instead.

74. Ministry requires a deliberate pacing of oneself for the journey. Take time out periodically to push back the chair and evaluate. Do not run yourself down spiritually, emotionally, psychologically or physically.

75. Ministry demands a covenant attitude of gratitude each step of the way. Thank God for where you are to activate God's hand for the next level. As you express gratitude for where you are and what you have, you commit God to take you to the next level. (Exodus 23:28-30) **Thankful people always have their tanks full**.

76. Ministry which originated as a divine mandate cannot be achieved by fleshly methods/effort or in the energy of the flesh. A heavenly calling therefore requires the question, 'What am I divinely mandated to do?'

77. Ministry is walking according to the will of God. Don't step into anything until you know for sure, that is the will of God for you: **Being set apart for the Master's use. Proverbs 4:18 says, 'The path of the just is as the shining light, that**

**shineth more and more unto the perfect day.'**

From Genesis 1, we discover: **God creates, God moves and God speaks and so does the Church. The church creates, the church moves and the church speaks.** If you can see it, you can have it. The quality of decisions we make is governed by the degree of information we have.

78. Sustained ministry requires praying without ceasing - strategic, spiritual warfare and all manner of prayer. (Ephesians 6; James 5:17-18)
i. Prayer eases the birthing of vision; informed prayer.
ii. It urges a manifestation of internal vision and foresight.
iii. We must have a greater understanding of prayer.
iv. Pray the promise, not the problem.
v. Prayer that is not praying the promise is ineffective prayer – pray the promise not the problem.
vi. Pray the promise. When we pray the promise we are boasting in God.
vii. Praying the promise activates angels on our behalf.

79. Ministry presents challenges and problems that must be solved.
- A Minister must develop a good attitude towards challenges/problems.
- Problems are normal in ministry terrain.
- Problems come in different shapes and sizes – in the form of people, things, issues, challenges, etc.

80. Timing is everything in ministry.
i. Never be in a hurry to acquire or achieve what heaven has not sanctioned. (Proverbs 28:22)
ii. Do not eat dinner too soon (in the morning). (Ecclesiastes 10:16-17)
- Anything you get too fast will definitely not last. [It leaves just as fast]
- Bid your time and allow the process to take its full course.
- Haste is hazardous.
iii. When greatness comes, it often does not come in the form you were expecting it. Often it is a hand in the sky or seed and not a forest. (e.g. Elijah's storm was first a little hand – 1 Kings 18:44)

81. Effective Ministry will require all that you have and all that you are.

82. Success in ministry is the implementation of set goals and tasks, such as a target of 10 to start, 20 by end, etc.

83. Success in ministry can be defined in the face of a clear assignment or purpose. Paul said, 'I strive for the mark of the high calling in Christ Jesus.' If there is no mark, you are striving in the wrong direction.

84. Success in ministry is not measured by comparison with others but with set goals such as how many of the set goals were achieved.

85. Greatness in ministry requires being controversial sometimes and criticized. REMEMBER: Greatness, criticism and controversial often go hand in hand. Do not be afraid of being controversial in the pursuit of greatness. The enemy's comments are irrelevant.

a. There will be times when you will be at odds with those who serve you. They will from time to time not see what you see (or hear what you hear). [Such as: Elijah saying, 'I hear the sound of an abundance of rain;' or Elisha saying to Gehazi, '……those with us are more than those against us;' or Joshua instructing 'let's walk round the walls of Jericho' or Moses stretching his rod in response to 'go forward into the Red Sea...'

b. God said to Abraham, 'I will make your name great'; (not title)
- **Greatness is intrinsic and not contagious.**
- **Greatness is released in steps and stages.**

c. Do not scuffle with those you are sent to teach. Servants/sons should be taught and trained to submit and be obedient without necessarily seeing or understanding it. The power of mantle/anointing transference is in seeing what I see. 'If you see what I see when I am taken from you.' (Elijah, Elisha).

d. Do not be fooled by what people SAY; be cautious to consider what people DO more importantly.

86. Ministry requires diligence, discipline, determination and

sacrifice. There are rules and there are regulations to fulfilling ministry and remember it is hard work.

87. In ministry there is no such thing as luck. Fools believe in luck whilst the wise believe in the principle or law of cause and effect.

88. If you are not called, ministry will be full of constant struggles. 1 Thessalonians 5:24 says, 'Faithful is he that calleth you, who also will do it.' If He called you, He will do it, but if He did not call you then you will do it or bring it to pass through carnal strategies.

89. Ministry is not fulfilled by intentions but by required actions. You don't sleep with vision - you run with vision just like prophecies don't fulfil themselves but prophecies are fulfilled through pursuit of purpose, focus, sacrifice, effective use and management of time, dogged determination, discipline, devotion, continuous learning, acquisition and application of the required skill, an addiction to excellence, being under an effective proven mentor, contention in warfare [battle] and hard, smart, creative work within purpose.

90. In ministry, God is only committed to what He commands. For example in Judges 6:14, 'And the LORD looked upon him, and said, Go in this thy might, and thou shalt save Israel from the hand of the Midianites: have not I sent thee?'

91. Ministry is not for Novices.

92. Ministry requires the right attitude – your attitude determines your altitude.

93. Guaranteed Provision for ministry begins with a certified call and sending. God pays for what He sends as indicated in Luke 22:35.

94. Ministry is not about pursuit of money or making money at the expense of others. It's about impact. 'MONEY DOESN'T MAKE MINISTRY - IT IS MINISTRY THAT MAKES MONEY.' - BISHOP OYEDEPO

95. Ministry is not about raising offerings but raising men.

96. Ministry requires a complete knowledge and understanding of what He said and is saying.

97. Ministry is not equal to ambition. Scripture says in Hebrews 5:4, 'And no man taketh this honour unto himself, but he that is called of God, as was Aaron.'

REMEMBER that In Ministry: One must never mistake ambition for vision. Ambition leads to frustration. Ambition has fatalistic outcome - it brings or is a cancer to ministry. Ambition says 'me' whilst calling says 'Him'. The proof that God sent you is in the supernatural results. Ambition is a desire to be seen. Ambition is what you want - vision is what God wants. Unfortunately, many mistake ambition for vision. Divine calling says God said and He will do it. Ambition says me and I will do it.

98. Ministry is embracing a divine agenda, not a personal or man-made agenda or ambition. With every suggestion and idea, ask yourself, 'Is this part of His divine agenda/mandate for me or not?' REASON: You will squander a move when you embrace a non-divine agenda.

99. Ministry is not just about going to collect a loan, hire a hall, fill it with chairs and musical instruments and see if people will come. No! It begins with a definite calling, preparation, equipment, sending, divine backing from the Sender, staying in touch with the Sender, operating as commanded and proven results. RESULTS PREVENT INSULTS!

100. Ministry requires paying the required price. - DON'T MAKE THE MISTAKE OF KEEPING YOUR EYES ON THE GLORY OF MINISTRY WITHOUT SETTLING DOWN TO UNDERSTAND THE STORY BEHIND THE GLORY.

101. Ministry will inflict scars on you and in you so, stay resolute. Success both in life and ministry is not only measured by what a man achieves/accomplishes, but by the opposition he has encountered, and the courage/fortitude with which he has maintained the struggle against overwhelming odds. REMEMBER: The measure of a man is the way he bears up under misfortune. IN MINISTRY PEOPLE WILL EITHER BE AN ASSET TO YOU OR A LIABILITY.

# BE COURAGEOUS AND FOCUSSED!

102. Effective ministry requires a persuasion of what you are equipped and empowered to accomplish. You are not equipped to do everything.

- Every church and Pastor has an emphasis. What is your emphasis?
- What is the vision, the mandate, the agenda of your ministry?
- You must have a revelation of what you are called to do. When they wake you up from bed, what springs out of you automatically? What is your core message? Ezekiel said, 'I prophesied as I was commanded.' What have you been commanded to prophesy and to who? You should know where you are sent. You don't go just anywhere. Jonah liked Tarshish but he was sent to Nineveh. The fact that you are an African and are from Africa does not necessarily mean you may be sent to Africa or called to Africans, e.g. David Livingstone, a white man was called to Africa, Reinhard Bonkke, a white man to Africa, Sunday Adelaja, a black man to Ukraine, etc.
- Your calling has a 'what', a 'where', a 'when', a 'who', a 'with whom', a 'when', a 'why', a 'which' and a 'way' or 'how'. Be careful how you apply them. It is not everything that is now. When you have and are preaching the sent word and your voice is blessed from heaven, people will hear you and want to hear you any day; they never get bored or tired of hearing you and they will look for you – they will come and find you. You will be a sought-out one – Isaiah 55 & 62.

103. Ministry requires all you are and all that you have and keeping your eyes single by sitting on your assignment. 'DON'T SUCCEED OUTSIDE AND FAIL AT HOME.' - ARCHBISHOP BENSON IDAHOSA

104. Ministry involves reformation and transformation. We are men on a mission to produce effective global spiritual, physical, economic, mental, transformation, translation, transfiguration and social reformation in every sphere of life. We are here to turn the world upside down with the right side up. Acts 17:6 says, 'And when they found them not, they drew Jason and certain brethren unto the rulers of the city, crying, These that have turned the world upside down are come hither also;'

**Revival is not what goes on in your building. Until your ministry has an impact on the outside world, you've not started ministry.**

105. Ministry requires as of necessity daily communion with God for fresh manna [revelation] and instruction.

106. Effective ministry requires full dedication.

107. Ministry is vision and mission – accomplishing a divine mission /mandate (Joel 2:7). Ministry is an army that does not break its ranks. Ministry has ranking and ranking is not the same thing as titles. Ranking is placement and sequence for collective good. Where they were placed, they stayed there. There will be different churches - all significant. Don't form

your church according to another's pattern. God will reward us for faithfulness to what He has called us to do, not according to size. Understand the vision of God for your church. Be yourself, not someone else. Don't copy people's calling; you have your own calling.

2 Corinthians 10:12 says, 'For we dare not make ourselves of the number, or compare ourselves with some that commend themselves: but they measuring themselves by themselves, and comparing themselves among themselves, are not wise.'

Come to God and ask him to tell you what to do. Whatever you do, don't copy someone's assignment.

108. Ministry is not a career or venture you embark on or about personal ambition or popularity but about fulfilling destiny which calls for great sacrifice for your assignment backed by focus, discipline, determination, diligence and dedication. 'To win without risk is to triumph without glory.' [From frontline leadership mini-book by Dr. Myles Munroe]

109. Effective ministry requires a zero tolerance for procrastination, time-stealers and time-wasters. The time is short. Make every day and every minute count now and for eternity. Be careful about the passage of time. Anything left to time stays the same. Procrastination is a deadly weapon of the enemy '...a little sleep, a little slumber, a little more sleep.... and poverty will come on you as an armed robber.' (Proverbs 6:10-11) Poverty is a lack of productivity, so, utilise your time

well. Don't allow time-wasters around you. If people don't respect your time, they don't respect you or your gift. Make daily decisions that have eternal value and consequences. [Get my book the Dangers of Procrastination)

110. Ministry is about setting yourself on fire and people coming to watch you burn and catching your consistent fire to go set others on fire for Christ, kingdom purposes and to pursue their assignments in life.

111. Lasting ministry is not built on bringing in guest speakers always – train the flock to know and heed your voice – Jesus said, 'My sheep know my voice.' - STOP INVITING GUEST SPEAKERS ON AN ONGOING BASIS TO MILK, HARASS AND ERAZE YOUR MEMBERS BY RAISING AND RAISING OFFERINGS THROUGH CARNAL, MARKETING AND PUBLIC RELATIONS STRATEGIES. YOU DONT BUILD A LASTING MONUMENTAL CHURCH ON GUEST SPEAKERS.

112. Ministry is about impacting your world, your generation within and without the four walls of the church and beyond [with posterity clearly in mind]. Revival and causing waves is not what goes on in your building only. Until your ministry has an impact outside the four walls of your church that cannot be erased, you've not entered or started ministry.

113. Ministry is fulfilled according to His pattern. You are destined for upward movement only if you will conduct

ministry His way–**according to the pattern** shown you.

Hebrews 8:5, 'Who serve unto the example and shadow of heavenly things, as Moses was admonished of God when he was about to make the tabernacle: for, See, saith he, that thou make all things according to the pattern showed to thee in the mount.'

114. Impactful and life-transforming ministry is initiated, not waited for. **The next move of God in your life is entirely up to you. Discard the doctrine of waiting for God; God is waiting for you to 'pay the price – the required price.'**

115. Ministry begins with and is sustained by an understanding of and a persuasive settlement of whether you are called into full-time ministry or part-time [helps and marketplace ministry] and staying with it.

116. Ministry must always begin with a certified and definite calling:

a. Without a calling, ministry is more or less like a curse because it will be devoid of divine backing because Jesus said, 'Without me ye can do nothing.' Embarking on any ministry-related enterprise without a calling is tantamount to unending struggles and heartaches.

b. So, ministry begins with an understanding of your calling either into pastoral or itinerant [travelling ministry].

117. Ministry begins, grows and expands essentially by understanding the following: The 'who', the 'why', the 'where', the 'whom', the 'which', the 'where', the 'what' and the 'how' [the way]. That makes the journey colourful and fulfilling.

118. Ministry is sustained by a vigorous no-nonsense pursuit of your purpose in life. Proverbs 27:8, 'As a bird that wandereth from her nest, so is a man that wandereth from his place.'

119. Ministry involves knowing, being persuaded of your originality, staying original and not compromising your originality by being a photocopy of someone else whilst catching the spirit and embracing the virtues / disciplines of your mentors/father in the Lord.

120. The strength of your ministry and the guarantee of your supplies lie in the depth of your commitment to your core assignment. (Luke 8:1-3; 22:35) The strength of any ministry therefore is not in its spread, but in its depth; so preach the Word in season and out of season. (2 Timothy 4:2) Do not let anything or anyone take you off your core assignment because that is what determines your overall success in ministry.

121. Ministry essentially means a minister bearing a message that meets the needs of mankind through the instrumentality of the Word. (Acts 6)

122. Preaching the Word is what makes ministry and ministry is what makes money. The WORD is what determines the

quality of your ministry which in turn determines the quality of life you enjoy.

123. Ministry is not for weaklings but fighters – warriors.

Remember the following:
- **MINISTRY IS NOT FUNFARE; IT IS WARFARE!**
- **MINISTRY IS NOT A PLAYGROUND BUT A BATTLEGROUND!**
- **YOU DON'T SLEEP WITH VISION OR PROPHECY – YOU RUN, WORK AND WAR WITH IT!**
- **LIFE DOES NOT GIVE YOU WHAT YOU DESERVE BUT WHAT YOU DEMAND THROUGH CONTENTION IN BATTLE!**
- **BATTLES ARE WON ON THE PREMISE OF CONTENTION!**

God told Moses in **Deuteronomy 2:24, 'Rise ye up, take your journey, and pass over the river Arnon: behold, I have given into thine hand Sihon the Amorite, king of Heshbon, and his land: begin to possess it, and contend with him in battle.'**

And in Daniel 10, Daniel had to war with the prophecy concerning their return to their homeland from captivity.

SO: **PROPHECIES DON'T FULFIL THEMSELVES.** They are warred into reality as instructed in 1 Timothy 1:18-19 with emphasis on vs. 18, "This charge I commit unto thee son

Timothy according to the prophecies which went before on thee, that thou by them mightest war a good warfare; Holding faith and a good conscience which some having put away concerning faith have made shipwreck;" (KJV)

AMPLIFIED VERSION says, "This charge and admonition I commit in trust to you, Timothy, my son, in accordance with prophetic intimations which I formerly received concerning you, so that inspired and aided by them you may wage the good warfare… …."

That by them – that in their power or in the power of them [those prophetic words that have been spoken over your life/ministry] son, Timothy, use those words and war or wage a good warfare or inspired and aided by those prophetic words you may wage a good warfare.

124. Ministry is not just a commitment; it is a commission.

125. Ministry is a divine appointment not a self-appointment.

126. Ministry demands a definite and clearly-defined message – that is the core assignment of one's ministry.

127. Ministry is Word-made and Word-based. At the centre of every great ministry is the Word. (Acts 6:1-7; 2:37-47; 4:4, 30-32)

128. Ministry requires heavenly approval and heavenly

partnership. If you have heavenly approval and heavenly partnership, all you need to accomplish the mandate God has assigned to you, will be provided so you definitely accomplish it – it is made possible by heavenly backing.

129. Success in ministry is not measured by the quantity of accumulated possession, neither is it measured by popularity but rather consists of the attainment of God's goals and purposes for one's life as God told the prophet in Jeremiah 29:11. Discovering your God-given assignment and pursuing it is what ministry is.

130. My father in the Lord said: 'MINISTRY: Is neither a dream nor a trance. It's not a church title or leadership position held in a local Church. It's not an organisation or an association but rather a divine assignment handed down to a person by God. It is stewardship – serving as a messenger to carry out the orders of your superior. It is not an idea, a feeling or a burden but carrying out a given task. It is harnessing divine resources to carry out divine assignments committed into a man's hand. It is not limited to pulpit or to preaching as it were but covers every area of human need - social, moral, spiritual, physical, mental, etc. So, wherever divine intervention is needed for the gospel of the kingdom to be enhanced, God always dispatches human agents to stand in for Him and on his behalf.' (Amos 3:7; Isaiah 44:26)

131. Ministry demands you look to God as your main Source. The day you start having human sponsors for your ministry is

the day God stops being your sponsor. Human sponsors will pocket and limit your ministry. No matter the needs of your ministry, God has all it takes to meet them all. **Your resources are not in the hands of men but in His hands.**

132. A successful ministry is highly dependent on a successful family life.

133. Behind every successful ministry is a successful family life.

134. The Level of Opposition you face in ministry reveals your strong position.

135. The reality of an Open heaven over a ministry/church requires the Pastor to be a covenant practitioner – i.e. to be a tithing and giving Pastor and the ministry to remain a tithing and giving ministry/church.

136. Ministry is impossible without the anointing (Isaiah 11:1-3; Zechariah. 4:6-7)

137. REMEMBER: **The most important thing in ministry is to love God. Don't love your vision so much that you neglect God.**

138. In Ministry, Love is the key. (Matthew 22:35-39)
a. Love is the overriding and motivating force.
b. Love for God.

c. Love for Jesus.
d. Love for His people.
e. Love for His purpose.

139. The Ministry has everything to do with people.
a. It is called 'The People's Business'.
b. There is no future for any leader or ministry who is out to use people.
c. Serving others makes a leader - serving self makes a slave.

140. IN CLOSING THIS CHAPTER REMEMBER THE FOLLOWING:

a. Ministry is about people, not you – **It's People-related Ministry.**

b. Raise men, not offerings/money and you'll have all you need.

c. Bless people with all your heart when you preach, teach or talk to them and minister to them; leave them blessed.

d. Your prayer must be, 'They must become better people. God show me something that will empower them to be better to walk in dominion.'

e. **Revelation comes to you when you have such a craving and desire for people to be blessed with truth.**

f. People will gather anywhere where the grass is green and remains green – Psalm 23.

g. Bless them from your heart and they'll come from everywhere to hear you.

h. Don't charge people or levy them financially; bless people.

i. Don't preach to impress people. Preach to bless and impact them. Neither you nor your ministry will ever lack if you give yourself for them.

j. Seek their welfare, not their stuff. Give your whole life to bless the people of God selflessly. 2 Corinthians 12:14 says, 'Behold, the third time I am ready to come to you; and I will not be burdensome to you: **for I seek not yours, but you**: for the children ought not to lay up for the parents, but the parents for the children.'

Paul said, 'I do not seek yours but you. I am not coming to ask for your stuff, but to seek your/their prosperity, success and progress.'

k. Stop going for your members' pockets. The Law of connection says, 'You touch a heart before you ask for a hand.' As we discovered in my leadership manual: 'Pastoral Leadership 101' if you touch them, they will in turn touch you.

l. God does not need men or money to execute His intentions.

He needs faith, [Hebrews 11:6] because without faith it is impossible to please [move] Him and when a man's ways please the LORD, he maketh even his enemies to be at peace with him. (Proverbs 16:7)

Luke 22:35, 'And he said unto them, When I sent you without purse, and scrip, and shoes, lacked ye any thing? And they said, Nothing.' The man by the pool said he did not have anyone to put him in the pool when the Word, Jesus was right by the pool. It begins by faith and men come and put it together. God has prepared a total stranger to come in and give towards that cause. Pastor, don't dream according to the paper computations. We must walk by faith and do exploits for the kingdom. You don't need partners to do the work of God – you need heavenly partnership.

CHAPTER FOUR

# MINISTRY ORACLES FOR DISCERNING YOUR SEASON AND STAYING IN THE MOVE

This is a prophetic word and apostolic empowerment. We are in a season of the prophetic and apostolic. IN MINISTRY YOU ARE EITHER IN THE MOVE OR ARE REMOVED! YOU ARE EITHER IN THE MOVE OR ON THE SIDELINES. This section is to empower you with oracles to stay in the move. Oracles are divine secrets that are downloaded for the next move of God. They are simple but relevant for the season in which we are in our respective nations.

Dimensional doors: Every time God wants to do something new in your life or a nation, He sends someone to you/them – a leader. Amos 3:7 says, 'Surely the Lord GOD will do nothing, but he revealeth his secret unto his servants the prophets.' When He wanted to do a new thing in the life of Elisha, He sent him Elijah. He did the same for Israel by sending Moses, David, Nehemiah, John the Baptist and Jesus. It was Elijah who opened the dimensional door. If you don't discern in your spirit, you will look at the appearance of those He sends to you and miss your opportunity for change; if you are not very discerning, you will look at their clothes like John the Baptist and miss your door. ADVISE: In this coming new season and beyond, look out for people that are empowered by God for you.

There are some oracles for the kingdom now. There are some things you can preach or teach but ultimately it is God that brings the increase. If instead of judgment like the thief beside Jesus on the cross, a man can be marked for righteousness, and his position and destination to hell is changed to paradise, I prophesy to you that you and I will be marked for a definite change of position, a definite change of name, a positive and clear change of status and a permanent change of story from this year. The way forward will be clear. God has marked you and I for the unusual. The sceptre shall not depart from Judah until Shiloh comes. We therefore sanctify our atmospheres and declare it as a habitation for the move of God in this new season. Prepare for seven times more which is the number of God - we are about to enter a season of rest and like we said, rest does not connote non-productivity but our faithful seeds will catch up on us in a great and mighty harvest and we shall accomplish far more with less effort for the set time for God to favour us has come.

Proverbs 4:7-9, 'Wisdom is the principal thing; therefore get wisdom: and with all thy getting get understanding. Exalt her, and she shall promote thee: she shall bring thee to honour, when thou dost embrace her. She shall give to thine head an ornament of grace: [divine favour] a crown of glory shall she deliver to thee.'

1 Chronicles 12:29-32, 'And of the children of Benjamin, the kindred of Saul, three thousand: for hitherto the greatest part of them had kept the ward of the house of Saul. And of the children of Ephraim twenty thousand and eight hundred, mighty men of valour, famous throughout the house of their fathers. And of the half tribe of Manasseh eighteen thousand, which were expressed by name, to come and make David king. And of the children of Issachar, which were men that had understanding of the times, to know what Israel ought to do; the heads of them were two hundred; and all their brethren were at their commandment.'

You are in the Lord's hands - God is in control. Wisdom is a divine system that delivers grace. Wisdom is the principal thing so get wisdom. You do not need to be an apostle to operate under an apostolic mantle.

Even though the children of Benjamin chose to stay with Saul, the children of Issachar on the other hand:
i. [They] had understanding of the times
ii. [They] knew what Israel ought to do.

Let us examine the attitude of the Sons of Issachar and Sons of Benjamin in a time of transition i.e. in a time of change in Israel. The whole nation was in a time of transition. **Staying in the same spot in a season of rapid change can be disastrous and detrimental to you!**

## 21 FACTS TO KNOW AND HEED ABOUT TRANSITION:

1. To be in a time of transition and not know you are in a time of transition is perilous. Every church will be in a season of change.

2. The fact that you started that way does not mean you will remain that way. Alvin Toffler said: 'The illiterates of the 21$^{st}$ century are not those who cannot read and write but those who cannot learn, unlearn and relearn.'

3. Everyone with divine assignments will have seasons of transitions - you cannot avoid it lest you be seen to be fighting against God.

4. God will shift not because He has changed but because He's moving you. In the realm of the Spirit, we are in a shift, new wine in new wineskins, not old wine in new wineskins.

5. Methods are for seasons. To not understand your season can be disastrous. In the above passage, they were supposed to be a whole lot more than 3000 but they remained loyal to the house of Saul. 3000 people had the opportunity to join a new move with David as the leader but chose to stay with what was dead and only 200 could discern the shift and move over to David's side.

6. To stay on a side that has been removed or rejected by God in

a new move is suicidal. While Saul was reigning as king, it was alright to be loyal to Saul, but Saul was now being moved yet they locked themselves in an old move. They stuck close. You must understand the times to know what to do. Your season has changed - stop flogging the dead horse.

7. YOU MUST STOP OR KILL IN YOU WHAT HAS THE TENDENCY TO STOP OR KILL YOU: PROPHECY: There are some things you did last year which you can't afford to do anymore this year. There are some things in you which you thought was dead in you which you have discovered that given the right opportunity resurrected in you and were not dead at all which you need to kill definitely this year before they kill you.

Romans 8:13 says, 'For if ye live after the flesh, ye shall die: but if ye through the Spirit do mortify the deeds of the body, ye shall live.'

Colossians 3:5, 'Mortify therefore your members which are upon the earth; fornication, uncleanness, inordinate affection, evil concupiscence, and covetousness, which is idolatry:'

It could be quick temper, anger, depression, lack of self control etc. kill it.

CAUTION: You need to revisit and redefine some relationships you have from destructive to constructive or break away. There are some close friends or associates you had last year that you should break away from this year or they'll break you. There are some people you must break away from before they break away from you and break your heart. As Charles Tremendous Jones said, "You are the same today as you will be in five years time except for two things - the books you read and the friends you move with."

There are some sins you need to deal with before they deal with you and you need to finish sin before sin finishes you. Spend more time developing you before developing others but don't stay too long there.

8. We shouldn't become passionate to his doings and yet be deaf to his change. Psalm 103:7, 'He made known his ways unto Moses, his acts unto the children of Israel.'

9. You must understand the times to know what to do. Your season has changed - stop flogging the dead horse.
a. Don't be married to something God has killed.
b. Find out what He is saying now not only what He said yesterday.
c. If you marry yourself to something God was doing, you will miss what He's doing.
d. Understand the times and seasons, hear what He is saying and not what He was saying. It is a thing that comes from bended knees - totally submitted to God - asking God 'what are you saying now?'
e. To never want to step into the unknown because you are used to the old is dangerous.

10. Understand what God is saying about where you are now otherwise you are not in ministry. Our prayer is that we shall not miss the time of our visitation for lack of knowing - i.e. having a visitation but not knowing what to do.

11. Avoid the danger of being humanly loyal but being divinely displaced - out of tune with the finger of God. This is a tragedy we read in 1 Chronicles 12. The bible locates a bracket for them.

12. House of Saul is something that ruled before but no longer has the mandate to rule. The house of Saul is not a person but a system.

13. In ministry today you must remain born again because ministry is about ministering the mind of God to people. How can you talk to people about a God you haven't spoken to? You can be a Pastor and be disconnected from God. For Example: Eli was a priest but couldn't hear God; so, you can still be a man of God and yet not be hearing GOD. To avoid all that, you must maintain a passionate intimate walk with God. **Be in love with God more than His stuff. He says 'I am interested in relationship with you - that first and your church will grow.'**

14. It is possible to be a pastor and yet not know your season. We therefore have a choice either to be sons of Benjamin or sons of Issachar. The question is: Are you a player or a spectator? At every given point in time in ministry, you are

either on the pitch playing or on the stands watching. Make a quality decision not to watch but to make things happen.

15. At every given point in time in ministry, you are either, in the move and also on the move or are removed. Make a quality decision not to be removed but to be both in the move and on the move – in movement.

2 Kings 2:7-9, 'And fifty men of the sons of the prophets went, and stood to view afar off: and they two stood by Jordan. And Elijah took his mantle, and wrapped it together, and smote the waters, and they were divided hither and thither, so that they two went over on dry ground. And it came to pass, when they were gone over, that Elijah said unto Elisha, Ask what I shall do for thee, before I be taken away from thee. And Elisha said, I pray thee, let a double portion of thy spirit be upon me.'

Fifty [50] men of the school of prophets were at a distance - they stood afar off. **It is tragic when people that are schooled for greatness stand afar off in the time of visitation - in a time of new things. They were schooled for greatness but stood afar off when the shift came.**

To be by-passed - They didn't miss God because of moral failure but because they chose to stand by and watch from afar. It was a choice - that is why God said through Moses to the children of Israel like the church today in Deuteronomy 30:19, 'I call heaven and earth to record this day against you, that I have set before you life and death, blessing and cursing: therefore choose life, that both thou and thy seed may live:'

Joshua also reiterated this to the children of Israel in his day in Joshua 24:15 in a time of double-mindedness and indecision on their part by making his stand clear, saying 'And if it seem evil unto you to serve the LORD, choose you this day whom ye will serve; whether the gods which your fathers served that were on the other side of the flood, or the gods of the Amorites, in whose land ye dwell: but as for me and my house, we will serve the LORD.'

16. This new move is not for people who are passive but people who choose to engage. Die for something than live for nothing - think about what happens when people stand by observing events than participating in events. Haven't you heard the saying about a lot of things that have been destroyed because people chose not to say anything at a time when it was crucial that they said something? God is looking for people that are intoxicated for his kingdom like David; people who ask: 'Is there not a cause? I elect to confront Goliath.'

**Evil is perpetuated because of the silence of good people.**

**Evil is perpetuated not because darkness is stronger than light but because those who have the light don't switch it on.**

People on the stands don't break their ankle - they don't jog for 2-3 miles and watch their diet. They go only when a match is being played.

17. We live in a season where we must give ourselves com-

pletely for a worthy cause and if you can't fulfil the cause, life is not worth living. Islam has no message; it is perpetuated by certain things. The display of our faith is in what we do not in what we have.

18. Die for a cause than live for no cause.

19. Do something for what you stand for - don't just speak about it. Pursue what you stand for - live for a cause. Do something for the cause you stand for - don't just speak about it. The 50 who stood afar off who were called; they were part of the original school of prophets; they stood afar off even though they had an idea that God was moving in a new way. May you not stand afar off in this new move and in this new season while things decay around you or great things happen around you without your active, willing involvement and full commitment.

20. Those that journey take risks. Elisha was not guaranteed what Elijah had. When he saw there was a shift, it did not matter what his identity was in the past or in the old order as a business man; he pursued his identity in the new order. A company of 50 pastors were locked into an old order instead of pursuing cities God wanted to build.

21. Be led by the glory of His voice in any transition. **ADVANTAGES OF BEING LED BY THE GLORY OF HIS VOICE – BY THE SPIRIT OF THE LORD:** Isaiah 48:17, 'Thus saith the LORD, thy Redeemer, the Holy One of Israel;

I am the LORD thy God which teacheth thee to profit, which leadeth thee by the way that thou shouldest go. O that thou hadst hearkened to my commandments! then had thy peace been as a river, and thy righteousness as the waves of the sea: Thy seed also had been as the sand, and the offspring of thy bowels like the gravel thereof; his name should not have been cut off nor destroyed from before me. Go ye forth of Babylon, flee ye from the Chaldeans, with a voice of singing declare ye, tell this, utter it even to the end of the earth; say ye, The LORD hath redeemed his servant Jacob. And they thirsted not when he led them through the deserts: he caused the waters to flow out of the rock for them: he clave the rock also, and the waters gushed out. There is no peace, saith the LORD, unto the wicked.'

Romans 8:14, 'For as many as are led by the Spirit of God, they are the sons of God.'

PROPHECY:
- You will not thirst if you are led by him through the deserts.
- When God leads you by his glorious and majestic voice, God will cause waters to flow out of the rock for you; he will clave the rock and the waters will gush out towards you while there is dryness in other places like the light that shone in Goshen in the same land of Egypt which was experiencing darkness.
- This season, waters will gush out towards you in your life, in your vocation, in your profession, in your ministry and in your business.
- Whilst the mockers are mocking, the Maker will make you.

Song: Speak to me, I shall not be dismayed, show me your love, for my life; Open my eyes, I shall see, the wonders of your word, for my life.

- Concerning where to go, what to do, grace for distinctive hearing from heaven, receive it now in the name of Jesus.

- No more trial and error or beating the air in the pursuit of your destiny in Jesus' name. Let the Assyrians be smitten down in the name of Jesus. This is going to be the greatest season in your life and your ministry - nothing in your hand is permitted to die in the name of Jesus. AMEN!

CHAPTER FIVE

# SECURING THE BLESSING OF GOD ON YOUR MINISTRY

## HOW TO SECURE THE BLESSING OF GOD ON YOUR LIFE AND MINISTRY

Proverbs 10:22, 'The blessing of the LORD, it maketh rich, and he addeth no sorrow with it.'

Psalm 127, '...Except the LORD build the house, they labour in vain that build it: except the LORD keep the city, the watchman waketh but in vain. It is vain for you to rise up early, to sit up late, to eat the bread of sorrows: for so he giveth his beloved sleep. Lo, children are an heritage of the LORD: and the fruit of the womb is his reward. As arrows are in the hand of a mighty man; so are children of the youth. Happy is the man that hath his quiver full of them: they shall not be ashamed, but they shall speak with the enemies in the gate.'

In this Psalm, he talks about three things – BUILDING, WATCHING and CHILDREN – and has his quiver full of them.

Seek God for what He wants to do. A voice must come first. You must ask, 'Where is the God of today?'

5 WAYS TO SECURE or GUARANTEE the BLESSING of God that enriches your ministry – as reminders and oracles, they don't fail.
- There is a divine move of God in the atmosphere.
- This will be spearheaded by a people who don't have a name.
- It's not in working harder – it's principles.
- God wants to deploy principles of enrichment.
- The Law of principles must be understood and embraced – it prevents shipwreck.
- Don't attempt to do anything without understanding the principles that undergird it.
- Our prayer as pastors shouldn't be 'Grow my church' rather it should be 'Grow me, teach me, show me the principles of ministry.'
- Until then God will keep you in one spot until you understand the principles.
- Whenever God wants to move you into another dimension of His glory, He deploys principles, covenants, insights and understandings e.g. Moses had to meet God in a fire – you will understand what you are doing.
- Incline your ear to hear - Saul of Tarsus, before he became Paul, had a Damascus road experience; God took him to the wilderness of Arabia and taught him.
- Jeremiah 33:3 – Answer us Lord and show us principles.
- Psalm 37:22 – If you are blessed by God no one can stop

you.
- Pull down on you the blessings of God.
- Psalm 107:38 - The blessing of God on you forbids decrease in your quarters because God does not allow decrease in your quarters – Jeremiah 30:19.
- What you need to understand is how to be blessed by God.
- Psalm 113:7-8 – To partake of the coming glory you must understand this.
- The BLESSING is like a spiritual credit card / cheque book.
- You cannot be blessed and look like everybody else.
- People that are blessed by God are exceptional / different.
- When you are blessed by God, people send for you to show you what you need to know and what you need to do to get to the next level of glory in your life e.g. Cornelius.
- Ignorance and darkness is a curse.
- Tectonic plates are shifting.
- There are some things we need to know – it's not in books – it's what we hear in our time with God.

**The question then is:**
**HOW DO WE WALK IN THE BLESSING OF GOD?**

**These are 5 TRUTHS THAT WILL TERMINATE YOUR STRUGGLE.** These are Time-Tested and Eternally-Tested Truths.

## 1. KNOW YOU ARE BLESSED BECAUSE OF WHO GOD IS.

- The Blessings of God rests on those who know it is God. (Daniel 11:32)
- You are about to be asked a question – the answer you give will take you to your next level.
- Joseph answered Pharaoh's question and his level was changed dramatically from a prisoner to a prime minister.
- Daniel answered King Nebuchadnezzar's questions and he was appointed the president of presidents and his three friends were also appointed as cabinet ministers, administrators and advisors.
- They will send for you and you will know it is God. It is a God-factor.
- There are certain things only God can script or do.
- God has an agenda and has the capacity to bless you beyond what you ever imagined.
- God can do anything He wants for anyone without anyone's permission.
- Your church gets blessed because of who God is.
- God can take a Jacob, Rahab, Esther, a failure and make you a brilliant person; he took Abraham and made him the father of faith. That's a God thing!
- Anything I am and anything I have and will be is a God-Factor.
- May the God-Factor speak for me.
- May the God-Factor attach itself to me.
- Church growth, finances, owning your own building is all a God-Factor. (2 Thessalonians 1:12)

- The God-Factor will work for me.
- Whatever does not reveal the glory in our life and ministry stops now.
- Anything that has legitimate pursuit of you in your past gives way now to God's unprecedented favour.
- Whatever has a legitimate right in your past to harm you, we release the favour of God and his mercy.
- I deploy a God-factor in your direction - we bury it in the blood; we release favour and mercy. Satan, the blood is against you – it is over!
- There are some things that God will do for you that has nothing to do with you - it is a God-factor; it is called the blessing of the Lord that maketh rich and addeth no sorrow to it. HE IS GOD!

## 2. GODLY LIVING unleashes the Blessing of God.
- Godliness is profitable in all things.
- Righteousness is a force in the spirit that provokes the blessing of God.
- Iniquity has a price and sometimes it's not obvious – it results in lost dominion.
- God is calling the church back to purity both in the pulpit and in the pew.
- Godliness is a principal requirement for power in ministry.
- Lasting success, continuous growth and effectiveness in ministry requires godliness.
- We must be able to say with Jesus the devil comes but hath nothing in me.
- Numbers 23 (Don't be lured by gifts – obey God)

- Adam and Eve lost a lot by the fall.
- The fact that you are getting away with it does not mean you are not paying for it.
- GREATNESS is in two categories: There's primary greatness and secondary greatness.
- Primary greatness is not what you did or can do – it is who you are and what you are while secondary greatness is visibility gift – gift to fame.
- Godliness addresses inherent greatness – it is who I am – it provokes the blessing of God.
- God-factor comes from the live-right factor.
- We must deal with any force or cycle of iniquity in our life before it deals with us – live right.
- Integrity – righteousness is a force that lifts.
- Whatever spiritual resource is required take it off and out of your suitcase now.
- Whatever requires off-loading resolve to offload it now.
- When you arrive there must be nothing - it is not about now it is about the arrival point, the checkpoint.
- When the light shines brighter, the flaws become obvious.
- Drink of the spirit of godliness.
- Stop it; deal with it; address it.

## 3. BLESSED BY ASSOCIATION

- Find people that are truly blessed; genuinely carrying the blessing – it is extremely contagious - E.g. Jacob–Laban; Potiphar–Joseph; Naomi– Ruth-Boaz
- How do you associate? Associate wisely – in a wise fashion.
- Embark on a journey of discovery and investment – find out

why they are blessed. HOW?

1. Learn and study them closely – carry their bible so you can observe watch them.
2. Sow into the association, financially, with time, service, prayer, put into practice what you learn from them - Be consistent about this association.
3. Disassociate from those who are not blessed – it is contagious too – if you are not careful what they carry will rub off on you – plug into the right socket – find the right plug.

**4. PLACE A DEMAND IN PRAYER TO BE BLESSED.**
- Private prayer will hand you blessing.
- Bent-over travail in the spirit opens the heavens.
- Makes things happen.
- Breaks the fallow ground.
- Provokes a move.
- Is the womb out of which comes miracles.
- Pray to the God of miracles.
- Until the angel over the ministry is prayerful nothing will happen, e.g. Elijah prayed until the heavens opened – Jabez, prayed until his name, status and situation was changed; Jacob prayed until the break of day... .....pray until... ... ......
- It is through the womb of prayer that the supernatural is birthed, souls are saved.
- Pray until every seat is filled in your spirit.
- Pray until you know God has heard your prayer.
- Bind the strongman.
- Your own prayer life – you the pastor (James 5:16)

## 5. MAKE SURE THAT YOU WALK, UNDERSTAND AND ARE UNDER SPIRITUAL AUTHORITY AND COVERING

- God blesses people who remain loyal to and stay in the family tree.
- Stay there.
- Don't end up like Lot in Genesis 13 or the prodigal son [You can order my book LEADERSHIP SECRETS for more insight from our website: www.houseofjudah.org.uk]

SUMMARY: 5 things to secure Proverbs 10:22
- Recognize that He is God – The God-Factor
- Live a holy life
- Associate with blessed people
- Pray deliberately for the blessing
- Find your spiritual authority and family tree and stay there

CHAPTER SIX

# 21 MAJOR DETERMINANTS OF LASTING SUCCESS AND LONGEVITY IN MINISTRY

IT IS WORTH REMINDING YOU OF THESE CRUCIAL STATEMENTS mentioned in chapter two as we begin this section:

The day a pilot is tired of checking his manual and stops reading or referring to his manual is the day he begins to dig his grave. Every pilot is married to his manual; it is impossible to embark on a flight without the manual in your bag. Every pilot is a bag carrier - he does not put biscuit or cake in his bag; he puts his manual in his bag. If he wakes up at night and is confused or not sure about something he refers to his manual before going back to bed, because you cannot fly on your opinions, you can only fly on valid instructions. That's why those who train pilots are called instructors not just teachers. Reason being, you can't fly on your feelings; you can only fly on valid instructions. His uniform is not as important to him as his manuals so, he lays it on his lap because he can't risk guessing - he can't depend on guess work, which button to press, so he keeps checking it. **It is only those who want to crash who stop doing what makes them fly.**

Every time you see a man who is tired of checking the manual he is heading for disaster that will culminate in destruction to both his life and that of his passengers. That manual is the guarantee, the security of your destiny. How familiar you are with the manual will determine how smooth your flight will be. That is why God told Joshua at the onset of his ministry in Joshua 1:8, 'This book of the law shall not depart out of thy mouth; but thou shalt meditate therein day and night, that thou mayest observe to do according to all that is written therein: for then thou shalt make thy way prosperous, and then thou shalt have good success.'

It is the only way to make your way prosperous - by observing to do, not observing to quote or observing to preach but you observe to do! You don't prosper on what you preach; rather, you prosper on what you practice. You don't get tired of reading this manual; when one is getting tired, worn out or old you renew it because you can't afford to miss one letter. You don't buy a new suit when your bible is torn or worn out; your suit is so they can have access to and listen to you.

THIS IS YOUR Number one wife in ministry so, you have to get married to it; you and your wife can crash without it, but with it you can't crash. Take this manual in your hand; Take this manual in your hand; the pilot does not decorate his library with it; he decorates his mind with it. This is how it is with the pilot; he puts the manual on his lap and looks out there at the sky and sees what is coming at him or what is approaching - the weather, rain, cloud, snow, turbulence, etc. at that time his focus is not on home - he does not think of his wife or children but rather how he can fly and get the plane back on land so he can go and see his wife and family. That's why scripture says in Isaiah 60:8, 'Who are these that fly' i.e. who are these that are married to the manual who are not preachers of the manual but are practitioners of its content? So, it's not just reading or quoting scriptures. Any one at all can quote!

Don't only focus on the gifts of the spirit because even a donkey, prophesied in the bible so you don't have to be saved to prophesy, because the ass wasn't saved yet it prophesied so focus on developing the fruits of the spirit than the gifts so that the gifts can be seen to be genuine and of God. So concentrate your energies on what matters. If you are determined to remain on this flight then be married to this manual - keep checking it, keep checking it. Know why everything happens, know why you are prospering; know why you are growing as a church so you keep doing it.

IF YOU LIVE YOUR LIFE ON CHANCE YOU DON'T HAVE A CHANCE. YOU HAVE TO LIVE IT ON FACTS! The manual [The Bible] is the security of your destiny; you cannot afford to decorate your shelf with it, you cannot afford to be quoting it and sweating on quotations; you have to begin sweating on the practice. These fundamental instructions are things that are considered fundamental if you are going to scale heights in the pursuit of and fulfil your divine assignment in ministry. Psalm 11:3, 'If the foundation be destroyed, what can the righteous do?'

## IGNORANCE IS NO EXCUSE!

In Luke 12:47-48, the fact that you don't know does not excuse you from what you have to suffer i.e. stripes. It may be reduced but you still have to pay for it. As we look at these fundamental instructions which are major determinants of our lasting success and longevity both in life and especially ministry it will help to mould our behaviour towards practical accomplishment of His purpose for our lives because ignorance is no excuse in the kingdom. We are told that the moon has no light of its own; rather all it does is to align itself at a particular angle to the sun and this glorious moonlight which is celebrated worldwide is nothing but a reflection of the light that comes from the sun. It does not generate its own heat but aligns itself to the heat of the sun and so reflects its light. In the same way the Sun of Righteousness generates the heat and the moon simply reflects the glory; so we are not created for heat generation. We are not programmed to go through a tough and tense life. Things are tough, rough and tense because of wrong alignment. He is the Sun of righteousness with healing in his wings so align and reflect His glory. He generates the heat that produces the light and when we are properly aligned we simply reflect the light.

## MINISTRY IS EASY!

# EASE IN MINISTRY

Jesus said come unto me all who are weak and are heavy laden and I will give you rest for my yoke is easy and my burden is light ... come and learn of me ... come and find out how to be correctly positioned and you'll find rest for your life for my yoke is easy and my burden is light - all you need to do is learn of me - Joshua 1:8. So ministry is intended for ease not for struggle, not for tension, not for perspiration, not for sweating, not for frustration but rest. So ministry is designed for ease, for my yoke is easy and my burden is light if you are ready to learn of me. If it's not easy then there are things you should have learnt and until you learn them you'll keep suffering the tensions. If I know what to do and put them to work I will experience the ease that ministry is designed to offer - my yoke is easy and my burden is light. MY ONLY YOKE I need to carry is to learn - learn of Him.

Carry the yoke of a learner - come and learn of me and I will give you rest for your soul for my yoke is easy and my burden is light. There is one glory of the sun and another glory of the moon and one star and one exceeds the other in glory; we are never called the sun; no, we are only identified with stars; and stars reflect the light from the sun just like the moon does so we reflect the light of the sun just as the moon does. So, we are to be reflectors not generators of heat and sweating all around because certain things are not being done right. Your paths must shine more and more unto the perfect day.

**REMEMBER:**
What you hear determines what you believe!
What you believe determines how you behave!
How you behave determines what you become!

**CORRECT POSITIONING:** So take advantage of all these teachings on ministry because it will largely determine what will become of you. If the foundation be destroyed what can the righteous do. Leave the Sun of righteousness to keep generating the heat and let us be correctly positioned to reflect the light. That's how easy it is so your correct positioning is vital to the realization of your destiny. The following determinants - fundamental truths therefore will help each of us to possess the correct perspective towards our work and towards the CALLER. It will go on to determine how far you go in your pursuit.

**WHAT SEEST THOU?**

He said in Jeremiah 1:11-12, 'Moreover the word of the LORD came unto me, saying, Jeremiah, what seest thou? And I said, I see a rod of an almond tree. Then said the LORD unto me, Thou hast well seen: for I will hasten my word to perform it.'

So, when you see well enough you enjoy great speed in your pursuit - YOU SEE WELL ENOUGH AND YOU ENJOY GREAT SPEED IN YOUR PURSUIT.

## 21 MAJOR DETERMINANTS OF LASTING SUCCESS AND LONGEVITY IN MINISTRY

LIFE IS NOT MEASURED IN DURATION [How long you lived] BUT IN DONATIONS. [The contributions you made to impact lives]

### 1. RECOGNIZE THAT YOU ARE NOT CALLED ON MERIT:

1 Corinthians 1:26-29, 'For ye see your calling, brethren, how that not many wise men after the flesh, not many mighty, [strong] not many noble, are called: But God hath chosen the foolish things of the world to confound the wise; and God hath chosen the weak things of the world to confound the things which are mighty; And base things of the world, and things which are despised, hath God chosen, yea, and things which are not, to bring to nought things that are: That no flesh should glory in his presence.'

So, if you are called into ministry, please recognize that you have not been called on merit. We have been called by mercy. It is only a grace of election because he said to Jeremiah in Jeremiah 1:5, 'Before I formed thee in the belly I knew thee; and before thou camest forth out of the womb I sanctified thee, and I ordained thee a prophet unto the nations.'

Then as recorded in Romans 9:10-16, there were two children Jacob and Esau in Rebecca's womb and before they were born,

God made His choice so you are HIS PRIVILEGED CHOICE, not a right - you are His Privileged Choice, so don't be proud as a minister. Scriptures state: 'And not only this; but when Rebecca also had conceived by one, even by our father Isaac; (For the children being not yet born, neither having done any good or evil, that the purpose of God according to election might stand, not of works, but of him that calleth;) It was said unto her, The elder shall serve the younger. As it is written, Jacob have I loved, but Esau have I hated. What shall we say then? Is there unrighteousness with God? God forbid. For he saith to Moses, I will have mercy on whom I will have mercy, and I will have compassion on whom I will have compassion. So then it is not of him that willeth, nor of him that runneth, but of God that showeth mercy.'

That was how you were chosen because He is the same yesterday today and forever [Hebrews 13:8]. While you were in your mother's womb he separated you and said I won't let him die - I will keep him as the apple of my eye because I have ordained him to serve in My vineyard so it was not on merit. Paul, the apostle said in Galatians 1:15, 'But when it pleased God, who separated me from my mother's womb, and called me by his grace,..'

So, you are not called on merit. That will help you, to keep a regular size for your head; your head will not blow up. If you are called, I called you because you are among the foolish, I called you because you are among the weak, I called you because you are not - not means zero - people that have no value and have no worth. So recognize that you have not been called on merit. Paul said in 1 Corinthians 15:9-10 'For I am the least of the apostles, that am not meet [even worthy] to be called an apostle, because I persecuted the church of God. But by the grace of God I am what I am: and his grace which was bestowed upon me was not in vain; but I laboured more abundantly than they all: yet not I, but the grace of God which was with me.'

I am not even worthy to be called an apostle, so, Paul was not called because he was a PhD in legal studies or a popular man in politics. Brethren, see your calling how that not many mighty men are called so you are not listed among the mighty at all. We are only called and separated by the grace of election. Knowing and being mindful of this will help to balance your approach to your duty, that you are not called on merit.

## 2. THOUGH YOU ARE NOT CALLED ON MERIT YOU ARE ALSO NOT INDISPENSABLE:

Jesus said to a man, 'follow me' and he said I won't follow you. After this incident, there was no reference to that issue anymore throughout scripture. That was how irrelevant his calling was. Jesus never reflected on it once. There were better neighbours on the line and he was selected but he refused and blew it big time. You are not called on merit; you are not indispensable. He said woe unto him that trusteth in man and maketh the arm of man his strength. So, the One who said don't put your trust in a man couldn't possibly have violated his own law by turning around and trust in a man to fulfil his program or purpose on the earth. So, your answering God's call is not to God's advantage and you are not doing Him or your leader a favour by answering the call or assisting in any ministry. YOU ARE DOING YOURSELF, YOUR DESTINY AND YOUR SEED A FAVOUR - SO GET ON WITH IT!

**Your answering the call is purely a privilege of your destiny.**

You are not called on merit; you are not indispensable. In Luke 19:40, Jesus said if these ones should keep quiet even the stones will take their place. In other words, my PROGRAM CANNOT BE GROUNDED because of anyone's refusal. I can get stones to take the place of human beings. My program cannot be hindered - delayed - cancelled - thwarted or limited by man's response. You are not called on merit; you are not indispensable! You are not called on merit; I am not called on merit! You are not indispensable; I am not indispensable!

In 1981, God told my father in the Lord Bishop Oyedepo, 'I have not called you because you are smarter or better or more intelligent than others. Should you abuse this privilege, there are 100's better neighbours of yours at the door.'

REMEMBER: **GOD IS NEVER IN SHORT SUPPLY OF HANDS. His crowns are transferable crowns - the crowns are transferable.** That's why He said to hold fast that which is in thy hands lest another man take thy crown. (Revelation 3:11) **The crown is made to fit – IT'S UNIVERSAL SIZE!**

When it falls off your head, someone else picks it. Who knows whether you are taking somebody's place right now? You are not indispensable. This will help your response to duty and your fellowship with God. God is not using you - you are the one using God i.e. what He has to make it. King Saul was told in 1 Samuel 15:28, there is someone better than you.

You and I are on the stage today as it were depriving a better person from doing what we are doing. God says when one falls I have a better reserve. In the world, in football they put their second best as reserves but God puts His best as reserves so when you play up they take over from you and end up doing a better job than you. They are on reserve, crying 'Lord, use me,' wishing that someone breaks his legs that they will come in. A better neighbour of yours! I have a better neighbour of yours who can accomplish what you've accomplished in 10 years, in five years. He said to Saul the kingdom has been torn from you not because the kingdom has now crashed but because you crashed. This perspective will help your balance. When people become proud, God gets angry with them and moves them out of the way - may you not crash. 'You think I'm using you, no, you are using me - you are blocking me from using someone better than you.'

## 3. THE WORD THAT IS EFFECTIVE IS THE ONE THAT HE GIVES:

So, when anyone claps from the effect of the words that you preach or teach from your mouth you must not mistake it for a clap and an ovation for you. The Lord gave the word and great was the company of them that published it - Psalm 68:11. Psalm 107:20 says, 'He sent His word and it [the word] healed them and [the word] delivered them out of all their destructions.'

So it is His word that is effectual in your lips - the word that He gives, He said the Holy Spirit will fill you up and show you what to say. You don't have to crack your head about what to say, I will be speaking those words through you. During Jesus' triumphant entry into Jerusalem, the donkey on which Jesus rode would have made a big mistake in developing a big head if he assumed that the Hosanna cheers from the crowd was for him. They were clapping for and because of Jesus and in the same way your hearers are clapping not because of you but because of the words that God put in your heart to preach from and with your lips. So, have a proper attitude, perspective and balance for the ovation that is coming from the congregation so it doesn't go to your head because He shares His glory with no man. When you find men rising in ovation, they are rising in ovation to the Source of the Word that is impacting their lives. The Lord gave the word and great was the company of them that published it; the Lord sent His word and it healed them and delivered them out of their own destructions.

**4. BE WARNED THAT WHETHER YOU ARE A FOUNDER, SENIOR PASTOR OR THE LEADER, YOU DON'T HAVE CAPACITY TO OWN THE CHURCH YOU PASTOR:**

No mortal man, no matter how anointed has capacity to own a church so to pose ownership is to depose yourself. The day you think you own the church you pastor is the day the OWNER will disown you. The gates of hell will not allow any church owned by a mortal man to survive. Jesus said in Matthew 16:18 'I will build my church and the gates of hell will not prevail against it.' That tells you why many churches that have crashed, had to crash. You can't own a church; it must never cross your mind for you to even say, 'My church or my members.' You must shiver at the thought of even saying that. When the church is growing you are not the one growing it because Paul the apostle said, in 1 Corinthians 3:6, 'I have planted, Apollos watered; but God gave the increase.'

God is the one that brings the increase, otherwise the growth will stop.

Psalm 127:1 says, 'Except the Lord builds the house, they labour in vain that build it.' Every house is built by some man but he that builds all things is God. Yes we have a part to play, yes, but after we've done our part, God is still the One who determines the increase. Paul is planting not that he is sleeping, Apollos is watering not that he is snoring but it is God that gives the increase. This perspective will help you in maintaining an ever-growing church in your various assignments. **You can't own a church.**

## 5. THE PEOPLE ARE NOT YOUR MEMBERS – YOU ARE ALSO A MEMBER OF THE BODY:

1 Corinthians 12:12 says, 'For as the body is one, and hath many members, and all the members of that one body, being many, are one body: so also is Christ.'

We are members one of another. If you see them as your members, you are likely to abuse them, misuse them and assault them. Verse 27 says: 'Now ye are the body of Christ, and members in particular.' So, we are members one of another. These verses clearly define the fact that the people in the church that we are serving or the church we are sent to begin must never be visualized as your members. It must not cross your mind thoughtless to the extent of passing through your mouth. They are not your members; we are all members of one body called Christ. If you see them as your members you are likely to abuse them.

**VERY IMPORTANTLY, LET'S EXAMINE HOW GOD QUALIFIES THE FLOCK:**

**REASON: Your attitude largely determines your altitude. The way you think is largely determined by the information that is available to you and also the level of your spiritual and natural understanding. So, when you have the correct information and revelation, it renews your way of thinking and your way of thinking renews the steps you are taking and the steps you are taking determines your speed [i.e. acceleration - how fast you are going] and how soon you get to your destination.**

## SUMMARY: They are not your members!

1 Corinthians 12:18 says, 'But now hath God set the [HIS] members every one of them in the body, as it hath pleased HIM.'

### WARNING TO BREAKAWAY PASTORS

Do you know why many breakaway pastors break away? It's because they think the people are their members. From their shallow understanding, they say things like 'I introduced them to the church and brought this number of people to the church so when am leaving they must follow me' or 'You know how many people I have brought to this church? I have added at least 500 people to this church so when it is time to move on and set up my own, they must come with me; you can't transfer me out of this town, I have about 450 members, where else will I go when I have about 1000 people that are my members here in this church I have helped to raise?' YOU "DON'T 'LOST' YOUR MIND!"

### THE KIND OR CALIBRE OF PASTORS THAT GOD LOVES/BLESSES

The calibre of Pastors that God loves dearly and keeps blessing and increasing are the kind that do not own the churches they pastor or serve - the kind that no matter what takes place in the churches they pastor, there is nothing that they have any internal stake in; they have no stake overtly or covertly in the churches they have been privileged to lead. They feel no pinch if God tells them to move out of that location. Because to them they did not do anything there - GOD DID IT! The moment you have a personal possessive view of His work, He deposes you. When you do that, He says He will collect His sheep from the pastors in Ezekiel 34. **God does not hide His feelings.**

Vs. 1-3: And the word of the LORD came unto me, saying, Son of man, prophesy against the shepherds of Israel, prophesy, and say unto them, Thus saith the Lord GOD unto the shepherds; Woe be to the shepherds of Israel that do feed themselves! should not the shepherds feed the flocks? Ye eat the fat, and ye clothe you with the wool, ye kill them that are fed: but ye feed not the flock.

- You eat the fat they produce and clothe yourself but don't feed them

Vs. 4: The diseased have ye not strengthened, neither have ye healed that which was sick, neither have ye bound up that which was broken, neither have ye brought again that which was driven away, neither have ye sought that which was lost; but with force and with cruelty have ye ruled them.

- They saw them and handled them as their properties.

Vs. 5: And they were scattered, because there is no shepherd: and they became meat to all the beasts of the field, when they were scattered.

Vs. 6: My sheep wandered through all the mountains, and upon every high hill: yea, my flock was scattered upon all the face of the earth, and none did search or seek after them.

Vs. 7: Therefore, ye shepherds, hear the word of the LORD;

Vs. 8: As I live, saith the Lord GOD, surely because my flock became a prey, and my flock became meat to every beast of the field, because there was no shepherd, neither did my shepherds search for my flock, but the shepherds fed themselves, and fed not my flock;

In all these God keeps saying my, my, my sheep, my flock, my......my flock, my.....my......my....... Not yours...but my.......but because you thought they were your own that is why you cruelly handled them. He said they are my sheep, my flock but see how you bastardize them......the shepherds have fed themselves instead of feeding my flock...lead them, feed them.....

**LISTEN TO THE WARNING BECAUSE OF THEIR ATTITUDES to God's Flock - the consequences:**

Vs. 9-10: Therefore, O ye shepherds, hear the word of the LORD; Thus saith the Lord GOD; Behold, I am against the shepherds; and I will require my flock [whose flock] at their hand, and cause them to cease from feeding the flock; [I will retire them] neither shall the shepherds feed themselves anymore; for I will deliver my flock from their mouth, that they may not be meat for them.

- God says, I will take my sheep from their hands - they won't have anybody to pastor again.

Mark the words: my...my flock my sheep my my...so when you begin to see them as or call them my flock or my members your wife can remind you 'This is not your flock, it is His flock'. In order that you don't take the wrong step which will end up with you unemployed, she will strongly remind you of what God the OWNER said in the manual of life - they are His flock, not yours. If you or your wife are insulting the members calling them stupid and telling them to go, etc., you can be reminded please don't let him take this church or ministry or these members from our hands; don't let Him retire us or else I will have nobody to pastor.

Have you not seen empty churches that were once filled or ministers who have gone into oblivion? Yes you have; so, don't mess with God or with His flock. They are not your members. They are not your flock. They are not your sheep. Those caught or who find themselves saying 'my members, my sheep, my church'... such people may not be around after a while. You should tell the staff, you are not my staff, I cannot engage you; the one who has the field is the one that owns and pays His labourers. So when someone says, 'my ministry, my ministry,' he's lost his mind - That you are employed in a vineyard does not make the vineyard your own.

From Matthew 20:1-6, 'For the kingdom of heaven is like unto a man that is an householder, which went out early in the morning to hire labourers into his vineyard. And when he had agreed with the labourers for a penny a day, he sent them into his vineyard. And he went out about the third hour, and saw others standing idle in the marketplace, And said unto them; Go ye also into the vineyard, and whatsoever is right I will give you. And they went their way. Again he went out about the sixth and ninth hour, and did likewise. And about the eleventh hour he went out, and found others standing idle, and saith unto them, Why stand ye here all the day idle?'

From the above passage of scripture, He saw us wandering and gave us employment. Most of us were wanderers when He called us. Do you now lay claim to something because you were the first one to arrive? You are only a foreman who just came before the others - a fore labourer. You came before the others but we are all labourers. You don't assume ownership because you were the first to arrive or because you arrived on-time. The people are not your people. When people join our churches we receive references from their former pastors; we ask them to go for a release but now what some ministers are doing is boldly telling people 'come, come, and join my church. I have a position for you; come and let me ordain you; I can do it easily without any checking or references' - no ethics.

**SOME ARE EVEN GETTING ORDAINED ONLINE AS PASTORS! Others are being lured with titles and position!** Why? **They are not conversant with the manual and so it's**

**so easy to crash.** No Reference! ADVISE: Don't send the members on errands at the expense of their family obligations except they volunteer without it affecting their job or family.

**WARNING:**
- They are not your members.
- They are not your flock.
- They are not your sheep.
- So, if you don't want the Owner to terminate you, terminate your employment or to retire you, prematurely, better change your disposition. You have no right to abuse God's honour in their life.
- If the members are not your members neither are the staff.

Vs. 11: For thus saith the Lord GOD; Behold, I, even I, will both search my sheep, and seek them out.

Vs. 12: As a shepherd seeketh out his flock in the day that he is among his sheep that are scattered; so will I seek out my sheep, and will deliver them out of all places where they have been scattered in the cloudy and dark day.

Vs. 13: And I will bring them out from the people, and gather them from the countries, and will bring them to their own land, and feed them upon the mountains of Israel by the rivers, and in all the inhabited places of the country.

Vs. 14-15: I will feed them in a good pasture, and upon the high mountains of Israel shall their fold be: there shall they lie in a good fold, and in a fat pasture shall they feed upon the mountains of Israel. I will feed my flock, and I will cause them to lie down, saith the Lord GOD.

So, when you continue to abuse them [His sheep], His flock, His members] He deposes you so He can reposition His sheep well and look for another shepherd for them [the flock]. I prophesy, No one reading this book will ever tell his story of when he was a bishop, pastor, minister, elder, deacon or leader [he used to be a pastor].

vs. 16: I will seek that which was lost, and bring again that which was driven away, and will bind up that which was broken, and will strengthen that which was sick: but I will destroy the fat and the strong; I will feed them with judgment.

**WARNING TO THE FLOCK/CONGREGATION**

Don't foul or destroy where you feed, eat from or draw your spiritual feed – be grateful or you will face my judgment:

Vss. 17-18: And as for you, O my flock, thus saith the Lord GOD; Behold, I judge between cattle and cattle, between the rams and the he goats. Seemeth it a small thing unto you to have eaten up the good pasture, but ye must tread down with your feet the residue of your pastures? and to have drunk of the deep waters, but ye must foul the residue with your feet?

Make it easy for others to come and draw feed, nourishment, strength and encouragement from His house:

Vss. 19-20: And as for my flock, they eat that which ye have trodden with your feet; and they drink that which ye have fouled with your feet. Therefore thus saith the Lord GOD unto them; Behold, I, even I, will judge between the fat cattle and between the lean cattle.

Don't mistreat each other or you will be judged:

Vss. 21-22: Because ye have thrust with side and with shoulder, and pushed all the diseased with your horns, till ye have scattered them abroad; Therefore will I save my flock, and they shall no more be a prey; and I will judge between cattle and cattle.

I will set up one pastor over them so they live in peace:

vss. 23-25: And I will set up one shepherd over them, and he shall feed them, even my servant David; he shall feed them, and he shall be their shepherd. And I the LORD will be their God, and my servant David a prince among them; I the LORD have spoken it. And I will make with them a covenant of peace, and will cause the evil beasts to cease out of the land: and they shall dwell safely.

## 6. THEY ARE NOT GATHERED UNTO YOU:

The people that come to your church, you did not bring them - your efforts did not bring them - God brought them and that is why you must take good care of them, lead them and feed them. I heard my father in the Lord say one day: "It's so interesting to know that Advertisement doesn't bring people to church. There are many advertising churches that don't have people." John 6:44 says, 'No man can come to me, except the [my] Father [in heaven] which hath sent me draw him: and I will raise him up at the last day.'

So when you see them or when they come, celebrate the SENDER who sent them or brought them. They are not gathered unto you, they are gathered unto the BRINGER - the One who drew them.

- Remember Genesis 49:10, 'The sceptre shall not depart from Judah, nor a lawgiver from between his feet, until Shiloh come; and unto him shall the gathering of the people be.'

You discover from the two scriptures that HE DRAWS THEM TO HIMSELF so you should approach them with fear and awesomeness in your heart.

See the people He has brought here as He, having brought them to HIMSELF for us to serve. He goes to the town where you are and has drawn those people and said to them, 'I have a shepherd here; I have appointed a shepherd here for you' according to His promise in Jeremiah 3:15, 'And I will give you pastors according to mine heart, which shall feed you with knowledge and understanding.'

NOTE: So, He brought them - so you didn't bring them. So,

don't pride yourself in how many of them came. He brought them where He is - where He has appointed. So, CELEBRATE THE ONE WHO BROUGHT THEM - HE BROUGHT THEM - HE BROUGHT THEM - You didn't bring them - HE DREW THEM!

**7. THE MONEY IN THE CHURCH IS NOT YOUR MONEY, NEITHER IS IT THE MONEY OF THE PEOPLE OR THE MONEY OF THE MINISTRY – IT IS GOD'S MONEY:**

It is not your money, it is not the people's money - it is not the ministry's money - IT IS HIS MONEY! People mess up because they don't have that perspective of the resources in the kingdom. It is used for His purposes under His directives. The moment you drop it, it becomes His. It is no longer the church's own; it's no longer the people's own, it's not the Pastor's own; it has become God's money. Many more people have lost their ministry to financial mishandling, financial mismanagement, financial carelessness and financial misappropriation than any other thing.

In Luke 16:1-12 he said in verse 2 'How is it that I hear this of thee? Give an account of thy stewardship; for thou mayest be no longer steward.' What is this I hear of you?

He said render an account of thy stewardship because he was told his servant was wasting the resources entrusted to him. Give an account of thy stewardship that your stewardship shall be no more. When you begin to deal carelessly with HIS MONEY, YOU ARE TOYING WITH YOUR MINISTRY [service] or the ministry He has entrusted into your hands. He will take the ministry from you because you are not effective in handling His resources - you are wasteful in handling his resources so he went around changing the figures in preparation for his downfall, so that when he falls, not if he falls they may receive him into their everlasting habitation - note: when ye fall....

**So, when you have a wasteful disposition towards His resources you do not only lack supplies, you lose the ministry.**

**When you are wasteful with His resources, you lose [the] your ministry.** Many people around the world today have lost their ministry due to financial misappropriation and financial indiscipline because they thought it was their money. You may ask, 'Is it not what we are preaching that is bringing in the money, so, why can't we spend it?' Because it is not our money, it is His. Get the receipts - keep detailed accounts as the final chapter of my book: GENERATING FINANCES IN MINISTRY will teach you.

NEVER FORGET THIS: Always remember that your financial stewardship has a lot to do with your sustenance in ministry. Many ministers who have crashed and no one knows where they live or are now, crashed because every offering that came in, they considered it as their offering especially those in freelance ministry. They have nothing in place to separate ministry money from their own - they bundle them all together - some are even not afraid and are so indisciplined that even when someone gives them their tithes to pay for them they squander it. Some self-appointed leaders are even so ignorant or shallow in their understanding that they say the money should be given to the people when they need it, after all it is the people's money. That is someone who lacks understanding - period.

**LISTEN: The money is not your own, it's not the members' own, it's not the church's own, the money is His own.**

Bible says in Hebrews 7:8, 'And here men that die receive tithes; but there he receiveth them, of whom it is witnessed that he liveth.'

Here, men that die [Pastors] operate as ushers who collect or receive your tithes but there [in heaven] He receiveth them.

So it is His - you don't toy with His money.
So you don't go about trying to rob Him of His money.
PROVERB: Only a fool goes about planning how to rob a lion of his resources when the bible says categorically in Genesis 49:9,10, 'Judah is a lion's whelp: from the prey, my son, thou art gone up: he stooped down, he couched as a lion, and as an old lion; who shall rouse him up? The sceptre shall not depart from Judah, nor a lawgiver from between his feet, until Shiloh come; and unto him shall the gathering of the people be.'

They ask you, 'Where are you going? And you say, 'I am going to the zoo.' What for? 'I have found a sack of gold near a lion and I am going to enter his cave while he is asleep and collect it from the lion' - that is an invitation to suicide. The lion may be snoring but when you get closer he will have you for dinner because whether a lion is asleep or awake - he is still a lion - king of the jungle - you don't go near it or what is his. Lions don't sleep at night. Don't play with lions. You don't play such games with lions, no matter what state they are in.

**JESUS IS DESCRIBED AS THE LION OF THE TRIBE OF JUDAH** - the tithe is His. That's why God says because ye have robbed me, ye are cursed with a curse. The money is not your own; keep accurate records and give detailed accounts with excitement. Don't wait to be reminded for your financial accounts, reports or returns. Get it ready and send it.

Don't touch God's money - Don't try it - Don't curse your life - don't curse your livelihood - don't play with your livelihood - don't play with His money. Any accursed thing in your possession puts you under a perpetual curse. It is never late to be right - so, fix it. Don't put God's stuff among your stuff like Achan did - if anything was wrong before now, make sure it does not happen again because it will cost you your ministry, not your job - this is not a job; you are not here on a job, you are here on a mission. If this mission is terminated, your life enters into an unending frustration - you can't afford to do that.

## 8. THE VIRTUE THAT FLOWS THROUGH YOU TO BLESS OTHERS IS HIS VIRTUE – NOT YOUR VIRTUE:

Jesus said, 'Who touched me, virtue is gone out of me.' When you are preaching or ministering it is His virtue that flows out of you through His word to the people so never say so much virtue has gone out of you because it is not your virtue; it was His virtue through you. Nothing comes out of you. So it is not your virtue - don't clap for yourself in secret. Bible says in Acts 19:11-12 'And God wrought special miracles by the hands of Paul: So that from his body were brought unto the sick handkerchiefs or aprons, and the diseases departed from them, and the evil spirits went out of them.'

It was God, who wrought special miracles by the hands of Paul.
Q: Who wrought? God wrought ... demonstrated
Watch what will start to happen in your life when you recognize that. Watch what God will begin to do and continue to do when you give credit where credit is due. When you recognize this, you won't be praying prayers that require ovation... it's not your virtue... it's His virtue. He says He has placed this treasure in earthen vessels. 2 Corinthians 4:7, 'But we have this treasure in earthen vessels, that the excellency of the power may be of God, and not of us.'

We are Vessels of clay so don't sit down in the office and say, 'you know a surge of power has gone out of me...' it's not your power, it is His power.

## 9. IT IS HE THAT CONFIRMS HIS WORD, NOT YOU:

The confirmation of His Word is what results in signs. He said in Isaiah 44:24,26, 'Thus saith the Lord thy redeemer… …. That confirmeth the word of his servant, and performeth the counsel of his messengers; that saith to Jerusalem, Thou shalt be inhabited; and to the cities of Judah, Ye shall be built, and I will raise up the decayed places thereof:'

Mark 16:20 says, 'And they went forth, and preached everywhere, the Lord working with them, and confirming the word with signs following. Amen.'

God also was working with them confirming the word they preached. So, He wasn't confirming the grammar or how articulate you were; he was confirming the word, HIS WORD, not your word. So, don't pose as if you are the one to confirm the word. Your responsibility is to declare the word and His is to confirm the word. So every time a sign erupts, acknowledge and recognize the CONFIRMER. He confirmed the word into performance. It is God that confirms the word that results in signs.

Hebrews 2:4, 'God also bearing them witness, both with signs and wonders, and with divers miracles, and gifts of the Holy Ghost, according to his own will?'

Acts 14:3, 'Long time therefore abode they speaking boldly in the Lord, which gave testimony unto the word of his grace, and granted signs and wonders to be done by their hands.'

## 10. RECOGNIZE THAT IT IS ALL OF AND BY GRACE:

Whatever gets accomplished is by reason of His grace that is made available. A great ministry recognizes that it is all of Grace. Because, where Grace fails, disgrace takes over. That is why Paul, the writer of two-thirds of the New Testament said, 'I am what I am by the grace of God.' Grace! Grace! 1 Corinthians 15:10, 'But by the grace of God I am what I am: and his grace which was bestowed upon me was not in vain; but I laboured more abundantly than they all: yet not I, but the grace of God which was with me.'

## SO: IT IS GRACE THAT MAKES GREAT!

1 Samuel 2:9, 'He will keep the feet of his saints, and the wicked shall be silent in darkness; for by strength shall no man prevail.'

That is why it is said: 'If you don't grow in grace, you will groan in disgrace.' **It is grace that makes great.**

Romans 9:16, 'So then it is not of him that willeth, nor of him that runneth, but of God that showeth mercy.'

It is grace that makes great. It is grace that makes great so celebrate the Giver of Grace for every level of result you are privileged to experience and enjoy for it is grace not strength, not skill, not expertise for …'I returned, and saw under the sun, that the race is not to the swift, nor the battle to the strong, neither yet bread to the wise, nor yet riches to men of understanding, nor yet favour to men of skill; but time and chance happeneth to them all.' - Ecclesiastes 9:11

## 11. WITHOUT ME YE CAN DO NOTHING – SO: WE NEED TO GET TO THAT POINT WHERE WE WILL NOT ATTRIBUTE ANYTHING TO OURSELVES IN THE PURSUIT OF OUR ASSIGNMENT:

'For it is He that is at work in you [us] both to will and to do of his own good pleasure.' - Philippians 2:13

So, everything about you and me is nothing but God at work. Whatever works in your life is a pointer to the fact that it is God at work in you. God is at work for you. God is at work in your assignment.

## 12. YOU OWE HIM ALL THE GLORY - GIVE HIM ALL THE GLORY:

He said: 'These commandments is to you O priests: Malachi 2:2-3, 'If ye will not hear, and if ye will not lay it to heart, to give glory unto my name, saith the LORD of hosts, I will even send a curse upon you, and I will curse your blessings: yea, I have cursed them already, because ye do not lay it to heart. Behold, I will corrupt your seed, and spread dung upon your faces, even the dung of your solemn feasts; and one shall take you away with it.'

You owe Him everything. When you don't acknowledge Him or His input in ministry, people ridicule you saying: 'I thought he used to be a minister and was in ministry; what has become of him now?'

## 13. REMAIN AN ADDICTED LEARNER - STAY STUDIOUS:

Have an insatiable thirst for knowledge. Don't wait to learn from experience. Learning by experience is the worst form of education; the cost is always too enormous, many times irrecoverable experiences. You don't learn to avoid accidents by having one; you may never have a second chance. He didn't say learn by experience, he said learn by the book. When God called Joshua, the first thing God said to him was be of good courage I have called you….but to succeed and make your way prosperous, This book shall not depart from your mouth, this book, this book shall not depart from your mouth…………..this book…Daniel said, 'I understood by the books…' The apostle Paul said, in 2 Timothy 4:13, 'The cloak that I left at Troas with Carpus, when thou comest, bring with thee, and the books, but especially the parchments.' I NEED THEM!

**Learning by experience is the slowest form of all and the most risky**. I refuse therefore to accept that 'Experience is the best teacher'; rather an insatiable crave for knowledge with the learning attitude required is the best teacher in life. Don't wait to experience death - there may be no way to return to share your experience. If experience is the best teacher then we must die first before we agree that there is heaven or hell. If you end up in hell, there is no way you will come back to tell your story so don't wait to learn from experience. One must give his life to Christ now and live for Him.

That gives you an idea of how best experience is as a teacher which is the philosophy of traditionalists; it may hold in the open market of knowledge but not in the kingdom. Great leaders are deliberate at learning - they are addicted learners. Leadership Expert, John Maxwell said in Leadership 101, 'Leaders are readers! Even those who don't read widely, read wisely. They often clip out articles and quotes to file for future use.' He continued, 'Long ago, I learned that if you want to quote like a leader, you must note like a leader.' SO: READ! READ! READ! STUDY! STUDY! STUDY! RESEARCH! RESEARCH! For he who does not read is no better than he who cannot read! Rick Warren said: 'The moment you stop learning, you stop leading.' Leaders are learners. Once a person feels they have a firm grasp on all the answers, they have quit being teachable and will soon cease from leading. Their thoughts and methods will become outdated, and eventually stale.

Good leaders are hungry for learning, all the way to the grave. 'It's what you learn after you know it all that counts.' - John Wooden

Someone once said, "We only learn what we already know." When we get beyond a superficial understanding of an idea or concept is when the truth really sinks in.

Everyone that is responsible for another person owes that person a leadership responsibility because he or she is influencing people daily with or without walls. Every parent is a leader leading their family with Grace or into disgrace. Every mother is a leader leading their children either into destruction or into distinction. Every head of the family, every father is the leader of his family driving the family vehicle with his wife, his children and his entire household. So his skilfulness and influence at the steering wheel of life determines the destiny of his home. If he drives rough and ends up in prison he leaves his family as destitutes. So he/she must be an in-depth wide reader and learner about his assignment both before and during his assignment and always be abreast and ahead, ready and equipped to answer tomorrow's questions today. King Solomon, the wisest man besides Jesus was himself an addicted learner and researcher as confirmed in Ecclesiastes 12:9-10, 'And moreover, because the preacher was wise, he still taught the people knowledge; yea, he gave good heed, and sought out, and set in order many proverbs. The preacher sought to find out acceptable words: and that which was written was upright, even words of truth.'

## 14. NEVER DESPISE THE DAYS OF HUMBLE BEGINNINGS OR LOSE YOUR HUMILITY:

Zechariah 4:10, 'For who hath despised the day of small things?

for they shall rejoice, and shall see the plummet in the hand of Zerubbabel with those seven; they are the eyes of the LORD, which run to and fro through the whole earth.'

READ: 2 Samuel 6:16-23

## 15. NO MATTER HOW SUCCESSFUL YOU BECOME IN LIFE OR MINISTRY, NEVER ENTERTAIN PRIDE:

Pride is an evil spirit - it's like an acid... Pride is as poisonous as cyanide. REMEMBER: one major common denominator of all the great people more especially ministers of the gospel who fell and never regained the level of success they previously attained was pride - they had come to a place in life where no one beside, above or below them could advise them anymore or speak into their lives, much more correct them. There are about 49 scripture references to the evil and destructive nature of pride and we are warned categorically against it and to stay far away from it. God Himself says in Leviticus 26:19, 'And I will break the pride of your power; and I will make your heaven as iron, and your earth as brass:'

Man's Pride invites the wrath of God: 2 Chronicles 32:26 says, 'Notwithstanding Hezekiah humbled himself for the pride of his heart, both he and the inhabitants of Jerusalem, so that the wrath of the LORD came not upon them in the days of Hezekiah.'

Pride keeps the wicked from seeking God: Psalm 10:4, 'The

wicked, through the pride of his countenance, will not seek after God: God is not in all his thoughts.'

Pride brings shame: Proverbs 11:2, 'When pride cometh, then cometh shame: but with the lowly is wisdom.'

Pride brings people low: Proverbs 29:23, 'A man's pride shall bring him low: but honour shall uphold the humble in spirit.'

The Proud are stripped of all their glory: Isaiah 23:9, 'The LORD of hosts hath purposed it, to stain the pride of all glory, and to bring into contempt all the honourable of the earth.'

Isaiah 25:11, 'And he shall spread forth his hands in the midst of them, as he that swimmeth spreadeth forth his hands to swim: and he shall bring down their pride together with the spoils of their hands.'

People don't acknowledge what you've done in their lives when they rise out of pride: Ezekiel 30:6, 'Thus saith the LORD; They also that uphold Egypt shall fall; and the pride of her power shall come down: from the tower of Syene shall they fall in it by the sword, saith the Lord GOD.'

Even after knowing and saying this, he became a victim of his own advice: Daniel 4:37, 'Now I Nebuchadnezzar praise and extol and honour the King of heaven, all whose works are truth, and his ways judgment: and those that walk in pride he is able to abase.'

Daniel 5:20, 'But when his heart was lifted up, and his mind hardened in pride, he was deposed from his kingly throne, and they took his glory from him:'

WATCH IT! PRIDE COMES FROM WITHIN:

Mark 7:21-23, 'For from within, out of the heart of men, proceed evil thoughts, adulteries, fornications, murders, Thefts, covetousness, wickedness, deceit, lasciviousness, an evil eye, blasphemy, pride, foolishness: All these evil things come from within, and defile the man.'

1 Timothy 3:1,6, 'This is a true saying, If a man desire the office of a bishop, he desireth a good work....Not [he must not be] a novice, lest being lifted up with pride he fall into the condemnation of the devil.'

1 John 2:16, 'For all that is in the world, the lust of the flesh, and the lust of the eyes, and the pride of life, is not of the Father, but is of the world.'

## 16. BE ADDICTED TO DIVINE DIRECTION AND DIRECTIVES:

Always follow Him and do as He says - Joshua 1:8 [don't only hear - also do]. David was an addicted inquirer of the Lord. No wonder he became the man after God's own heart. Prosperity follows those who are addicted to inquiring at the hands of the Master.

1 Samuel 23:2, 'Therefore David inquired of the LORD, saying, Shall I go and smite these Philistines? And the LORD said unto David, Go, and smite the Philistines, and save Keilah.'

1 Samuel 23:4, 'Then David inquired of the LORD yet again. And the LORD answered him and said, Arise, go down to Keilah: for I will deliver the Philistines into thine hand.'

2 Samuel 5:19, 'And David inquired of the LORD, saying, Shall I go up to the Philistines? wilt thou deliver them into mine hand? And the LORD said unto David, Go up: for I will doubtless deliver the Philistines into thine hand.'

## 5 ADDITIONAL MAJOR DETERMINANTS ON HOW TO FINISH WELL FROM KING SOLOMON [ECCLESIASTES 12:1-14]

These unavoidable words of wisdom from King Solomon, the wisest man that ever lived besides Jesus in his great finale sound like the lecture of an experienced mentor attempting to counsel an emerging leader; trying to keep him or her from making some of the same mistakes he made:

### 17. DON'T LOSE SIGHT OF THE 'BIG PICTURE' – YOUR DESTINATION ESPECIALLY WHEN YOU ARE YOUNG IN MINISTRY [Young Ministers]:

Ecclesiastes 12:1-4, 'Remember now thy Creator in the days of thy youth, while the evil days come not, nor the years draw nigh, when thou shalt say, I have no pleasure in them; While the sun, or the light, or the moon, or the stars, be not darkened, nor the clouds return after the rain: In the day when the keepers of the house shall tremble, and the strong men shall bow themselves, and the grinders cease because they are few, and those that look out of the windows be darkened, And the doors shall be shut in the streets, when the sound of the grinding is low, and he shall rise up at the voice of the bird, and all the daughters of music shall be brought low;'

Bible says of Jesus who for the joy that was set before him endured the cross despised the shame now……......

## 18. DO WHAT IS RIGHT BEFORE IT IS TOO LATE TO CORRECT YOURSELF:

Ecclesiastes 12:5-8, 'Also when they shall be afraid of that which is high, and fears shall be in the way, and the almond tree shall flourish, and the grasshopper shall be a burden, and desire shall fail: because man goeth to his long home, and the mourners go about the streets: Or ever the silver cord be loosed, or the golden bowl be broken, or the pitcher be broken at the fountain, or the wheel broken at the cistern. Then shall the dust return to the earth as it was: and the spirit shall return unto God who gave it. Vanity of vanities, saith the preacher; all is vanity.'

## 19. USE YOUR WORDS LIKE TOOLS TO SHEPHERD AND ADD VALUE TO OTHERS:

Ecclesiastes 12:11, 'The words of the wise are as goads, and as nails fastened by the masters of assemblies, which are given from one shepherd.'

## 20. DON'T TRY TO MASTER EVERYTHING IN LIFE – JUST WHAT'S IMPORTANT AND MATTERS WITHIN YOUR PURPOSE:

Ecclesiastes 12:12, 'And further, by these, my son, be admonished: of making many books there is no end; and much study is a weariness of the flesh.'

## 21. TRUST AND OBEY GOD - HE IS THE ULTIMATE JUDGE:

Ecclesiastes 12:13-14, 'Let us hear the conclusion of the whole matter: Fear God, and keep his commandments: for this is the whole duty of man. For God shall bring every work into judgment, with every secret thing, whether it be good, or whether it be evil.'

CHAPTER SEVEN

# 17 FUNDAMENTAL LAWS FOR FULFILLING YOUR MINISTRY

Colossians 4:17, 'And say to Archippus, Take heed to the ministry which thou hast received in the Lord, that thou fulfil it.'

That you have received a ministry does not mean you will fulfil it. Take heed - get to know what you are called to do, what you must do and what it takes or what it requires and give it all it takes to fulfil the ministry you have received from the Lord. Remember, it must be a ministry you have received from the Lord that you fulfil, not a ministry you designed for yourself but a ministry delivered from the Lord - what He gave you. If the vision is not from the Lord you will be the one to fulfil it. Calling yourself into ministry is a self-inflicted curse. If it is Him, you position yourself, doing what He tells you to do and He steps in to fulfil it so we don't mistake ambition and impressions as vision. That you see a need does not mean God has called you to fulfil it - Are you the one sent to fulfil it? **A need is not equal to a calling on your life. That there is a need is not equal to a calling on your life. There are needs every day. An open door is not equal to an open vision.**

So, fulfilling your vision begins with knowing it's from the Lord. If it is not from the Lord it will not be fulfilled. God said to the prophet in Jeremiah 27:15 says, 'For I have not sent them, saith the LORD, yet they prophesy a lie in my name; that I might drive you out, and that ye might perish, ye, and the prophets that prophesy unto you.'

In the above passage, God said of some, I have not sent these prophets yet they run; I have not sent them yet they prophesy. So, there are people running a race they have not been assigned like Ahimaaz in 2 Samuel 18. Psalm 32:9 says, 'Be ye not as the horse, or as the mule, which have no understanding: whose mouth must be held in with bit and bridle, lest they come near unto thee.'

Get your definite calling, definite instructions, specific message and specific location for its fulfilment from the Manufacturer before stepping out. The purpose for leadership and ministry is not the maintenance of followers but the production of more leaders/ministers/ministries so you must be equipped to do so. 2 Peter 1:10 says giving all diligence - give it all it requires. There are requirements you must meet to fulfil that ministry to make your calling sure. There are vital forces you must engage to fulfil your ministry. Ministry cannot fulfil itself no matter how good it appears. There are rules and there are regulations to fulfilling ministry and remember it is hard work. Hard work is the only way to become a high flier. Jesus said, 'I must work the works of him that sent me for the night cometh when no man can work.'

Ministry is not a calling into laziness; it is a calling into doing what is more than normal: i.e. EXCELLENCE. Paul said in 1 Corinthians 15:10, 'I laboured more abundantly than them all.'

**SO, NO LAZY MAN HAS A FUTURE IN MINISTRY.**

There are fundamental laws that you must obey to fulfil your ministry. **Fulfilment is not so much about getting results; it's much more about getting results to match or meet the aspirations and the expectations of the Caller or Master [the One who called you].** So, it's important to stay spiritually awake. Unto whom much is given, much is required. He will require of you to the level that He has put in your hand. So: Concentrate; put all your eggs in one basket, and watch that basket. As Liz Ashe said, "Don't try to be great at all things. Pick a few things to be good at and be the best you can." **Focus! Leaders are individuals who have declared independence from the expectations of others.**

So let's examine: The FUNDAMENTAL LAWS THAT WILL ENHANCE OR GUARANTEE FULFILMENT OF MINISTRY i.e. LAWS TO ENGAGE IN, IN FULFILLING YOUR MINISTRY i.e. the rules and regulations you must comply with which will help to add to the rate of the amazing results we are attracting. He said, 'my yoke is easy and my burden is light.' **If it is not easy it is not his yoke.** That you have a ministry doesn't mean you will fulfil it. Pursue it skilfully and intelligently. God is leaving you with the responsibility to fulfil it. Unto whom much is given, much is required.

If God has assigned you to pastor a church of 2000 and you are pastoring a church of 1000 you have not fulfilled your ministry. Everyone might be clapping for you but much more than that is expected of you. We are learning to adapt to those rules and regulations that will enable us fulfil his mandate on our lives. There are rules, there are regulations that will help you arrive at your destination - if you don't mind them, then you are selling off your birthright. REMEMBER: **It takes a studious man to secure a glorious destiny. So,** 'Study to show thyself approved unto God, a workman that needeth not to be ashamed, rightly dividing the word of truth.' (2 Timothy 2:15)

**Only those who obey rules become rulers and only those who comply with laws become lords.** So, for you to fulfil your ministry indeed, you must enjoy the laws of scriptures. Every law of scriptures is a law of life. He has delivered us from the law of sin and death through the law of the operation of the law of life in Christ Jesus.

**Anchor Scripture: 2 Timothy 2:3-5,**
'Thou therefore endure hardness, as a good soldier of Jesus Christ. No man that warreth entangleth himself with the affairs of this life; that he may please him who hath chosen him to be a soldier. And if a man also strive for masteries, yet is he not crowned, except he strive lawfully.'

Another translation says: 'No athlete wins the prize except he does it according to the rules - by applying himself to the rules of the game.'

Every calling into ministry requires everything that you are and everything that you have. **Ministry is fulfilled by abiding by the following laws some of which [*] originated from the book/teaching: EXPLOITS IN MINISTRY (A book I highly recommend) by my father in the Lord, Bishop David Oyedepo and my manuals - PASTORAL LEADERSHIP 101, MINISTRY 101:** [You can order copies of Exploits in Ministry from www.dphstore.co.uk and our manuals from www.houseofjudah.org.uk].

**I. The first is law is what I call the Law of DEFINITIVENESS OF PURPOSE:**

A discovery of your purpose and that of your ministry from God is crucial and non-negotiable in fulfilling your ministry and your destiny. Why are you here? What is your ministry called to do? EVERYTHING STARTS WITH YOUR SOURCE and your PURPOSE. Proverbs 27:8, 'As a bird that wandereth from her nest, so is a man that wandereth from his place.'

**Definitiveness of purpose is the starting point of fulfilment of destiny, impact in life and all wealth.** IT IS SAID THAT: THE GREATEST TRAGEDY IN LIFE IS TO BE ALIVE AND NOT KNOW WHY YOU ARE ALIVE!

'As a bird that wandereth from her nest, so is a man that wandereth from his place [purpose/assignment].'

To fulfil destiny, you must discover your assignment in life which empowers you to decide exactly what you want, write it down and then make a plan for its accomplishment. Leaders know that they possess the capacity to be leaders within the sphere of the purpose for which they were born. Discover and fulfil your ministry – don't wait; know and do your part. Mother Teresa put it this way: "I am a little pencil in the hand of a writing God, who is sending a love letter to the world." Singleness of purpose is one of the chief essentials for success in life, no matter what may be one's aim. As Kalvin Clause Witz said, "Pursue one great decisive aim with force and determination."

## REMEMBER:
## DESTINY IS NOT DECIDED;
## DESTINY IS DISCOVERED!

## THE IMPORTANCE OF PURPOSE: (21 keys)
1. **Where purpose is unknown abuse is inevitable.**
2. Everything must begin with a purpose.
3. Where there is no bearing life becomes a burden.
4. Anyone who lacks bearing, purpose or direction in life becomes a burden on his family, on people, society and the nation. Proverbs 27:8, 'As a bird that wandereth from her nest, so is a man that wandereth from his place or purpose.'
5. The greatest tragedy in life is to be alive and not know why you are alive and the greatest form of waste is wasted potential due to a lack of discovery of your 'wiring' or why you are 'wired'/gifted the way you are.

6. Most people who are frustrated in life are those who have not as yet discovered their purpose or are not pursuing or fulfilling their purpose in life.
7. LIFE IS NOT MEASURED BY DURATION BUT BY DONATION, i.e. contributions made for the benefit of others and society motivated by purpose.
8. Purpose gives you a reason for living and a drive to succeed in life.
9. Purpose is what gives one a reason for living, not one's job. 'For I know the thoughts that I think toward you, saith the LORD, thoughts of peace, and not of evil, to give you an expected end. – Jeremiah 29:11
10. YOU WILL ONLY FIND FULFILMENT IN YOUR GOD-GIVEN, GOD-ORDAINED AND GOD'S PREDESTINED PURPOSE. (Jeremiah 1:5-10)
11. Your purpose in life must be something you are ready to live and die for like Esther. (Esther 4:13-14)
12. When you discover your purpose, you don't settle for the status quo or negative statements of people around you or the dictates of the economy - you rise up and get violent at the expense of your life.
13. Without purpose life is just an existence.
14. When you discover your purpose, you are ready to die for it.
15. Your purpose is the reason for your life.
16. Your purpose is the reason for which God has given you a lease of life.
17. Those with no purpose did not show up here.
18. UNTIL YOU ARE READY TO DIE FOR SOMETHING,

YOU ARE NOT READY TO LIVE FOR ANYTHING.
19. The greatest achievers in life are those who discovered the purpose for which they were willing to die.
20. Your PURPOSE IN LIFE IS WHAT MAKES LIFE MEANINGFUL. A discovery of your purpose in life gives you meaning, focus and fulfilment.
21. When someone has a purpose for which they are ready to die and you have a purpose for which you are not ready to die, don't compete with him. When you have a purpose you are not ready to die for, you back out at the slightest challenge and crisis or hard times. What are you here for? What meaning do you give to your own life? The value of life is not in how long a person lives alone, but in how that life was lived in pursuit and fulfilment of its God-given purpose.

**II. The second law is the Law of DISCOVERIES:**

Discovery brings recovery. Discover your purpose, your strengths, your weaknesses, your potential – gifts and talents – what you do best with ease backed by proofs even without training and add skill, excellence and diligence for maximum productivity and discover opportunities in which to use them. Life is not fulfilled by intentions but by deliberate action. Anything left to chance does not stand a chance. Jeremiah started off by making discoveries about his purpose and 'wiring' by meeting with God to introduce him to himself and his assignment in life. Jeremiah 1:5, 'Before I formed thee in the belly I knew thee; and before thou camest forth out of the womb I sanctified thee, and I ordained thee a prophet unto the nations.'

Get to know what you are here for before stepping out. Discover your potential – who you really are but no one has seen yet; what you are capable of becoming, doing and achieving but haven't become, done or achieved yet. You do this by meeting with and making discoveries from God who is your Source and your manufacturer and then adding skill and value to what I call your 'wiring' - your gifts and strengths to use it to add value to people to fulfil your ministry and thereby create your wealth. Discover where you are sent and with what message and stay there.

**REASONS:**
**From** Genesis 26:1-6, 12-14, we discover that you prosper and become synonymous with prosperity when you go to, sow into, work at and stay at the appointed place irrespective of who was there before you got there. Like Isaac, you begin to prosper, continue to prosper and become very prosperous to the extent that the philistines [the indigenous people, the original citizens who were there before you arrived] envy you in your appointed place both of worship and assignment. But you are thrown out of the boat and end up in the belly of a whale as your accommodation like Jonah when you go where you choose.

**God is not an anyhow God - God is a covenant-keeping God!**

**Divine assignment can only be accomplished in a place of divine appointment!**

**REMEMBER THE FOLLOWING VITAL TRUTHS:**

YOU ARE ONLY A SIGN WHERE YOU ARE SENT - YOU STINK WHERE YOU ARE NOT SENT
YOU SHINE WHERE YOU ARE SENT - YOU ARE DIM WHERE YOU ARE NOT SENT
YOU ARE A MIRACLE WHERE YOU ARE SENT - YOU ARE A RIDICULE WHERE YOU ARE NOT SENT
LIGHT SURROUNDS YOU WHERE YOU ARE SENT - WHILST DARKNESS ENVELOPES YOU WHERE YOU ARE NOT SENT
YOU ARE FAMOUS WHERE YOU ARE SENT - YOU ARE 'SHAMOUS' WHERE YOU ARE NOT SENT
YOUR FAME SPREADS WHERE YOU ARE SENT - YOUR SHAME SPREADS WHERE YOU ARE NOT SENT
YOU ARE FULL OF GRACE WHERE YOU ARE SENT - YOU ARE DISGRACED WHERE YOU ARE NOT SENT
YOU ARE CELEBRATED WHERE YOU ARE SENT - YOU ARE TOLERATED WHERE YOU ARE NOT SENT
YOU ARE A CELEBRITY WHERE YOU ARE SENT - YOU ARE A NUISANCE WHERE YOU ARE NOT SENT
YOU MAKE NEWS WHERE YOU ARE SENT - YOU MAKE NOISE WHERE YOU ARE NOT SENT
YOU ARE ACCEPTED WHERE YOU ARE SENT - YOU ARE REJECTED WHERE YOU ARE NOT SENT
YOU ARE A POSITIVE INFLUENCE WHERE YOU ARE SENT - YOU ARE 'INFLUENCED' NEGATIVELY WHERE

YOU ARE NOT SENT

YOU ARE AN ANSWER ONLY WHERE YOU ARE SENT - YOU ARE A QUESTION MARK OR ARE QUESTIONED WHERE YOU ARE NOT SENT

YOU HAVE PROOFS OR RESULTS WHERE YOU ARE SENT - YOU LACK PROOFS OR RESULTS WHERE YOU ARE NOT SENT

YOU ARE A BLESSING WHERE YOU ARE SENT - YOU ARE A BURDEN WHERE YOU ARE NOT SENT

YOU PROSPER WHERE YOU ARE SENT - YOU ARE A PAUPER WHERE YOU ARE NOT SENT

YOU GIVE WHERE YOU ARE SENT - YOU BEG WHERE YOU ARE NOT

YOU ARE AN AMAZEMENT WHERE YOU ARE SENT - YOU ARE AN AMUSEMENT WHERE YOU ARE NOT SENT

YOU ARE FULL OF FRAGRANCE WHERE YOU ARE SENT - YOU ARE A STENCH WHERE YOU ARE NOT SENT

YOU ARE BLESSED, UNMOLESTIBLE, UNHARASS-ABLE, IMMOVABLE, UNTOUCHABLE, UNHARMABLE, UNSTOPPABLE, WHERE YOU ARE SENT BUT YOU ARE CURSED, MOLESTIBLE, HARASSABLE, MOVABLE, TOUCHABLE, HARM-ABLE AND STOPPABLE WHERE YOU ARE NOT SENT

YOU ARE A WONDER WHERE YOU ARE SENT - YOU ARE A WANDERER WHERE YOU ARE NOT SENT.

That is why when the crowds saw what Paul had done, they shouted in the Lycaonian language, "The gods have come down to us in the likeness of men." (Acts 14:11) compared to Acts 21:38, '................art thou not that Egyptian who stirred up trouble...' Then in Acts 28:4-6, 'And when the barbarians saw the venomous beast hang on his hand, they said among themselves, No doubt this man is a murderer, whom, though he hath escaped the sea, yet vengeance suffereth not to live. And he shook off the beast into the fire, and felt no harm. Howbeit they looked when he should have swollen, or fallen down dead suddenly: but after they had looked a great while, and saw no harm come to him, they changed their minds, and said he was a god.' YOU AMAZE PEOPLE WHERE YOU ARE SENT - YOU AMUSE PEOPLE WHERE YOU ARE NOT SENT - Daniel and three Hebrew boys amazed people in their place of assignment while the sons of Sceva amused people going where they were not sent.

Your appointed place is your only place of accomplishments - 2 Samuel 7:10, 'Moreover I will appoint a place for my people Israel, and will plant them, that they may dwell in a place of their own, and move no more; neither shall the children of wickedness afflict them anymore, as beforetime,'

Psalm 125 says in your appointed place, you become immovable. There is no comparing the planting of God with the planting of men – (Isaiah 61) The appointed place is your place of security, safety, peace, joy, provision, divine supply, stability, blessing, accomplishment and fulfilment.

## III. The third law is the Law of VISION

**a. You must have vision** - Proverbs 29:18, 'Where there is no vision, the people perish: but he that keepeth the law, happy is he.'

**You must have the vision for your assignment.. - Why?**
1. Where God isn't, there is no vision.
2. Where there is no vision, the people perish.
3. Where there are no willing, skilled, trained, equipped, available, loyal, faithful, determined, dedicated and devoted people to carry out the vision in cooperation with God and the leader, both the people and the vision will perish.
4. Vision is the seed for growth; nothing grows that is not first of all conceived. So the conception for church growth or your ministry is vision - until you conceive it you cannot see it. Until you imagine it, you cannot actualize it.
5. Leaders have vision – leaders are visionary - Knowing:
6. Vision breeds persistence.
7. Vision is the capacity and ability to capture the future before it arrives knowing that the thoughts that we have today will become the realities of tomorrow.
8. It is vision that makes a leader, not the other way round.
9. Vision is capacity to see; so rub minds with people who see - go where it already works – go after those who have proofs - those who have obtained the promise, not those who make promises.
10. Vision is capacity to see success even in failure; to see success in someone who is failing.

11. Vision is the ability and capacity to see tomorrow in today.

12. Vision is the ability and capacity to see an adult in a child, a man in a boy, a woman in a girl and possibilities in the midst of impossibilities.

13. 'Vision is foresight based on insight with the benefit of hindsight.' – George Barna, Management consultant

14. Vision is the ability and capacity to see the stars whilst in the gutter.

15. Your future lies in your vision and can be predicted by your daily routine. Until you visualize it you cannot realize it; what you believe is what you see. So, a Pastor's vision is his limit; your vision is your limit. Your future lies in your vision. God said to Abraham, 'Lift up now thy eyes as far as you can see, I have given to you' - which means all you can see I have given to you - in other words what you cannot see I cannot give to you - so you get what you see.

God is unlimited but man's limit is man's vision. So the Pastor/Minister must have a vision for his desired destination - a desire for it - a goal, a projection - he must have vision for what he's looking forward to. To be goalless and aimless is to hit at nothing.

**IV: The fourth law is the Law of PASSION**

**You must have passion:** REASON: The future of every vision is passion-determined; the moment you lose your passion, you lose your power to achieve. God will give you several things but there are a few things God will not give you such as passion. It is man that supplies the passion, the drive to see to the accomplishment of his vision and that's why Habakkuk 2 said He gives you the vision but it is you that does the running; that is where the difference comes in terms of the output and results. We need people with a passion - strong emotions. We are building a people who are passionate about our assignment to add value to others, raising and developing selfless impactful leaders to make impact in every sphere of life.

**Differences in results are a function of applied passion, not just passion; but applied passion. PASSION IS THE VEHICLE IN WHICH VISION RIDES TO ITS DESTINATION! Where passion stops is where vision stops. The output of your vision depends on PASSION. Do you have passion? Do you have drive? What drives your actions?** What are the programs put in place to see to the effective progress of the church you pastor or ministry you lead? It is your passion that moves you to put profitable programs in place beginning with outreaches and various church and specialized services, programs/seminars that are being organized to ensure the growth of the church/ministry. **It is Passion which culminates in a desire for Personal growth** or personal development for the fulfillment of your assignment. This is very important as John 1:16 reveals. 'And of his fullness have all we received, and grace for grace.'

SO, PEOPLE COME TO RECEIVE OF THE PASTOR'S FULLNESS:

- An empty Pastor cannot fill a church.
- A pastor that's full inside him cannot continue to Pastor an empty church.
- What fills him and is full in him is what flows out of him to the people.
- No church ever grows beyond the growth of the Pastor.
- That is to say if a church must grow then of necessity the Pastor must grow.
- It is the growth of the Pastor that sets the pace for the growth of the church.
- If you give a church of 1000 to a Pastor with the capacity of 100, the church will dance down to 100; in the same vein if you give a church with a capacity of 100 to a Pastor with a capacity of 1000 the church will jack up to 1000.
- Where your personal growth stops is where your church growth stops.
- Of his fullness have we all received - so a Pastor must develop his capacity for growth; he must enlarge his heart for growth. IT'S ALL ABOUT CAPACITY!
- The size of your heart will determine the number of people you can accommodate. Acts 6:4, 'But we will give ourselves continually to prayer, and to the ministry of the word.'
- RESULTS: Acts 6:7, 'And the word of God increased; and the number of the disciples multiplied in Jerusalem greatly; and a great company of the priests were obedient to the faith.'
- SUMMARY: So, the Pastor is the number one factor;

the vision will begin to drive him and the true evidence of your vision is your passion.
- A church grows off the altar of the PASTOR.
- A growing pastor grows a church.
- The Pastor is very crucial to why people are leaving the church and he is the reason why many people are coming and staying.
- When a pastor stops growing his church stops growing.
- A growing pastor will always lead a growing church.
- You can't convince anyone you have a vision when you don't have a passion to back it up.
- When passion goes to sleep vision goes to rest.
- Every vision hangs in the grave when passion is absent - that passion will propel him to fast, propel him to pray, to study, spend quality and quantity of time preparing his messages, cry out in the middle of the night for souls, etc.
- So you see, there are things that when you have a vision and a passion for, you will not be told to do; you do them of your own volition because you know it is mandatory for the fulfillment of your vision and realization of your goals.
- There are things that you just find yourself doing because of your passion.
- For instance the reason a Pastor has to be advised to fast and pray for his church to grow is because he does not have a passion.
- There are things that just occur in a natural sequence because of your passion.

- You organize programs that are orchestrated towards growing the church and of course in the process you are also growing yourself.
- As he grows himself God begins to fill up the place.
- Where a Pastor's growth stops is where the church or ministry stops.
- God is more bothered about your preparation of yourself than about filling the room - it is as you prepare yourself that God will begin to fill it up.

**V. The fifth is THE LAW OF TOTAL ABANDONMENT***

This is where you abandon your all on the altar of sacrifice to fulfil His mandate. The apostles asked this fundamental question in Matthew 19:28-29, 'We have left all and followed thee, what will we get in return?' Ministry is fulfilled through the Law of Total Abandonment - total sacrifice. There are many ministries that have left nothing yet want to fulfil the ministry that God has given them. (Mark 10:28-30; Luke 18:28-30) Until you abandon yourself to the Caller, and lay all on the altar, Ministry will not be realised. The disciples said, 'We have left all and have followed thee, what shall we have then?' Don't go outside what you are sent to do or else you will sink. Until you have left all, you may never fulfil your ministry. Until your life becomes a seed, the fulfilment of your ministry is not in view. Until you are totally abandoned to your calling, you cannot fulfil it. Until you are addicted to God and your assignment, the fulfilment of your Vision is not in view. **THIS IS TOTAL DEDICATION!**

## VI. The sixth law is the Law of ABSOLUTE DEPENDENCY ON GOD*

i.e. making God your only Source for accomplishing His mandate in your life. God is your only Source. This law is built on three scriptural philosophies.
1. Whatever God cannot do, let it remain undone.
2. Whatever God cannot give me, let me never have it.
3. Wherever God cannot take me to let me or may I never get there.

So, at every point in my life and whatever happens in my life, it is traceable to God. Every time you share His glory with anyone, you annoy God. Thank the One who is using them not them. **You are not sent by the people; you are sent to the people.** Don't go outside what you are sent or you will begin to sink. Faith taps into the Omni-potency of God in dealing with the limitations of man; faith is a universal currency delivering at the same rate or value all over the earth. God is big enough to meet all the needs of the ministry He has given us. That's why He told the disciples expressly to 'Greet no man on the way; salute no man, lobby around no man's resources; no core group in your church; carry no purse or scrip, not even your leaders.' - Luke 10:4; 22:35

God is big enough to meet all the needs of the ministry he has given to me. (Philippians 4:15-19)

## VII. The seventh law is the LAW OF DIVINE COMMANDMENT*

We do nothing except it is commanded - that is how you get things done cheaply in life and ministry. OPERATING AS COMMANDED! ONLY OPERATING AS COMMANDED! In Ezekiel 37, the prophet said, 'I prophesied as commanded', just did as commanded and God went into action. Ezekiel 37:7, 'So I prophesied as I was commanded: and as I prophesied, there was a noise, and behold a shaking, and the bones came together, bone to his bone.'

Ezekiel 37:10 says, 'So I prophesied as he commanded me, and the breath came into them, and they lived, and stood up upon their feet, an exceeding great army.'

**When you operate as commanded, you are always in command.** The Commander is always backing you. OBEDIENCE TO WHAT GOD SAYS TO DO WITH THE WORD IRRESPECTIVE OF WHAT'S GOING ON IN YOUR LIFE OR AROUND YOU is all that matters with God and all that God requires of you to make you a living star. IT IS ONLY THOSE WHO OBEY COMMANDS WHO EMERGE AS COMMANDERS. IT IS ONLY THOSE WHO RECEIVE COMMANDS WHO GIVE COMMANDS - you cannot obey commands and not end up a commander. IT IS ONLY THOSE WHO OBEY RULES WHO BECOME RULERS. **You cannot obey rules and not end up a ruler.**

IT IS ONLY THOSE WHO RECEIVE INSTRUCTIONS WHO ALSO BECOME INSTRUCTORS [GIVE INSTRUCTIONS]. YOU CAN'T BE UNDER A GIANT AND END UP AS A DWARF - where the elephant eats is where it gathers its strength; you cannot eat elephant's food and end up as a cat. IT'S ONLY THOSE UNDER AUTHORITY WHO EVENTUALLY EXERCISE AUTHORITY OVER OTHERS!

It's only those who are under the tutelage and mentorship of lords who also become lords. Jesus became the Lord of lords [us] who submit to His lordship [ownership and rulership.] Revelation 5:9-10 reads: 'He hath redeemed us.......and hast made us unto our God kings and priests: and we shall reign on the earth.' You only move as He commands. Lamentations 3:37, 'Who is he that saith, and it cometh to pass, when the Lord commandeth it not?' If it's not commanded by God, no man can bring it to pass. I do as I see my father do. If you don't want to be stranded, operate only as commanded. Operating as commanded is what puts you in command. We took over the second floor of our office premises because He commanded from Isaiah 54:1-17 and because He commanded it, He has been paying for it and sustaining it ever since. You don't move your ministry to another city or country just because you think it is greener there.

ITS GREENER ONLY WHERE YOU ARE SENT AND WHERE YOU WATER IT! BECAUSE YOU ARE ONLY A SIGN WHERE YOU ARE SENT – YOU SHINE THERE!

## VIII. The eighth law is the Law of MENTORSHIP*

A close observation over the years has revealed that African leaders are only recognised after they are dead; it is an evil spirit. Leaders in Africa are only recognised after they are dead. By inheritance, they are victims of castigations, character assassinations, etc. That is why most people in Africa don't have mentors; nobody seems qualified to mentor them so they lead a mentor-less life and by leading a mentor-less life they never reach their fullest potentials because God has arranged men on your path to bring the best of you out of life. No man is an island in himself. Jeremiah 6:16, 'Thus saith the LORD, Stand ye in the ways, and see, and ask for the old paths, where is the good way, and walk therein, and ye shall find rest for your souls. But they said, We will not walk therein.'

**- Show me any man without a mentor and you will never be able to trace leadership aura on his life.**
**- Every great leader is an offspring of another leader.**
**- Every great leader's making is traceable to another great leader. If you don't have any man that you are following, there may not be any man following you.**

**GOOD LEADERSHIP IS BORN OUT OF GOOD FOLLOWERSHIP. GOOD FOLLOWERSHIP LEADS TO GOOD LEADERSHIP.**

Hebrews 6:12 reads: 'That ye be not slothful, but followers of them who through faith and patience inherit the promises.'

The passage of scripture above shows us how to correctly identify a plausible positive mentor for our life. People have obtained what you are striving for or you want to obtain; look out for them, and try to uncover their secrets, follow them and engage those secrets in the pursuit of your own destiny. Despite his eighteen hours vision encounter with God, my father in the Lord was told categorically, "I will not have you go as others have gone; I will have hands laid on you according to Deuteronomy 34:9, 'And Joshua the son of Nun was full of the spirit of wisdom; for Moses had laid his hands upon him: and the children of Israel hearkened unto him, and did as the LORD commanded Moses.' and you shall be filled with the spirit of wisdom, i.e. don't lay hands on yourself - send for Adeboye. He will lay his hands on you and you shall be filled with the spirit of wisdom."

Despite the eighteen hour long vision and talking with God, God still connected him to a human source through which he could receive those deposits. 20 years after he had been following Kenneth E. Hagin's ministry, God said to him in a vision, 'Pattern your ministry after this man, - Kenneth Hagin.' Over the years, he had desired, 'Whatever makes Hagin, Hagin, I want it. I want the serenity, calmness, the noiselessness and proofs of this man and his ministry.' Eventually at a campmeeting in Tulsa, while he was on the balcony, he heard, 'My son David, the baton has been passed over to you.'
King Solomon said in Ecclesiastes 1:9, 'The thing that hath been, it is that which shall be; and that which is done is that which shall be done: and there is no new thing under the sun.'

There is no race you are running that someone else is not holding the baton of already. Where Hagin stopped is where Bishop Oyedepo took over. Hagin had the faith movement of the first order and the faith movement of the second order was passed to my father in the Lord, Bishop Oyedepo because you believe in their God and what they carry. (2 Chronicles 20:20) Identify the carriers of what you need, go after them, learn from them, believe in them, their ministry and personality, receive them, sow into them and their ministry, pray for them and then partake of their grace. **The law of mentorship must be recaptured again. If you don't have a mentor today, we cannot be sure of your future tomorrow. Mentorship guarantees the future of everyone.** ASK: Fresh oil! Fresh oil! Lord. Let not my head lack oil. Isaac Newton said, 'If I have seen further it has been by standing on the shoulders of those who went ahead of me.'

## IX. The ninth law is the Law of FOCUS*

Matthew 6:22, 'The light of the body is the eye: if therefore thine eye be single, thy whole body shall be full of light.'

1 Kings 20:39-40, 'And as the king passed by, he cried unto the king: and he said, Thy servant went out into the midst of the battle; and, behold, a man turned aside, and brought a man unto me, and said, Keep this man: if by any means he be missing, then shall thy life be for his life, or else thou shalt pay a talent of silver. And as thy servant was busy here and there, he was gone. And the king of Israel said unto him, so shall thy judgment be; thyself hast decided it.'

'As I was busy here and there he was gone.....'

STAY FOCUSSED ON YOUR ASSIGNMENT. Don't be lured into the trap of: 'This is what they are preaching now, so, let's do the same.' Lack of focus can make you lose your ministry. The more focussed you are, the more fruitful your ministry becomes. Kenneth Hagin stayed with 'Go teach my people – Faith' to the last day. Billy Graham has stayed with the message on salvation for over six decades and abandoned the suggestion to build a university even though the resources were going to be given him on a silver platter. Oral Roberts stayed with the Healing message till the last day and despite the vogue of church ministry he never deviated to become a pastor. Because of the impact Jesus had on people, they tried to crown him king. When Jesus noticed they were coming to crown him king he walked through them and stayed in his assignment. He stayed with the one reason for which he came, 'I am sent to the lost ones of the household of Israel' and so did John the Baptist. When he was asked if he was the messiah, he replied categorically, 'I am not.' These examples should help you and I to realign our priorities and remove every distraction.

**FOCUS IN RELATION TO YOUR MENTOR:**

Keep your eyes on your mentor/father in the lord if you want to stay focussed. 2 Kings 2:10, 'And he said, Thou hast asked a hard thing: nevertheless, if thou see me when I am taken from thee, it shall be so unto thee; but if not, it shall not be so.'

1 Kings 20:40, 'And as thy servant was busy here and there, he was gone.

Stay on your assignment remembering that it is kings who run after priests not priests running after kings; so, don't run after politicians, they should run after you. You can't be a great pastor going everywhere. Sit on your job. Proximity does not matter - it's heart to heart that matters. Fathers are coaches most times telling you what you don't like. Be ready to accept shocks. A father can disown a son but a son cannot disown his father. **Fathers can be Harsh but be right**. Anyone who talks against his boss it's because it's not his own father. Philippians 3:13, 'Brethren, I count not myself to have apprehended: but this one thing I do, forgetting those things which are behind, and reaching forth unto those things which are before,'

## ENEMIES OF FOCUS:

**1. Ambition mixed with vision**
Peter lost focus when he went back fishing. Ambition is what you want while vision is what God wants. This is like mixing oil and water. (Matthew 4:1-11 - shortcuts) The world must know you for something. They wanted to make Jesus a king but He run right through them. They asked John the Baptist, 'Are you the Messiah; his answer was 'I am not.'

**2. Wrong company/Bad associations**
Not everybody at the bus stop or airport is travelling so not everybody in ministry is going somewhere. Proverbs 13:20, 'He that walketh with wise men shall be wise: but a companion of fools shall be destroyed.'

- 1 Corinthians 15:33, 'Be not deceived: evil communications corrupt good manners.'
- **Iron sharpens iron, not wood.**
- Proverbs 27:17, 'Iron sharpeneth iron; so a man sharpeneth the countenance of his friend.'
- Psalm 1:1-3, 'Blessed is the man that walketh not in the counsel of the ungodly, nor standeth in the way of sinners, nor sitteth in the seat of the scornful. But his delight is in the law of the LORD; and in his law doth he meditate day and night. And he shall be like a tree planted by the rivers of water, that bringeth forth his fruit in his season; his leaf also shall not wither; and whatsoever he doeth shall prosper.'

**3. Ignorance of the contents of your assignment.**
- Your prosperity is in your purpose/assignment so focus on your purpose/assignment.
- Find out what God revealed to you and stay with it.
- Ministry begins with and is sustained by receiving four major instructions. You must of necessity receive these instructions from God before you embark on your journey/enterprise in ministry:

They are namely:
**a. Description**
**b. Inscription**
**c. Prescription and**
**d. Subscription.**

The statement: **WRITE THE VISION DOWN** in Habakkuk 2 means:
1. **Describe it**
2. **Inscribe it**
3. **Prescribe for it and**
4. **Subscribe To it.**

**SO:**
- 1$^{st}$ of all **describe it – define clearly what the vision is.**

- 2$^{nd}$, **inscribe it – write it down so you don't keep changing it because of circumstances/opinions,** so it cannot be erased.

- 3$^{rd}$, you must **take a prescription from God as to the How!** God said you will pastor a church of 10,000 - you have the steps. Now, **wait on Him to tell you how. This is what you need to do so what I said will come to pass.** For you to be what you should be, take this prescription twice or thrice daily, hold this or that event weekly, monthly or yearly.

- 4$^{th}$, **subscribe to it** - after you've received the steps and prescription, **act upon it; do it; subscribe to the prescription.**

- This ensures you don't sway from the original path.

**SO YOU MUST BE CONVERSANT AND FULLY PERSUADED OF THE FOLLOWING:**

**1. THE WHO:** Who is the target? Who are you called to? Who is to be involved? Genesis 11:6, '....and the people is one; nothing will be restrained from them which they have imagined to do' and 2 Samuel 6. Also, who have you been called to? – Paul to the Gentiles (Acts 26:14-19) Peter to the Jews.

**2. THE WHAT:** What is the assignment? What is the target? And all this must reflect His image and bring Him glory. The project of Nimrod and those in Babel was nullified because it was for self; it was aimed at bringing them the glory and not God. That is why God came down and interrupted their program.

**3. THE WAY:** [how to achieve it]. In 2 Samuel 6, King David initially employed the wrong way to carry or bring the ark back to Jerusalem even though there was a prescribed way as stated in 1 Samuel 5-7 which should have been studied by David the king before employing natural, physical, trial and error means using a cart to transport the ark resulting in Uzzah in trying to stop the ark from falling by touching it – helping God, being killed. King David eventually repented, wised up, found and followed the right way to bring the ark back. SO: Find the divinely prescribed way or you'll end up using a blunt axe, exerting human effort and energy to accomplish little [Ecclesiastes 10:10] wearing everyone out or even killing yourself or others.

**4. THE WHY:** Why did God make you a king, Saul [1 Samuel 9 & 10]? Why did God give you the vision you have? Why are you doing what you are doing? Why did He give you that assignment? For example, He said to Moses to tell Pharaoh, 'Let my people go that they may serve me, worship me and sacrifice to me in the wilderness.' - Exodus 4, 8, 9, etc.

Solomon's reply to God's question in 1 Kings 3:3-9, 'Ask me what you will' 'Give me an understanding heart' – Why? '..that I may judge thy so great a people.' There is always a 'why' to everything God asks you to do - find it. It helps make the journey great, significant, fulfilling and keeps you focussed when others doubt and criticise you. It is because they don't know what you know or see what you see - the end of the tunnel - the eventual outcome and the number of people that will be blessed by your obedience. Hebrews 12:2 says, '... Jesus, who for the joy that was set before him, endured the cross, despised the shame and is now set at the right hand of majesty.' On the cross when Jesus beheld what they were doing to him and saying of him and to him, said to the Father, 'Father, forgive them for they know not what they are doing.' If only they knew and in the epistles, Paul the apostle said 'if only they had known, they wouldn't have crucified the Lord of glory'. He also said of himself on his conversion that he persecuted the Christians out of ignorance; he did not know that in persecuting the Christians he was actually persecuting Christ. **Ignorance is a killer!** That is why we should know the why.

Genesis 2:5, 'And every plant of the field before it was in the earth, and every herb of the field before it grew: for the LORD God had not caused it to rain upon the earth, and there was not a man to till the ground. But there went up a mist from the earth, and watered the whole face of the ground.'

There was no rain because there was no man to till the ground. There is always a reason for everything that God does. If certain things are not in place, God doesn't do certain things because there is time for everything as stated in Ecclesiastes 3. In Genesis 2:5-6, because, there was no man to till the ground God sent a mist out of the ground to water the ground.

**5. THE WHEN:** There is a when to every vision that God gives to every man. [Habakkuk 2 – though the vision tarries, wait for it, for it shall surely come to pass]. E.g. Esther in the palace; Moses in the wilderness with Jethro – the Midianites; David in the wilderness; Joseph sold into slavery ending up in prison for the preservation of life [posterity] - Ecclesiastes 3:1-3. The timing and environment must be right for the manifestation of the vision or promise. Find out when. When the fullness of time came, God sent his Son.

**6. THE WHERE:** Where is God going to bring the promise to pass? In the accomplishment of very vision, all these six points or characteristics must be seen or satisfied just as it was in the scenario in Genesis 11.

- The who: Come let us – all of them of one language [vss.3&4]
- The what: let us build a city [vs. 4]
- The way & how: they had brick for stone and slime for mortar [vs. 3]
- The why: for a reason - we will not be scattered abroad [vs. 4]
- The when: let us build now [vs. 4]
- The where: a plain in the land of Shinar where they dwelt [vs. 2]

Don't enter ministry without a specific personal and ministry covenant with God. When you understand the covenant you have, you have confidence and boldness to summon your covenant to deal with demons and hindrances that stand in the way of the fulfilment of your divine assignment. If you are sent, you must know the covenant that comes with your sending. Moses knew 'I am that I am' was with him to back up his words. The apostles knew He would confirm the words they preached with signs and wonders. Jesus knowing He was sent by God was bold enough to say, 'the works I see him do is what I do also', etc.

In conclusion, I repeat: Ministry begins with and is sustained by receiving four major instructions and knowing the 6 'w's and 1 'h'.
**a. Description**
**b. Inscription**
**c. Prescription and**

**d. Subscription.**

**e.** Know the following six crucial points: The 'who', the 'what', the 'way', [the how] the 'why', the 'when', and the 'where'.

Rudyard Kipling said: "I keep six honest serving men (They taught me all I knew); Their names are What and Why and When And How and Where and Who."

You must of necessity receive and familiarize yourself with these instructions from God before you embark on your journey/enterprise in ministry:

**4. Know how to deal with your prophet.**
- Don't desire to be physically close, rather let your heart be close.
- You may have too many people but not many sons; many follow but not many are sons. Only Elisha was a son out of all those students in the school of prophets. 2 Kings 2:7, 'And fifty men of the sons of the prophets went, and stood to view afar off: and they two stood by Jordan.'
- Don't offend them and if they shout on you stay humble - don't change.
- Focus on the man you are following. Your attitude should be: 'I am here to serve and learn and receive from him all I need to get to my destination.
- Don't get excited at Gilgal, Bethel or Jericho. Follow your leader to Jordan. That is where you are asked 'What would you have me do for you?' and that is where you have access to the mantle and double of what your father is carrying.

## X. The tenth law is the Law of CONTINUOUS LEARNING*

– Those who learn more, earn more. Today a Reader, Tomorrow a Leader. 1 Timothy 5:17, 'Let the elders that rule well be counted worthy of double honour, especially they who labour in the word and doctrine.'
- It takes a studious life to secure a glorious ministry.
- It takes a studious life to secure a glorious career.
- It takes a studious life to secure a glorious destiny.
- Schooling gives you a certificate and credentials but learning makes you a leader and a fortune.
- Schooling makes you literate but continuous investment in literature makes you an impactful leader and creates your future.
- If you are not studious you are heading for shame. Paul said in 2 Timothy 2:15, 'Study to show thyself approved unto God, a workman that needeth not to be ashamed, rightly dividing the word of truth.'
- A preacher who is not a reader will soon preach himself out. Romans 11:33, 'O the depth of the riches both of the wisdom and knowledge of God! how unsearchable are his judgments, and his ways past finding out!'
- That is why he said 'study'. Nobody ever comes to an end of a studious life. The greatest Pastor on earth today David Yonggi Cho of South Korea said he spends 75% of his time studying, searching, preparing messages whilst others keep chatting and walk dry to the platform. **It is important for us to know that it takes a studious life to secure a glorious ministry.**

Paul said in 2 Timothy 4:13, 'The cloak that I left at Troas with Carpus, when thou comest, bring with thee, and the books, but especially the parchments.'

'.....but especially my notes, my parchments, my books.'
- He was a learner, a student of the word.
- If you are not a learner you never become a leader.
- Everyone who is taking the lead is a committed learner.
- If you cannot see beyond what others have seen, nobody will follow you. There are those who read the Bible for fun while some read to learn. If you are not a writer you are not a learner - the lessons you learn must be documented. If you want to enter into rest in your ministry then you must labour in the word of God, the anointed books around you, you must invest in resources in expanding your knowledge base. Some have said if you want to hide something from a black man put it in a book. This became a common saying among the whites. Unfortunately many have never read a book since they left school and we must enforce a change in that mentality. Schooling gives you a certificate, a job and credentials. But, Continuous learning makes you a leader and a fortune. **What you do after school determines who and what you become. Without a functional library you cannot generate extraordinary results or live an extraordinary life.**

Jesus was a perpetual learner. Isaiah 50:4, 'The Lord GOD hath given me the tongue of the learned, that I should know how to speak a word in season to him that is weary: he wakeneth morning by morning, he wakeneth mine ear to hear as the learned.'

He was constantly learning at the feet of the Father. If you must become a great leader then you better become an addicted learner. The man Daniel even though endowed by God with wisdom, was an addicted learner. He said in Daniel 9:2, 'In the first year of his reign I Daniel understood by books the number of the years, whereof the word of the LORD came to Jeremiah the prophet, that he would accomplish seventy years in the desolations of Jerusalem.'

If you are not a friend of books, you cannot go far; do not be slothful. Have a functional library, not a decorational or decorative library. Have an appetite for knowledge. Have and maintain an insatiable crave for knowledge. If you are not a hard worker, you cannot be a high flier. You can't eat your cake and have it. There are too many lazy people in the pulpits today, who are only just having fun with religion and are not impacting any lives because they are not willing to pay the price. NOTE: The price determines the prize. THE PRICE YOU PAY=THE PRIZE YOU EARN!
Engage the Law of tireless learning - addiction to knowledge - an addiction to learning. If you are not a reader, you cannot be a leader. What you do not have, you cannot give. It is said that TL Osborn in his latter days, turned his swimming pool into a library while Kenneth Hagin always had a book on his table before he went to be with the Lord; he was always reading. **What you don't have you cannot give - so sit up. There is no future for an idle man, no not in the ministry.** Double honour is a product of double commitment to a studious life. The more committed you are to a studious life, the more

glorious your ministry becomes. A disciplined life orders his life. It was George Washington who said, 'Discipline is the soul of an army; it makes small numbers formidable, procures success to the weak and confers esteem to all.'

## XI. The eleventh law is the Law of DISCIPLINE*

"Self-discipline is the ability to make yourself do what you should do, when you should do it, whether you feel like it or not." - Elbert Hubbard, author and lecturer

Looking at the life of Paul the apostle, a profound leader, we see a clear display of the virtues of self-discipline. He said in 1 Corinthians 6:12, 'All things are lawful unto me, but all things are not expedient: all things are lawful for me, **but I will not be brought under the power of any.**' Then in 1 Corinthians 10:23, he said, 'All things are lawful for me, but all things are not expedient: all things are lawful for me, **but all things edify not.**' [**Not all things are beneficial**]

The word expedient is described as appropriate: appropriate, advisable, or useful in a situation that requires action or advantageous: advantageous for practical rather than moral reasons. **So, some things don't have to be morally wrong to be the wrong thing to do.** It's just inappropriate, inadvisable, not useful or advantageous for practical reasons more than moral reasons.
- A disciplined life places greater value on essentials.
- It orders its priorities intelligibly.

- It operates by schedule.
- It functions without requiring supervision.
- It makes the most of his time.
- It takes discipline to be distinguished.
- If you leave your life to chance, you don't have a chance. "Without discipline there is no life at all." - Katharine Hepburn
- If you operate by whatever comes your way, you don't get anything accomplished by the end of any day. Discipline runs a schedule that tells him what time he gets up, what he does between the first and second hour, what he does between the second and third hour, the third and fourth hour, fifth and sixth hour, etc.
- A disciplined person RUNS A SCHEDULE THAT CONNOTES A MAN ON A MISSION! Someone once asked my spiritual father, 'How do you get time to read?' He answered with a question, 'How do you get time to eat?' He continued, 'How can you schedule your eating time without scheduling your reading time or praying time or study time?' Discipline puts you on a lifestyle of schedules. You know what each day is supposed to deliver and you work at it conscientiously. So no matter where you are today, discipline can transform your destiny. The students who fail in school, fail not because they are poor, they fail because they are disorganized, they are disorderly, don't have an orderly program and do things as it happens. You never find a distinguished man who is not disciplined. It takes an orderly life to enjoy progress. Paul said I will remain committed only to what things are expedient. I will do only those things that are expedient. That is the law of Discipline.

## XII. The twelfth law is the Law of DILIGENCE - HARD WORK*

Proverbs 22:29, 'Seest thou a man diligent in his business? he shall stand before kings; he shall not stand before mean men.'

Observe closely a man who is diligent in his business work, he shall stand before kings – not ordinary men - he has a place on top, not at the bottom. **So to move from where you are to a higher plain you have to take a flight of diligence.** That simply translates as hard work. Jesus said, 'I must work the works of him that sent me.' John 5:17 says, 'But Jesus answered them, My Father worketh hitherto, and I work.' Paul said, 'But by the grace of God I am what I am: and his grace which was bestowed upon me was not in vain; but I laboured more abundantly than they all: yet not I, but the grace of God which was with me.' (1 Corinthians 15:10)

You cannot get out of life more than what you are willing to invest into it. Paul said I laboured more abundantly than them all. The Law of Diligence is the only way to gain prominence in your field. Whatsoever a man sows, that is what he would reap.

Galatians 6:6-10, 'Let him that is taught in the word communicate unto him that teacheth in all good things. Be not deceived; God is not mocked: for whatsoever a man soweth, that shall he also reap. For he that soweth to his flesh shall of the flesh reap corruption; but he that soweth to the Spirit shall of the Spirit reap life everlasting. And let us not be weary in well doing: for in due season we shall reap, if we faint not. As we have therefore opportunity, let us do good unto all men, especially unto them who are of the household of faith.'

So: Don't just carry a title, accomplish your task.
- There is no entitlement in titles.
- There is only entitlement in accomplishments.
- Don't just carry a title; Strive to accomplish your mandate.
- Your mandate is more important than your title. Too many people are too relaxed to fulfil their ministry. Amos 6:1 warns, 'Woe unto them that are at ease in Zion.' Strive for mastery in your field - It is the only way. Luke 12:49-50 says, 'I am come to send fire on the earth; and what will I, if it be already kindled? But I have a baptism to be baptized with; and how am I straitened till it be accomplished!'
- How am I stretched until it is accomplished! If your ministry does not stretch you, it will not impact lives because it is the stretching of your mandate that impacts the people under your ministry. The Law of diligence simply means hard work. Every minister you see who keeps moving about every day greeting people in the corner, they don't make much out of life. It is time to stretch yourself to deliver your mandate. There must be a Baptism of Labour. There is no way to give birth as a woman without going through the labour ward. You can't deliver your mandate without passing through the labour room of your ministry; you must pass through the labour room before you can deliver. Your mandate will remain as pregnancy until you go to the labour room. (Isaiah 66) Jesus said, 'I must work the works of him that sent me....'

Paul said I laboured more abundantly than them all and the effect of his labour in his ministry is still speaking today. If Jesus tarries may the effect of your labour in ministry still be felt and be speaking four generations after you. John D. Rockefeller said, 'When work goes out of fashion, civilisation will totter and fall.' That is: when work goes out of fashion, when people devise short cuts to getting results outside work, advancements will cease. It takes work for things to keep working. I laboured more, but not me but grace. It takes grace to make the most of your time. We receive the grace to work and fulfil our mandate. (Proverbs 14:23; 12:24; 13:4) If you are not a hard worker today, you are sure to become a beggar tomorrow. My father in the Lord made this statement: "One disease that God has not cured in my life is the disease of being busy. Everybody even my enemies and the devil knows I am very busy and my being busy is not to be regretted. Receive that grace today in the name of Jesus. I have seen proofs. We have crossed the $1,000,000 mark as wages today in Africa. In all labour there is profit. He that tilleth his land shall be satisfied with bread. Stay on your job. God is all you need to have all your needs met. If you don't want to become a beggar, please become a genuine worker." (Psalm 1:1-3)

## XIII. The thirteenth law is the Law of SPIRITUAL IMPACT*

- This is the source of your wages in the ministry.
- This is the source of your income in the ministry.
- This is the source of your livelihood in the ministry.

## How Does A Minister Secure His Sure Continual Flow of Wages?

Romans 15:27, 'It hath pleased them verily; and their debtors they are. For if the Gentiles have been made partakers of their spiritual things, their duty is also to minister unto them in carnal things.'

**1. Make your hearers partakers of your spiritual things i.e. what you teach and he will make it their duty to also minister to you out of their material things.**

So, when you impact people spiritually, God makes it their duty to respond to you materially. Deuteronomy 25:4, 'Thou shalt not muzzle the ox when he treadeth out the corn.'

1 Corinthians 9:9, 'For it is written in the law of Moses, Thou shalt not muzzle the mouth of the ox that treadeth out the corn. Doth God take care for oxen?'

1 Timothy 5:18, 'For the scripture saith, Thou shalt not muzzle the ox that treadeth out the corn. And, The labourer is worthy of his reward.' The ox that is threshing the corn is entitled to the proceeds. The quality of your spiritual impact is what determines the material returns that gravitate to you.

**2. Preach and show the glad tidings**
Luke 8:1-3 records what happened in Jesus' Ministry. 'And it came to pass afterward, that he went throughout every city

and village, **preaching and showing** the glad tidings of the kingdom of God: and the twelve were with him, And certain women, which had been healed of evil spirits and infirmities, Mary called Magdalene, out of whom went seven devils, And Joanna the wife of Chuza Herod's steward, and Susanna, and many others, which ministered unto him of their substance.'

Because their lives were spiritually impacted, Mary Magdalene out of whom seven demons were driven out and the others ministered to Jesus out of their own substance, not their leftovers. So, it takes spiritual impact to enjoy material comfort. So if you must have your wages, bible says the labourer is worthy of his wages, labour in the word, labour in prayer, impact the lives of men positively and they will respond gladly by investing in the ministry God has given you and invest into your life. All biblical laws are universal - they deliver at the same rate everywhere; whether you are in a village or city it will still work. It is a law. It takes a spiritual man to impact people spiritually. A carnal man cannot impact people spiritually. It takes spiritual men to impact people spiritually - it takes spiritually-minded people to impact people spiritually. That is why the Bible says to be spiritually minded is peace and to be carnally-minded is death.

You are either spiritual or carnal - you cannot be neutral. A Pastor who is stealing church money, how spiritual is that? A pastor planning how to break the church - how spiritual is that? A pastor who never prays or reads his Bible, how spiritual is that? A pastor who is doing politics or is involved in gossip with the congregation or creating factions or tribalism, how spiritual is that? Therefore every minister is his worst enemy. There is nobody that is against you as much as you are against yourself. When you do what you must do, you will see how weak the devil is. Therefore, there is nobody who is doing you - you are doing yourself. So invest in yourself and in your ministry - read, study your bible, prepare and eat your messages before you dish it out to others. In 1987, God said to my spiritual father, 'Don't raise money; raise men and you will have more money than you will ever require for ministry.' Today the vogue is about raising money, bringing in 'Experts' in raising funds. If your ministry is a men-raising ministry you will never lack money or resources. Put these things before your eyes, and as you do these things and live by these laws, your 100 members will become 200 then 400 then 1000 then 10,000 then 20,000.

**The testimonies of changed lives are the cheapest way to grow a church.** It is interesting to note that: Publicity does not grow a church - it is transformation [of lives] that grows a church. Raise men - the law of spiritual impact. They must have seen enough proofs to convince themselves that where the church is located is not far. There is no scientific strategy for growing a church. Once I was blind, now I see and that is why you must strive to impact the people spiritually and as changes occur in their lives, you find members of their family coming in, friends coming up, colleagues coming in and then the church is filling up. It is the Testimony of changed lives that grows a church, not, radio, newspaper or TV adverts.

The growth of the church is effected by the members of the church whose lives have been touched and they go and tell others, 'come and see, we were all on the floor together but we are different now, come and see.' So, go every morning when you are going to minister to the people with a heart willing to impart to impact the people and you will see how the church will be growing. They go and tell the others, 'come and see' and that is enough TV advert.

**3. Stay with your assignment** – (Proverbs 27:8, 23-27)
Proverbs 27:8, 'As a bird that wandereth from her nest, so is a man that wandereth from his place.'

**4. Know the state of your flock:** Proverbs 27:23-27, 'Be thou diligent to know the state of thy flocks, and look well to thy herds. For riches are not for ever: and doth the crown endure to every generation? The hay appeareth, and the tender grass showeth itself, and herbs of the mountains are gathered. The lambs are for thy clothing, and the goats are the price of the field. And thou shalt have goats' milk enough for thy food, for the food of thy household, and for the maintenance for thy maidens.'

**5. FEED THEM the Word - Preach and show the glad tidings of the kingdom.** Galatians 6:6 says, 'Let him [them] that is taught in the word communicate unto him [them] that teacheth in all good things.'

The amplified version reads, 'Let him that receives instruction in the word of God share all good things with his teacher [contributing to his support.]'

So, the people are only permitted to minister of their material substance to those who teach good things. Not to come out of church downcast but rather lifted, because light has shined from heaven and their prison bands have been broken, walking free. So it is God who moves men. He said, 'If they minister to you spiritual things, it is your duty to minister to them of your physical or material things.' **So, you must generate spiritual impact in order to enjoy material supplies.** (Romans 15:27; 1 Corinthians 9:11)

## QUALIFYING FOR, PROVOKING AND ENJOYING HEAVENLY SUPPLIES
## – 21 THINGS TO NOTE AND DO:

1. If you want to enjoy heavenly supplies, you must constantly generate spiritual impact.
2. If you minister to them spiritual things, He makes it their duty to minister to you of their carnal or material things.
3. If you make it your duty to minister to them spiritually, God will make it their duty to minister to you of their carnal or material substance or blessing.
4. That is why a man of God should be fully set for his meetings; people have real problems. FACE REALITIES: ASK yourself, 'Am I imparting the people spiritually or am I just having fun; am I getting at the people, are they being transformed and is it

being backed with signs and wonders in their lives?'

5. You must be so prepared, fed and set for your meetings that when you get there they can see the freshness.

6. Be forever committed to your preparations; as you appear and whilst you are teaching, eat the things you're teaching because you've been in strong fellowship with the Holy Spirit in preparing yourself to be an agent that will meet the needs of the people.

7. They must see God through what you are teaching, preaching and showing - that takes a lot of responsibility on your part.

8. Great men and women of God package their lives to affect the people they are going to minister to. Package your life to affect the people you are going to minister to. Don't carry fun all about. Be in league with God. Be in link with God. Be in touch with Heaven so much so that within 15 minutes of your ministering, things begin to happen in the form of transformation of lives and manifestations of the Holy Spirit in the form of signs and wonders.

9. Spend time with Him before ministering. Wait on your ministry.

10. LIFE DOES NOT GIVE YOU WHAT YOU DESERVE BUT WHAT YOU DEMAND AND WORK FOR. Life comes with a great responsibility. Am I touching the people? If I am not touching them, they won't touch me. Everyone in our various ministries today are great potentials for the kingdom depending on how we are touching them with truth and indeed. Touching them with spiritual values and that continues to enhance their values in life.

11. Prepare and Minister with great responsibility that people will be so committed by what they experience that they would want to stay till they die in your church.

12. Preaching and showing will continue to multiply the number and multiply the resources. Acts 6:7, 'And the word of God increased; and the number of the disciples multiplied in Jerusalem greatly;............'

13. Preaching and showing - A ministry of proofs commanding divine provisions and divine supplies. You may say, 'I don't have the gift of miracles, signs and wonders.' God has given you a word. You are a steward of spiritual things. Every minister has been given the word; let that word begin to transform the lives of the people and they'll begin to touch your ministry in very unique fashions.

14. These spiritual truths will work anywhere. Some say, 'O the people in this nation are……..' If it is the word, it will work everywhere. It cannot be broken by climate or colour. The scriptures cannot be broken. Deuteronomy 2:36 confirms this: 'From Aroer, which is by the brink of the river of Arnon, and from the city that is by the river, even unto Gilead, **there was not one city too strong for us: the LORD our God delivered all unto us:**'

15. **NO NATION IS TOO STRONG TO RESIST THE POWER OF THE GOSPEL** (Romans 1:16). Our master responsibility is our commitment to the Word of God because it is the baseline for transformations and the baseline for manifestations. Mark 16:15-20 says, '….God was working with them confirming the WORD with signs following.' It is the word that transforms and it is the word that is also confirmed

to generate miracles.

16. THEREFORE: Preach the word in season and out of season and then you will enjoy great supplies for every heavenly mandate that you secure. Facilities are built or purchased through money and money doesn't drop on the altar or pulpit or on the floor; money always drops through human hands and it drops through human hands as they are touched. HUMAN SPONSORS HIJACK AND LIMIT THE MOVE OF GOD!

17. Ministry is not financed by any marketing strategy; you can't market the church through getting public relations experts to use carnal strategies to market the church. He came and flushed out all who were buying and selling. You can't market the church; you can only operate by the truth to command results. Stop looking for carnal strategies to obtain spiritual backing.

18. THIS IS THE TRUTH: If you touch the three people, they will soon become ten and if you touch the ten, their lives will change from one pound to ten pounds and if you touch the ten, their lives will change from ten pounds to hundred pounds and as you keep touching them they keep multiplying in number and multiplying in favour and your ministry begins to go up and up. The strategy hasn't changed - the word of God liveth and abideth forever. The same strategy – the same Lord over all is rich unto all (Romans 10:12). As we remain in covenant with God and with each other, our stories will get brighter and brighter by the day, Amen! Go and preach and show; the iron bars will not stop us. RESULT: GOD WILL COMMAND ANGELS, ANIMALS, FISHES, MEN, ORGANISATIONS, PEOPLE WHO KNOW OR DON'T

KNOW YOU, people who love you, hate you or dislike you to give to you. God commanded a raven and widow to feed Elijah, Joseph of Arimathaea giving his tomb for Jesus' burial; Luke 8:1-3; Abimelech and Abraham, Lydia; 1 Cor. 9. So, God is responsible for His servants' upkeep and wellbeing. (Luke 22:35)

19. The Holy Spirit will make it His responsibility to command and employ the ones you touch, impact, feed, lead, teach, care for, the members to bless you financially with monetary gifts. (1 Timothy 5:17 amplified version) This is an area where many Christians miss God completely, because they view the giving of financial gifts as a loss instead of the opportunity to attract prosperity that He designed it to be. Some don't even consider that their minister is spiritually employed, and as such deserving of wages, gifts, honorariums and bonuses. It is amazing to me that when these advantages are given in the corporate sector no one murmurs or complains. However Christians very often begrudge the man of God the right to benefit financially from preaching and teaching the Word. (1 Timothy 5:18)
20. Those who labour as shepherds tending Christ's sheep should be paid by God through those they lead. Just as you would not close up the mouth of the ox labouring to tread the corn (thus preventing him from eating) – neither should you stand in the way of your pastor benefiting financially from those whose spiritual needs he ministers to. As one in covenant with God, understand that when God tells you to do something, it's meant for your benefit and the area of giving is no exception. When you sow a seed into the life of your man of God, you

are sowing even more seed into your own life. How? First of all when you give, the bible clearly states in Luke 6:38 that it shall be given back to you again, good measure, pressed down, and shaken together and running over. It's truly beneficial for you to plant your seed (finances) into good soil (your man of God) because in obeying the word of God you will definitely reap a harvest.

21. In 1 Corinthians 9:7-14, it's absolutely clear that men of God are supposed to prosper, so don't look down on them when they start to do just that. When you begin to sow and plant into their lives, you too will begin to prosper. Does your pastor preach the word with understanding, so that you can get a hold of those things God wants you to know? Does he preach what you need to know in order to be a fruitful Christian and fulfil destiny? If so the Bible says that man is worthy of the finances he receives. To hold back on financial blessing or monetary gifts is to go against the word of God and hinders your blessings in the process.

**6. Teach the members to receive you as a gift from God** – Ephesians 4:7,8,11-12; Matthew 16:13-end. Jesus gave you to them as a gift. James 1:17 says, 'Every good gift and every perfect gift is from above, and cometh down from the Father of lights, with whom is no variableness, neither shadow of turning.'

**7. They must know you as their Pastor and know your wife** – they must study your lifestyle as a Christian leader and follow your faith. [What you've been able to achieve with your faith] – 1 Thessalonians 5:12; 2 Timothy 3:10

**8. They must Esteem you very highly in love and be at peace among themselves.** – 1 Thessalonians 5:13

**9. They must Pray for you daily both in the spirit and intelligently using God's word** that you will behold wondrous things from God's word, [Ps. 119:18] that you will be delivered from them that do not believe, that signs and wonders will be wrought through you as you minister God's word and that the word will have free course and great impact. – 2 Thessalonians 3:1; 1 Thessalonians 3:2; Acts 12:1-17 [Peter delivered from prison] (Order my book: How to Pray and Why You Must Pray For Your Pastor and Your Church daily from www.houseofjudah.org.uk)

**10. Teach them to Communicate to you personally** – give to you willingly and of their own accord and corporately as a church and arrange occasional surprises for you. They endear themselves to God and you that way because a man's gift makes room for him and brings him before great men. They must stand with your ministry without reservation. (Galatians 6:6; 3:7; Hebrews 7:5; Philippians 4:14-17; Luke 8:1-3)

**11. Teach them to imitate you as you imitate Christ** – be faithful to follow you. (1 Corinthians 11:1; Hebrews 6:12; Philippians 4:9; 2 Kings 2:1-15) Hosea 4:9, 'And there shall be, like people, like priest: .............., and reward them their doings.' … … … …..Like priest like people.

**12. Teach them to obey your teachings in order to be transformed** - in the process, they will sow into your life – God will ensure it. (Acts 20:28-32; 1 Corinthians 11:1-2) A Pastor's number one ministry is the word and prayer, not running around. (Acts 6:1-7) As they serve Jesus and their Pastor well, Ephesians 6:1-3 shall be their portion. If the church will allow the Pastors to stay in the word and prayer, they will behold wondrous things and the members will increase, multiply in number and be blessed.

**XIV. The fourteenth law is the Law of SOWING AND REAPING*** [seedtime and harvest]:

- The Law of seedtime and harvest is Key to **ENJOYING AN OPEN HEAVEN OVER YOUR LIFE AND MINISTRY** [Genesis 8:22; Galatians 6:6-10; Deuteronomy 8:17-18; Job 36:11]
- **PROSPERITY IS POSSIBLE IN THE MIDST OF SCARCITY.**
- The Ministry's prosperity is different from the Pastor's prosperity.
- What the Pastor sows, he reaps like any member of the church and it is what the ministry sows that determines what falls on the ministry.
- The subject of sowing and reaping in relation to ministry has not been taught extensively.
- Many ministries are not involved in seed-sowing at all and that is why many ministries are financially strangulated.
- Many ministries are under financial pressures because they have not discovered the mystery of ministry seed-sowing.

On the 4th of September, 1987 at Sheraton hotel in Lagos, my father in the Lord stumbled on a mystery command in Hebrews 7:7 'And without all contradiction the less is blessed of the better.' When he asked what it meant, God told him, 'Let the ministries begin to sow seeds into higher ministries and as they sow into higher ministries, they'll begin to move higher in their pursuits. Begin to sow into higher ministries and see what I will do in the ministry.'

- **There are things you do as a matter of convenience but there are other things you do as a commandment** – this is not sowing into ministries in need but into higher ministries **because the less is blessed of the better i.e. having an established approach to seed-sowing to reap consistently by deliberate provocation motivated by purpose.** REASON BEING: **THE COVENANT WILL PREVAIL IRRESPECTIVE OF THE CLIMATE!**
**THE COVENANT IS SUPERIOR TO ANY CLIMATE!**
**OPEN HEAVENS IS NOT BY CHANCE!**
**OPERATING UNDER OPEN HEAVENS IS NOT GUESSWORK OR BY TRIAL AND ERROR!**
**- IT IS CONSCIOUSLY AND DELIBERATELY PROVOKED!**

## DOES YOUR MINISTRY PAY TITHES?

Leviticus 27:30 says, 'And all the tithe of the land, whether of the seed of the land, or of the fruit of the tree, is the LORD'S: it is holy unto the LORD.'

**All the tithe of the land is the Lord's, it shall be holy unto the Lord; you shall not take an aught of it.** Malachi 3:8-12 instructs, 'Will a man rob God? Yet ye have robbed me. But ye say, Wherein have we robbed thee? In tithes and offerings. Ye are cursed with a curse: for ye have robbed me, even this whole nation. **Bring ye all the tithes into the storehouse, that there may be meat in mine house,** and prove me now herewith, saith the LORD of hosts, if I will not open you the windows of heaven, and pour you out a blessing, that there shall not be room enough to receive it. And I will rebuke the devourer for your sakes, and he shall not destroy the fruits of your ground; neither shall your vine cast her fruit before the time in the field, saith the LORD of hosts. And all nations shall call you blessed: for ye shall be a delightsome land, saith the LORD of hosts.'

Deuteronomy 12:14, '**But in the place which the LORD shall choose in one of thy tribes, there thou shalt offer thy burnt offerings, and there** thou shalt do all that I command thee.'

Malachi 3 says, bring ye all the tithe into the storehouse............... and Deuteronomy tells you ...............bring it where I shall choose...

## THE REALITY OF THE WINDOWS OF HEAVEN BLESSINGS

Enjoying an OPEN HEAVEN DIMENSION OF BLESSING OVER YOUR MINISTRY comes through tithing out to higher ministries and ministries you are instructed to give to. Our ministry sows ten percent of its income upward into higher ministries and senior men of God, spiritual mentors and my father in the Lord and their ministries that are higher than us and we attract the grace on them for speed and divine accomplishments. What you have to understand is the higher ministries you are authorised to give to don't need your seed - you are the one who needs and requires the grace upon them to fall upon you. Going around preaching to collect offering will not bring offering into your ministry. Stay on your assignment and the provisions will flow in. Start now - don't wait! Without an open heaven, your ministry will stagnate and suffer - that is the only way to increase - start now. That is how God has built himself ministries that are debt-free. Everything is debt-free and a proof of an open heaven.

**Do you really want to experience an open heaven?**
**Then: KNOW AND DO THE FOLLOWING:**
- Sowing into higher ministries takes you higher.
- Sowing into higher ministries opens financial fortunes to your life.
- Sowing into higher ministries opens you up into a new dimension of financial fortune.
- Sowing into higher ministries empowers you to attract their grace.
- Sowing into higher ministries makes you attract their happenings, i.e. what is happening in their ministries.
- Sowing into higher ministries entreats the favour they enjoy.
- Sowing into higher ministries opens major doors of ministry

to both your life and your ministry.
- Sowing into higher ministries brings speedy growth to your ministry.
- Sowing into higher ministries makes you attract what they attract.
- Tithing the resources of your ministry opens the heaven over it and you cannot be living under an open heaven without people noticing.
- Make sure you also give very good and worthy love offerings or honorariums to your guest speakers. It is absolutely essential, mandatory and crucial to the blessing that comes and remains on your life, ministry and members.
- There are Pastors who don't pay tithe. Pastors must pay tithes. The law of tithing is for everyone including pastors.

Galatians 6:6-10, 'Let him that is taught in the word communicate unto him that teacheth in all good things. Be not deceived; God is not mocked: for whatsoever a man soweth, that shall he also reap. For he that soweth to his flesh shall of the flesh reap corruption; but he that soweth to the Spirit shall of the Spirit reap life everlasting. And let us not be weary in well doing: for in due season we shall reap, if we faint not. As we have therefore opportunity, let us do good unto all men, especially unto them who are of the household of faith.'

- IF YOU ARE NOT A TITHER, AND YOUR MINISTRY IS NOT TITHING, I AM NOT SURPRISED THAT THINGS ARE TIGHT FOR YOU!

- IF YOU ARE NOT A TITHER YOU ARE NOT PERMITTED TO PROSPER!

- ALL THE SELF-PROCLAIMED 'MELCHIZEDEKS' MUST REPENT AND START TITHING NOW IF THEY KNOW WHAT IS GOOD FOR THEM!

Our prayer is that no one reading or studying this book will end up a beggar. I decree that every financial struggle both in your life or ministry comes to an end now as you practice this covenant of sowing and reaping. **Remember, it is not those who preach prosperity who enjoy prosperity; it is only those who practice the covenant of prosperity - seed time and harvest** (Genesis 8:22; 12:1-3; Deuteronomy 8:17-18; Luke 6:38; Philippians 4:14-19; Job 36:11; Psalm 37:4-6) **who enjoy prosperity.**

**SECRETS:**
1. Don't raise or receive offerings with an empty hand - an empty hand will reap an empty result.

2. If you are not a giver you are not permitted to prosper.

3. Stop raising offerings and start raising men and you will have more than you need to fulfil the ministry.

4. Obey these spiritual laws and you will be in command. Tithe!

5. The truth is that without money you cannot fulfil your

ministry and without an open heaven there will never be enough money to fulfil it. If money was crucial to Jesus and He needed a bag of money carrier [treasurer] to fulfil His mission, as anointed as He was, then you and I need it and the way to get it is by covenant practice.

6. You are a giver as a minister and a giver as a ministry [i.e. your ministry is a giving ministry too].

7. You are a tither as a minister and a tither as a ministry. [your ministry is a tithing ministry too].

8. The heaven will remain open and everything will begin to work and continue to work.

9. ADVICE: You should either give worthy honorariums to guest speakers or don't invite them at all; wait till you are ready or have an agreement with them before they agree to come and minister for you but don't promise and not deliver or abuse their gift. Let them know your size.

As a testimony: In our ministry, House of Judah, we set aside and sow fifteen percent of our income as a church to specific higher ministries and ministers and as love offerings and the results are evident each week. There is no stress in or on our ministry financially. God said after tithing, prove me now and I will open the windows of heaven and pour you out a blessing such as there will not be room enough to receive it. Grace to apply these treasures to your life – receive it now!

## XV. The fifteenth law is the LAW of ENVISIONING [VISIONEERING] OR THE LAW OF IMAGINATION:

No matter your area of calling, what you cannot see today never becomes a reality in your life tomorrow. In Genesis 13:14-17, He said to Abraham, 'And the LORD said unto Abram, after that Lot was separated from him, Lift up now thine eyes, and look from the place where thou art northward, and southward, and eastward, and westward: For all the land which thou seest, to thee will I give it, and to thy seed for ever. And I will make thy seed as the dust of the earth: so that if a man can number the dust of the earth, then shall thy seed also be numbered. Arise, walk through the land in the length of it and in the breadth of it; for I will give it unto thee.'

Many people have received visions from the Lord but they are not able to perceive the extent of that vision and if you are called the seed of Abraham, you are called to do the works of Abraham. **Whatever will become real in Abraham's hand tomorrow, he is required to see it today.**

The question then is what seest thou? What do you see? What future do you see in the ministry that God has given to you? God said to Jeremiah, 'What seest thou? He said I see a rod of an almond tree. He said thou hast well seen I will hasten my word to perform it.' What you are not able to see, God is not committed to perform. What do you see? (Jeremiah 1:11-12) After the establishment of his heavenly vision in verse 3-7 he is called upon to visualize what he can see so he can become

- what he cannot see he cannot have. We live in a dreamers' world - without a dream, destiny is doomed.

What you cannot dream you never dare! It is the dreamers' world. Until you become a dreamer no matter how heavenly your vision is, it will be limited. The extent to which you can see is what will determine what will become of your vision. The law of imagination '......though thy beginning was small thy latter end shall greatly increase.' (Job 8:7) That becomes your ultimate. So, a dream is a spiritual requirement for creating your desired future. See yourself talking to presidents, prime ministers, ministers of state well ahead of time. **A dream takes you into the reality of your future before you arrive there - it is so intoxicating that it takes you there. It takes a sanctified dreamer to fulfil his ministry. It takes a sanctified dreamer to fully deliver the mandate of God upon his life. It takes a sanctified dreamer to make a full proof of his ministry.**

- Sanctified dreams, revelation-provoked dreams, spiritually responsible dreams you have committed to make happen. There are many idle dreamers, there are people who dream of prospering without doing anything or what it takes to make it happen; so be responsible. Those are all idle dreams, balloon dreams.

- **What you see today is what you become tomorrow.** Declare what you want to see in your life and future. The future you cannot see, you never live in the reality of it. **A dream is the mental picture of your future.** He said in Genesis 11:6 '........

and this they begun to do and now nothing can be refrained from them of what they've imagined to do.'
- **So your imagination is what determines your destination.** It is your imagination that determines your destination - destiny. '......for as a man thinketh in his heart so is he.' – Proverbs 23:7
- So what you think determines what you take.
- Whatever is too big for your mind is too big for your hand.
- Whatever your mind cannot handle, your hand will never realize.
- Whatever becomes of your tomorrow begins with your mind - it begins with your mind - it begins with your mind.
- Whatever is too big for your mouth to say will be too big for your hands to handle. **Some people are so busy thinking 'poverty' there is no way they can mistakenly step into prosperity. They think of poverty so much that poverty becomes their natural companion.**

In 1986, just about the time his ministry started, my father in the Lord was asked by an American, 'What needs have you in your ministry?' His answer was, 'Our ministry has no needs - we only meet needs.' He said he gave that answer because he just couldn't identify with the thoughts of poverty because his royal mentality had overtaken him. Nothing could be made to make him think poor. He said recently, 'The minimum seed we sow to other higher ministries is $5000.' **You can't think poor and mistakenly become rich.** For as a man thinketh in his heart, so is he. I am full of that mentality of stewardship under the King of kings and Lord of lords. **Until you can see a crown on your head, you can never wear one. Until you can**

**see a crown on your head, you will never live to wear one.** I see you set free from day-dreaming; you are rather dreaming your dream from the Bible or day-dreaming. Jesus is the Sun of righteousness so whatever you can see from Genesis to Malachi to Revelation you are permitted to dream it; that is what is called sanctified dreams, i.e. dreams that are born out of revelation from the truth from God's word. 'Seest thou a man that is diligent in his business he shall not stand before mean men.' (Proverbs 22:29) As a committed tither, there has not been one day that my tithe was missing in God's account since 1989, so I can only dream of open heaven blessing. If you want to walk in kingdom prosperity, you must walk in the reality of covenant prosperity through covenant practice. Do your part and commit Him to do His part. If you want to avoid shame in your ministry, then study, study, study, tithe, tithe, tithe, give, give, give and remain diligent, grateful, thankful, praise-full, God-full and you will become wonderful. **You can't be sleeping and expect to be enthroned. No!**

So, if you do not want to see shame, study, read, think, dream big, envision, be diligent, sacrifice, focus, be excellent and give it all you've got. That is the kind of sanctified dreams we are talking about. What has God said is obtainable and what has He said you should do to actualize it i.e. to make it happen. When you do what you must do, God's integrity is committed to make it happen. Don't be praying when you should be acting responsible. Destiny is a race of responsibility. If you don't want to end up a liability, accept responsibility today.

## XVI. The sixteenth law is the Law of THINKING POSSIBILITIES

This law involves using your mind to create possibilities. **Think the word, think testimonies and think possibilities for as a man thinketh in his heart, so is he. (Proverbs 23:7)** Look around you and use [engage] your mind. Everyone has a future but you have to begin to imagine it - see it. The mind of man is the birthplace of wisdom which culminates in wealth.

**People are not poor because of the colour of their skin; no, people are poor because of the colour of their brain [they haven't decorated their mind with what it takes to create wealth.**

'I don't pray for money because I have prayed for wisdom which culminates in wealth creation (1 Kings 3:3-14; 4:29-34).' - Pastor David Ibiyeomie

Wisdom is the custodian of wealth any day, anytime, anywhere. Proverbs 8:18-21; Deuteronomy 8:18; Haggai 2:6; Jude 1:25)

Bishop David Abioye said the following:
i. The mind can be described as putting your brain to work.
ii. You cannot become a head until you put your head to work.
iii. Those who use their heads cannot end up as tails.
iv. If you find yourself as a tail the only thing to do is start using your head. It is your head that puts you ahead.
v. Every slave remains in slavery until he begins to put his head

to work - use his head.

vi. The cheapest way to terminate slavery and begging is to put your head to work. Use your head - use your brain.

vii. Sonship does not guarantee you automatic rulership. You have to be a son with a brain at work. (Proverbs 11:29; 17:2)

## VARIOUS LAWS OF PRODUCTIVITY:

**THE LAW OF CAUSE AND EFFECT**: Everything happens for a reason. For every cause there is an effect, and for every effect, whether you know it or not, there is a specific cause or causes. (Proverbs 26:2) There are no accidents. You can have anything you want in life if you can first decide exactly what it is, and then do the things that others have done to achieve the same result.

**THE LAW OF MIND:** All causation is mental. Your thoughts become your realities. Your thoughts are as creative. You become what you think about most of the time. Think continually about the things you really want, and refuse to think about the things you don't want.

**THE LAW OF MENTAL EQUIVALENCY:** The world around you is the physical equivalent of the world within you. Your main job in life is to create within your own mind the mental equivalent of the life you want to live. Imagine your ideal life, in every respect. Hold that thought until it materializes around you.

**THE LAW OF CORRESPONDENCE:** Your outer life is a reflection of your inner life. There is a direct correspondence between the way you think and feel on the inside and the way you act and experience on the outside. Your relationships, health, wealth and position are mirror images of your inner world.

**THE LAW OF BELIEF:** Whatever you believe, with feeling, becomes your reality. You do not believe what you see; you see what you have already chosen to believe. You must identify and then remove the self-limiting beliefs that hold you back.

**THE LAW OF VALUES:** You always act in a manner consistent with your innermost values and convictions. What you say and do, the choices you make - especially under stress are an exact expression of what you truly value, regardless of what you say.

**THE LAW OF MOTIVATION:** Everything you do or say is triggered by your inner desires, drives and instincts. These may be conscious or unconscious. The key to success is to set your own goals and determine your own motivations.

**THE LAW OF SUBCONSCIOUS ACTIVITY:** Your subconscious mind makes all your words and actions fit a pattern consistent with your self-concept and your innermost beliefs about yourself. Your subconscious mind will move you forward or hold you back depending on how you program it.

**THE LAW OF EXPECTATIONS**: Whatever you expect, with confidence, tends to materialize in the world around you. You always act in a manner consistent with your expectations, and your expectations influence the attitudes and behaviours of the people around you.

**THE LAW OF CONCENTRATION:** Whatever you dwell upon grows and expands in your life. Whatever you concentrate upon and think about repeatedly increases in your world. Therefore, you must focus your thinking on the things you really want in your life.

**THE LAW OF HABIT:** Fully 95 percent of everything you do is the result of your habits, either helpful or hurtful. You can develop habits of success by practicing and repeating success behaviours over and over until they become automatic.

**THE LAW OF ATTRACTION:** You continually attract into your life the people, ideas circumstances that harmonize with your dominant thoughts, either positive or negative. You can be, have and do more because you can change your dominant thoughts.

**XVII. The Last and most important Law needed for us to fulfil our ministry indeed is the LAW OF LOVE\* or THE LAW OF AFFECTION or THE LAW OF COMPASSION.** It is also the law that puts us in command of all other commands (Matthew 22:35-39). Jesus finished a meeting and before sending the people away, he noticed they may faint on the way as they go in John 6:5-11 so he decided let's give them something to eat before they go. He said I have compassion for the people. His ministry was always riding on the wheels of compassion for the people. **Faith can get things done, Hope can inspire the people but only Love can truly impact people. Faith can get things accomplished, hope can get them inspired but only love can impact them.**

The 3 powerful forces in 1 Corinthians 13 are faith, hope and love but the greatest of them is love. **People don't care what or how much you know as much as how much you care. You can inform them with faith, you can inspire them with hope but you can only impact them with love. It is only impacted people that can impact the ministry they belong to - only blessed people can bless the ministry where they belong. If the people you are pastoring are not positively impacted, they cannot positively impact your ministry.**

Only blessed people can be a blessing. He said to Abraham in Genesis 12:1-3, 'I am going to bless you so that you may be a blessing.' Except people are blessed they cannot be a blessing. It is compassion that draws out your soul to another man or for another man's blessing. Jesus was always full of compassion. If you are operating with compassion, you keep enjoying expansion. e.g. As you are preaching, get one of your associates to observe people, those feeling rejected, dejected, in pain and bring them to see you after the service - share with them what the church has. Until you do these you can pray till you die; they won't come near. Without a heart for people you cannot attract them. You cannot love people without them knowing. If you love them, they will know, because love is a spirit. God has not given us a spirit of fear but the spirit of love; people can pick it, because humans are spirits; they can always identify where love is. **Only compassionate ministers end up with great ministries**. People that lack compassion are not entitled to expansions. Jesus had compassion for the people. He saw them as sheep scattered without a shepherd (Matthew 9:36) so, he went in and healed the sick. (Matthew 14:14) He would not let them go and faint on the way. Compassion will always culminate in supernatural manifestations.

It is the compassion in your heart that works out the miracles by your hands. That was how bread and fish came alive. Compassion will always produce miracles. You cannot have compassion and lack miracles. In the days of John Alexander Dowie, people were dying in his time and he was burying people in his church daily. He went into his closet and cried out to God, 'Lord enough' then Acts 10:38 exploded in his spirit and one of the greatest healing ministries begun.....**If you don't have compassion you are not entitled to unction. It is compassion that entitles you to the flow of unction.** There are too many compassionless ministers in the streets. Too many compassionless ministers using people to meet their personal needs and that is why they are always in need.

If you won't stop using people, they will soon leave you. Stop using people; if you stop using people, they will stop leaving you. If you don't have a heart for people they will soon leave you. A leper came to Jesus He touched him and soon leprosy left him. If you don't have compassion, you will use scientific facts to keep people deaf and dumb - keep people in their same state. Compassion provokes the flow of unction. Compassion guarantees expansion. If you don't want your ministry to suffer stagnation, then let compassion rise in your heart. Love is not a gift - love is a choice. Love is the choice of the wise. The greater your love for God, the greater your destiny becomes. The greater your love for people, the greater your ministry becomes. Love is a choice – a decision. After His resurrection, Jesus asked Peter, 'Simon, lovest thou me more than this?' His answer was: 'Lord you know that I love you' - so love is a choice. The greater your love for God the greater your future as a person. The greater your love for people, the greater your ministry becomes … there is no in-between out there. Paul's heart: 1 Thessalonians 2:7-8 reveals the heart of Paul the apostle. 'But we were gentle among you, even as a nurse cherisheth her children: So being affectionately desirous of you, we were willing to have imparted unto you, not the gospel of God only, but also our own souls, because ye were dear unto us.'

If people are not dear to you, you cannot go far in ministry. Your attitude should be: we are not just out to teach you, we are here to pour our soul to you … … … … …..because you are dear to us. - That is what builds a great ministry. As a pastor of pastors, I see many pastors who don't have a heart for people; they are professional pastors who will halt anyone to have their way - the way they lead the ministries shows. You don't go far without a heart for people. Our attitude must be: we are not out there to take from you; rather, we want our souls to be transferred to you; we want what we see to be what you see. We want you to be higher than where we are; we want you to know God the way we know God.

Someone asked my father in the Lord: '**What is the secret of the prosperity of your ministry?**' His answer was: 'When I bless the people, I bless them with the whole of my intestines; everything inside me is blessing them. God, if you will not bless these people, stop blessing me. We don't want to be called a fake prophet - so a ministry where only the minister is being blessed is a fake ministry. They are blessed people so they can be a blessing. It's a Church of blessed people. They are dear unto our heart.' If people are not dear to you, you don't go far in ministry.

Pray, 'Let them have it; let them touch God more than I touch him now.' That will give you access to unlimited ministry. That may not be modern day ministry but that is bible-based ministry. Do you really have a heart for the people or are you taking advantage of them? When you have made a choice to love His people, the Holy Spirit empowers you to love more and more; the love of God is shed abroad in our hearts by the Holy Spirit. (Romans 5:5) 'I want the people I minister to, to be dear to me. Lord, cause the love of God to erupt in my heart - I want the people I serve to be dear to my heart. Let your love spread out to people. Holy Spirit, cause the love of God to erupt in my heart afresh. Cause the love of God to spread to your people, Holy Spirit.'

**Prophecy**
- I see you and your ministry step into the realm of unlimited expansion. I see your ministry ushered into the realm of unlimited expansion.

God has no problem working when there is no one there stealing the glory. It takes meekness to experience true greatness and growing greatness. Whatever we have seen God do in the ministries of our fathers, the living legends and also desire, we will see it duplicated in our churches and ministries and nations. It will erupt in our cities and nations. Amen!

CHAPTER EIGHT

# HOW TO BE PRESERVED FOR YOUR ASSIGNMENT

(Making Eternal Transactions – transactions that count both now and in Eternity)

There is a sound of an abundance of rain. There is going to be an unprecedented crystallizing move of the Spirit of God in this land that will spill over into Europe. (Matthew 4:8-10; 1 Corinthians 15:34 – awake to righteousness)

Life is not a right; it is a privilege. If you cannot keep your tongue, God cannot open your eyes to see mysteries. Those of us who stay alive should know that it was only God who kept us alive. Something has to shift for what God wants to do – the will of God be done on the earth. There is a recruitment taking place in the spirit realm. AWAKE TO KINGDOM PURPOSES – not morality per se, even though that is crucial and must definitely be observed. HIM ONLY WILL YOU SERVE. The only reason why you are alive is to serve him only. We are sons of the kingdom but we are also servants. Judge your life in the context of eternity – Say to Him, 'you've given me one life only, what do you want me to do with it?'

## MOVE TO HIGHER GROUND.

1. MOVE TO HIGHER GROUND – a wave is coming: EARTHLY and ETERNAL TRANSACTIONS. It is time to make the kind of transactions and deposits that will count in eternity and this comes by investing in kingdom business as commanded from above. There is a shift of plates [tectonic plates] and the same wave that will deliver Israel, will destroy Egypt.

In every wave, there is an element of judgment. We must abandon what is not of God in our ministries. We must make eternal transactions as opposed to earthly transactions. Eternal transactions are transactions that will count in eternity – where neither moth nor rust do gather. Matthew 6:19-20 puts it this way: "Lay not up for yourselves treasures upon earth, where moth and rust doth corrupt, and where thieves break through and steal: But lay up for yourselves treasures in heaven, where neither moth nor rust doth corrupt, and where thieves do not break through nor steal:"

And continues in verse 21,
'For where your treasure is, there will your heart be also.'

Paul talks about heavenly funding that comes from making eternal transactions in Philippians 4:17-19, "Not because I desire a gift: but I desire fruit that may abound to your account. But I have all, and abound: I am full, having received of Epaphroditus the things which were sent from you, an odour of a sweet smell, a sacrifice acceptable, wellpleasing to God. But [and] my God shall supply all your need according to his riches in glory by Christ Jesus."

The AMPLIFIED VERSION says:
"Not that I seek or am eager for [your] gift, but I do seek and am eager for the fruit which increases to your credit [the harvest of blessing that is accumulating to your account] ... and my God will liberally supply (fill to the full) your every need according to his riches in glory in Christ Jesus."

Matthew 6:24-25 & vs. 33 says:
"No man can serve two masters: for either he will hate the one, and love the other; or else he will hold to the one, and despise the other. Ye cannot serve God and mammon. Therefore I say unto you, Take no thought for your life, what ye shall eat, or what ye shall drink; nor yet for your body, what ye shall put on. Is not the life more than meat, and the body than raiment?"

Matthew 6:33,
'But seek ye first the kingdom of God, and his righteousness; and all these things shall be added unto you.'

Once you are taking care of kingdom business and making eternal transactions, your earthly supply is guaranteed; you don't have to go after it.

## What is the difference between earthly transactions and eternal transactions?

EARTHLY TRANSACTIONS end here!
ETERNAL TRANSACTIONS await us!
Where we are now is not home; it's an opportunity to do business; so, make tangible transfers into eternity. Faith has been converted to currency from the earth. The new wave will sweep those making earthly transactions and empower and bless those making eternal transactions.

HOW TO MAKE BIG DEPOSITS ON ETERNITY: Ask yourself the question: 'What does God celebrate?', and celebrate the same.
NOTE:
- The only way you can make an eternal deposit is by hearing eternal instructions.
- If it was not eternally instructed, it does not have eternal relevance or recording. Did heaven instruct it?
- The blueprint of his house is in His hands. (Psalm 127)
- Most are not receiving and following eternal instructions. All we do must be eternally recognised – where we go, what we say, what we do, what we sow, where we sow must all be with eternal instruction for it to have an impact on eternity. All we do must be eternally relevant for us at the end to hear God say, 'Well done thou good and faithful servant.' Matthew 6:2 says, 'don't do it before men or to influence men.'
- Give under heavenly advisement. To obey is better than sacrifice – it's our obedience that eternity records.

- Today is another day for you to fulfil your assignment as eternally instructed.

## 2. HAVE A SPIRITUAL GENEALOGY - SPIRITUAL PARENTHOOD

- The first breath of life came from God through the instrument of both parents. 'Children obey your parents in the Lord; Honour your father and your mother that it may be well with you....and that you may live long on the earth.' – Ephesians 6:1-3

DANGER: I will dishonour you if you dishonour your father and mother and you will not live long on the earth. Stay connected to your parentage – source. I am still the God of Abraham, Isaac, and Jacob till now.

- Everybody needs an Abraham to circumcise them.

NOTE:
i. It's not about individuals – it's about our genetic transfers.

ii. It's about covenant – continual [ium] my covenants perpetuate themselves – operate in genealogies of covenant. In covenant and genealogy, it's the father that matters. YOU ARE CALLED, YES, BUT IS THERE A COVENANT CONTINIUM? In Exodus 2:23-25, when Israel cried out to God, God heard their groaning and remembered His covenant-continium with Abraham, Isaac and Jacob and that is why He came through for them.

iii. It's about humility and openness to God – if you cannot receive your father you cannot go far.

iv. It's about covenant protection and provision – you can't give what you don't have. 3,000,000 men ate and were clothed in the wilderness not just because of themselves but God remembered the covenant He made with Abraham, Isaac and Jacob.

Exodus 2:24 says, 'And God heard their groaning, and God remembered his covenant with Abraham, with Isaac, and with Jacob.' – They were fed because they had a father who had a covenant with God – Abraham. Many times you hear God say I will spare ....for my servant David's sake or Abraham's sake. He was willing to spare Sodom and Gomorrah for the sake of ten righteous people in the land triggered by Abraham's negotiation with, prayer intervention and intercession to God.

- In this coming move, some people will not stay alive because they are not covered. God said: I am raising principalities in the earth - territorial principalities. There's more to fathering than having a big church.

**Who is a real spiritual father? (Refer to next CHAPTER)**

a. They will be territorial authorities whom God has given the blueprint of His plans. Fathers can't be blind. As in Genesis 18:17, 'And the LORD said, shall I hide from Abraham that thing which I do; …..'

From that point he was released into fatherhood without a congregation.

b. They will have angelic and human collaboration – it won't be by size. You can't be a father without knowing how angels operate. In Genesis 28:10-22, when Jacob erected that altar, he erected a connection between earth and heaven… it became a contact point which resulted in angels ascending and descending bringing results.

You are not and cannot be a priest without an altar. A priest must have an altar from which pronunciations are made which come to pass. You need angelic hosts. The angels assigned to me and my assignment will go and bring things that are not around me yet even for the fulfilment of my assignment. (Hebrews 1:14)

OUTREACH: deploy the people for outreach with an advancement of angels because of the princes of Persia out there.

- I have set a hierarchy so fathers will have sons and sons will have fathers.

- We must move together as a force; we as ministers - as fathers, we are priests and kings.
- Psalm 119:18 our eyes must be open first. TEA CUP-

SAUCER Illustration: My right connection with the teacup ensures that I as a saucer receive the drip-over tea. With Joshua and Caleb, Joshua was the leader, Caleb was the fighter; Joshua was chosen but Caleb was the one who fought. Life is not a right, it is a privilege.

There are things God wants to provoke in the earth - there are altars God wants to erect in the earth. The closer you are to the blueprint from God the closer the interaction from God. [How associate pastors kill their pastors]

'I surrender all and ask what do you want me to do today? Whatever you ask me to do I will do.' Hagar was asked to return to submit to someone who was deliberately tormenting her; reason being it wasn't Sarah she was submitting to but Abraham the one who gave the instructions in the first place.

3. ASSIGNMENT and PURPOSE
- Don't invest your life in the pursuit of worldly things and carnal gains that is outside eternal significance.

- Every investment you get involved in must have eternal ramifications. It must count in eternity.

- You mustn't be healthy and irrelevant; rather be unhealthy and relevant.

- Your marriage and children is for help, for your assignment must be relevant to eternity. Wealth, fame, health must all be relevant to eternity. Even influence must be put in the context of eternity.

- Why am I a pastor? What am I supposed to do with it to make an impact on eternity?

***THIS Subject has even affected our members – they earn more but give less. TITHE: they work 40 hours and give God only 4 hours of their salary that is those who pay their tithe; they are not awake to their purpose. Your life is like currency from the word current, tide, flow. – Ezekiel 47

THERE IS A CORRELATION BETWEEN LIFE, MONEY and ETERNITY. God says, 'I gave you currency to make contributions to eternity. I expect my people battered or new or dirty money to still make purchases for eternity. Whether your money in your hand is dirty or new, you still use it for purchases so whether you are poor or in need or have more than enough, despite your status, still make purchases for eternity. The best thing that can happen to you is to pursue your assignment.'

When Isaac was in the wilderness and there was famine, he meditated on his covenant with God. His deliberation was not on the famine, it was on the covenant. How do we know? He did what you don't do during famine – He sowed!

4. INTIMACY WITH GOD – Walk with God. (Refer to Chapter One)

Pastors/Ministers: **Don't become intimate with the work, rather, become intimate with God.**

**What to do to keep a walk with God**: If you want to see a real move of God, have a real walk with God – be a genuine article. How can you go to bed without a pen and paper or book by your bedside? Aren't you expecting a visitation from GOD? EVERY TIME YOU STAND TO SPEAK, YOUR ALTAR SHOULD BE SPEAKING. What you sacrificed behind the scenes, laid on the altar either in prayer, praise, worship, word investment, money, seed or intense preparation all should be speaking for you and backing you up. Is there any acceptable sacrifice burning on the altar which is a sweet fragrance, odour before God's nostrils moving Him to ask you, 'what do you want me to do for you?' 'I am not looking for perfect people. I am looking for willing and available people. Walk with me and you'll be perfect.'

5. CURRENCY, CASH and CHANGE – Money matters
- Life and death is money. Jesus said, 'you cannot serve God and money.'
- Money is a powerful force and it tells me and God who you really are.
- If you want to know who you are, go to your bank statement
- IT IS A SERIOUS PROPHECY OF WHO YOU ARE – You are Your Bank statement!
- In this life you are either making eternal transactions or earthly transactions.
- A lot of people are serving mammon and don't know it. GOD

measures you to a large extent on how much you are spending on HIM/KINGDOM.
- Most of the time we give, many are giving God CHANGE. We give God the left-over instead of the CURRENCY.

HOW MONEY IS OUR CONTACT TO ALTARS: In the Old Testament, they brought doves to the priest and sacrificed. How you direct your money determines what you call on from the altar.

- YOU CANNOT PULL FROM AN ALTAR IF YOU HAVEN'T PUT ANYTHING ON IT.

- YOU CANNOT PULL FROM AN ALTAR WHAT YOU HAVEN'T PUT ON IT.

- TO DIVERT YOUR LIFE INTO ETERNITY, YOU MUST DIVERT YOUR MONEY.

**TO CHURCH MEMBERS:**
- Give sacrificially and you will get returns here but don't give just for that purpose.
- Because there is nothing on the altar, so priests cannot invoke or command certain things for you.
- The wise men opened up their treasures to the KING. The church is not giving their currency to the KING; they are giving him change. The reason God was angry with Israel in Exodus when they made the calf wasn't necessarily about the calf they made but because they served and worshipped

the calf. The gold and jewellery from Egypt was for serving Him and building Him a sanctuary so they'll worship him there. Many are worshipping the calf – the wrong system. Don't worship the calf. Don't build monstrosities and serve and worship them. Cash and Currency are for serving and worshipping God.

## 6. RIGHTEOUSNESS, GODLINESS and CHARACTER

You will be judged by the same standards our flock will be judged by and ours will even be stricter because we are their teachers. (James 3:1) One of our biggest problems as leaders is character including time-keeping, jealousy, lust, competition, gossip, envy, pride, covetousness, etc. We must not be quick to judge, we must tamper judgment with mercy. We must honour and respect just as we expect our members to honour and respect us. Your relationships with your mentors must continue. Go to God and ask Him who your mentor/spiritual father is. Who is the person ordained by God to be my spiritual father, covering, mentor?

PASTORS: Note: Not everyone attending the church I pastor is my son, some are members, attendants, visitors, etc. Beware how you relate to people - each one of them.

[Order my book/Manual: LEADERSHIP SECRETS AND LEADERSHIP 101 for more information on who sons are from www.houseofjudah.org.uk]

YOU HAVE TO BE AWARE OF THE ALTARS OF YOUR

FATHERS AND PULL FROM IT. The following chapter will show you how.

CHAPTER NINE

# RIDING ON THE WINGS OF SPIRITUAL FATHERS AND MENTORS

## 50 ROLES AND RESPONSIBILITIES OF SPIRITUAL FATHERS:

The book of Malachi closes with a fathering gap: Malachi 4:5-6, 'Behold, I will send you Elijah the prophet before the coming of the great and dreadful day of the LORD: And he shall turn the heart of the fathers to the children, and the heart of the children to their fathers, lest I come and smite the earth with a curse.'

In this chapter broken into two sections, we will be examining and answering four principal fundamental questions that are absolutely vital for taking every form of toiling and struggle out of your life and ministry:

Firstly: Who a spiritual father and mentor?

Secondly: How do I discover or identify them i.e. what are the characteristics that will enable me to recognise them?

Thirdly: What is the role they play in both my life and ministry in empowering me to secure a glorious future in ministry stress-free, toil-free, struggle-free, gimmick-free culminating in a fruit-bearing, fruit-producing, fruit-maintaining and ever-growing ministry?

Fourthly: What are my responsibilities to them and why must I maintain my relationship with them?

**REMEMBER:**
Spiritual fatherhood has nothing to do with chronology. It could be someone who is younger than you but older than you in the things of the spirit. It has nothing to do with chronology or age.

### SECTION ONE:

1. **WHO IS A SPIRITUAL FATHER?**

2. **WHAT IS THE ROLE OF A SPIRITUAL FATHER TO ME AND IN RELATION TO MY MINISRY?**

**A Spiritual Father:**
1. Is a person whose spirit you're connected with - When the prodigal son was out of home nothing went well but when he returned home to the father, everything else fell in place.

2. Is necessary for stability, for realisation of set goals and the knowledge of the cross; if you must be stable in the call of God on your life. If you must follow a goal and direction in life, you need a father in your life you can look up to in the things of the spirit and say they taught me, they fathered me. Anyone can preach as long as they can talk. Scripture says, 'Obey them that have rule over you and submit yourselves; for they watch over your soul with… …that they may do it with joy.' – Ephesians 6:1-4

3. Shares with his son what he needs to hear or what a son must hear not what he wants to hear because your father is a coach, a mentor, your trainer who challenges you to help you become a better person; he sees what you need to do to become what you must be; what you need to become. Paul said in 1 Corinthians 4:14, 'I write not these things to your shame, but as my beloved son I warn you.' 1 Corinthians 15:34, 'Awake to righteousness, and sin not; for some have not the knowledge of God: I speak this to your shame.'

A father can look at you and with just one look knows whether what you did, how you preached or spoke was out of pride or not…he looks at your body language and knows whether you are in pride or humility, offended or appreciative at correction… even in basic announcements. A father tells you, you don't have to be angry at everybody. Young ministers make the mistake of using the pulpit as a place to fight their battles and lash out or launch out at people.

REMEMBER, the only person who can have many people in his church is a pastor who doesn't get angry; or who doesn't get angry easily and doesn't use his pulpit to address or solve private issues. He uses his pulpit to download God's mind and heart and ministers to the people's hurts, needs and gives them hope, comfort encouragement and direction. In every family there are different kinds of children; those who suck their thumb, adults who wet themselves, are rude, etc. but a true father carries everyone along.

4. Helps you to reach where you ought to get to – 1 Corinthians 4:15, 'For though ye have ten thousand instructors in Christ, yet have ye not many fathers: for in Christ Jesus I have begotten you through the gospel.'

5. Takes the time and effort to tell you to grow up and tells you when you are being proud. Sometimes the most difficult people to talk to are younger ministers who have seen 200 +. Recognise the place of a father.

6. Sees what you don't see and motivates and helps you get there. Don't be proud despite your success.

7. Is one under whose ministry you receive revelation to go further in your destiny, ministry, career, profession, relationships, marriage, etc.

8. In his company and under his ministry, your vision, your destiny manifests, and your life makes sense and gets into leaps and bounds.

9. Under his ministry teaching, training, mentorship, fatherhood and influence, you end up not on the same level with your contemporaries because you are older than your age as a result of the secret downloads from your father because of the wealth of knowledge, insight, wisdom and understanding you've gained and keep gleaning from him. You are not compared with your mates.

10. When you are with your father, you receive more than anyone is receiving and become distinguished. Some are in church but have no father; there is no connection why – Everybody claims someone to be their spiritual father but there is a way the sons distinguish themselves - by their actions, their love, devotion, dedication, loyalty, faithfulness, service attitude, response, by their contributions to their father, by their reaction, the way they draw from their father, the way they move at the blink of his eye; they know what the pastor is saying without him saying a word – they are excited to serve the vision of their father – because you can be in a crowd and distinguish yourself. May you be distinguished!

Genesis 5:4-32 onwards lists those who distinguished themselves as sons and those who didn't …it goes like this………..After he begut Seth …………..he had sons and daughters……..he had sons and daughters - what is their name - we don't know - we only know Seth lived 105 years and begut enosh…….vs. 5,6 …………. vs. 9 Enosh distinguished himself; lived and begut Canaan who distinguished himself ………… Mahalaliel had sons and daughters ……..vs. 18………… Enoch walked with God and was not for God took him………. those whose names are not mentioned did not distinguish themselves….Methuselah…had sons and daughters. These men here distinguished themselves that's why we know them by name out of all their father's children – may you be distinguished, may the call of God be very clear on your life and as you connect with your spiritual father - may there be an outflow of his grace into your life [from him to you] and from you too, may a greater mantle explode and expand.

1 Corinthians 4:15 says, there are so many teachers and instructors but very few fathers spiritually in every community whom you can say, 'This man is a father' - it's not by the size of their church or the size of the car or what they do. There aren't many fathers but you need to be sure you have a father in your life.

11. Brings you into a life-changing revelation of the word of God. When you meet him, you just find that your life is on a fast track you begin to see clearly; all the things that were jumbled and was without form in your mind begins to make sense; your life that seemed to be going nowhere you begin to find direction, purpose and meaning to your life.

12. Travails for you until Christ is formed in you and until the purpose of God is established in you. From Galatians 4:19, where Paul said, 'My little children of whom I travail in birth again until Christ be formed in you.' We discover that:

13. Is not necessarily the man who led you to Christ or the

first church you went to but loves you more than every other teacher would do.

14. Helps you to mature, to grow. Under such a person you are motivated to mature, possess the kingdom, take over the economy and do extraordinary things.

15. Guides you into all truth and into your vision as you draw from them. It's not the degree you get and acquire but it's the light available to you and who you are connected to who brings you that light. - Isaiah 60:1-3 - Arise and shine...; Psalm 127

16. The blessings pronounced from them makes you rich, wealthy in every way. Proverbs 10:22, 'The blessing of the LORD, it maketh rich, and he addeth no sorrow with it.'

17. Calls, comforts and corrects whom he loves - Proverbs 3:12, 'For whom the LORD loveth he correcteth; even as a father the son in whom he delighteth.' You need a spiritual father because you need correction. Sometimes you think you are alright but if you have no one to draw the line, you go the wrong way, in the wrong direction.

18. Helps you in your choices – your choice making - they are people you can submit your vision to who have no problem in believing in your vision or envious or jealous of your becoming great.

19. Is not in competition with you; you can report to them, you tell them the secret of your life and it's not broadcast on

television – a lot of emptiness comes from ministries without fathers; don't just send your dues - associate with people you can relate to - not associations or societies.

20. Protects you from the real destroyer because sometimes you may not realise that what you are doing is about to destroy you but a true spiritual father protects you from that destruction. He protects you from the wolves ...deliver your soul from death and to keep them alive in famine – there are wolves in ministry, false prophets, those who want to come and hold meetings for you in your church and take your members who pay tithes away – holding special seminars - those are people who have a ministry without ethics. You must reach a place in ministry or business where some values are important to you.

21. Prepares you to receive generally from God – By the time Paul was leaving the Ephesian church, he sat down with them and exhorted them, '... ... ... as a father how I kept back nothing that was helpful to you ... and taught you publicly from house to house.'

22. Is not in your life for what they will get from you but for what to add to your life to empower you to fulfil destiny. They see your future and want to get you there. He is not there for what he will get from you but what they can give you, what can make you a better person, build your life, how they can impact your life because they see your future not your past or present. Acts 18-20 is all about the two years Paul spent in Ephesus. The Ephesian church is the only church he did not correct any error. He spent two years with them; when he got there they

were demonic and by the time he left the demons had left. It's a book about a mature church – Ephesians 1-6.

23. Keeps back nothing from you, he loves you genuinely and wants you to progress.

24. Will warn you particularly when you are about to make an error or go wrong - ask yourself whose son am I? Paul said, 'I write these things not to shame you, but as my beloved sons to warn you … ….' You must have someone in your life whom you give account to.

25. Knows what is going on in your life.

26. Gives you all the word of God you need to make progress.

27. Crosses and corrects your ego before you destroy yourself. A fellow-mate will not correct your ego so as not to offend you but a father will to make you better. Those who reject correction sail out on their own sea and end up struggling.

28. Teaches you not to preach at people but to preach to people and minister to them.

29. Believes in you, in the gifts on your life and the grace of God in your life and encourages your gift to be manifested.

30. Doesn't necessarily hang around you all the time - they help you to be who God has called you to be, release you into your grace without over-fathering you.

31. Shows he cares by carrying the weights and challenges. Paul said in 2 Corinthians 11:23-25, 'Are they ministers of Christ? (I speak as a fool) I am more; in labours more abundant, in stripes above measure, in prisons more frequent, in deaths oft. Of the Jews five times received I forty stripes save one. Thrice was I beaten with rods, once was I stoned, thrice I suffered shipwreck, a night and a day I have been in the deep;.....'

Sometimes ministry is weight and challenge, it's a weight and it's a pain, it's a challenge if you have to carry people along. So honour such a person because they carried weights, people and things for you, they've even been embarrassed for you and paid certain unnecessary and avoidable bills and expenses for you, they covered you at one time or more and probably still do.

32. Shares his experience to protect you from mistakes to promote you for fulfilment.

33. Helps you to read your emotions and handle your feelings. There are times you want to quit; there are times you want to give up, you feel it is just too much, the attacks are too much, it seems as if the enemy wants to destroy you but he sees what you can't see, hears what you can't hear, feels what you can't feel and so encourages you and strengthens you to fight the good fight of faith, to keep the faith by running the race and can read your emotion to motivate you to continue in your calling so that you don't crash your ministry but finish well.

34. Sees what can short-circuit your life and stop you prematurely. Some people's behaviour, their attitude can short-circuit them; some people have an attitude problem; some people have insecurity, some people think when you rebuke them, you have rejected them so they say you don't like them. I rebuke my children not because I hate them but because I love them. Who is warning you? Who has corrected you recently? Who has called you recently to talk to you or put you in order? Who have you opened your life to? Who have you said, 'Sir, I can't say this to everyone, I need to talk to you; I am tired in my life, I am struggling in this area of my life - this is what is going on in my life? Etc.'

35. Gives you an example you can follow. Paul said, '… … be ye followers/imitators of me as I am of Christ.' Jesus said, ' ….follow me and I will make you fishers of men.' Following the footprints of a spiritual father will help you learn from their examples.

Paul writing to Timothy his son, said, 'The things you have heard and seen of me, the same commit thou to faithful men who will be able to teach others.'

36. Teaches you how to get out of impossible situations and difficult problems. There are times in ministry when you tell other ministers how to solve problems and what the reactions of the people they correct will be after you've advised them about how to handle a situation in their churches and after they have obeyed and implemented your advice they call you

back to ask how you knew? Fathers know because of:

i. The work of the Holy Spirit

ii. The ability to hear the voice of the Holy Spirit; and

iii. From Experience....because they have been through that before.

37. Demonstrates the anointing. Paul said, 'For this cause have I sent you Timothy... who will bring you in remembrance of my ways which be in Christ...' Elisha, a successful businessman followed, observed and served Elijah faithfully for twenty years just pouring water on his hands and at the end of Elijah's ministry he asked for a double portion of his anointing which he got.

38. Confronts error and pride in your life - he should be able to talk to you, correct you and confront pride in your life. He confronts pride in your life because you may not realise that there is pride in your life until the Holy Spirit confronts it and points it out in your life through your spiritual father

39. Makes you aware that **aspiration for office does not give you ordination for office.** Those without spiritual fathers will be carried away by strange doctrines, ideas that do not establish them. Without a spiritual father, you are likely to build on sensationalism and not the word of God. A spiritual man discerns spiritual things. When you have a spiritual father in your life, he tells you, you don't have to do all that – employing carnal strategies and gimmicks to make your ministry prosper - very soon you'll be found out. Wait! They will say because

God will prosper your work in due time. From my father in the Lord, I learnt 'Don't raise offerings - raise men and you will have all the money you need for your assignment' – it is working like hot knife through butter in our ministry.

**A true spiritual father will teach you that aspiration for an office does not give you an ordination for it.**

40. Tells you to slow down, to grow, to move from one level to the other beyond what they are desirous of. Some people have desired to want to go and launch my 'own thing' unaware that some are not called to be front-line ministers REMEMBER: it isn't anything less to support another person's ministry - that is your calling - that's your gifting and when you do it with all your heart God will bless your work, he will prosper your ministry because you are called at that time to be in support. When you first start ministry your message is often 'fire and brimstone messages, repent or perish, sinners in the hands of an angry God' – even if you will lead an apostolic independent work tomorrow, don't rush!

- THE NUMBER ONE KILLER OF YOUNG MINISTERS ARE - IS MEMBERS. **They will puff you up and make you think that as for you, butter will never melt in your mouth.** They say to you if you preach like that if you start your own the whole of the city will be there to support you; they won't tell you all the bills you must pay, the expenses, etc. Particularly in the charismatic movement, we are not like the orthodox churches who have been around for years and have structures and systems to manage, structure ministers and systems - they have been around for a long time - don't criticize them they have proper systems to manage what they are doing – You can expose yourself to all manner of danger if you have no fathers – you don't outgrow spiritual fathers.

According to Bible scholars, when John the apostle was 98 according to church history they'll put him in a chair and he'll preach – 1 John 1–3 John and after him came those who were referred to as the EARLY CHURCH FATHERS like Father Polycarp, Tertullia. We need fathers and the charismatic churches need fathers not just various associations, especially when the rubber hits the road, you must go to your specific fathers who will speak into your life what God is saying. In your season of battle, in your state of emotion those people speak into your life in a very special way. The pastors wear the coat of the set-man because Leviticus says the sons of Aaron shall wear the coat of Aaron. The anointing you respect is the anointing you attract; the anointing you have and see determines what comes to you.

ABOUT SPIRITUAL FATHERS: Spiritual fathers are chosen by God, both son and father: As people bless you, pass on and pray for them; bless them and tell them to go and enjoy what you enjoy. It is at the latter stage that children give and not before. Fathers provide. A real daddy will do everything to ensure his son prospers.

**Place Yourself Under Authority:**

Make your life easy. Jesus said, 'I do what my father tells me to do.' Elisha, beholding the departure of his spiritual father Elijah said, 'My father, my father.' When you link with a father or a mentor you tap into what the fathers have. It is: 'who is fathering me?' the transmission of spiritual genes. NOTE: There are certain demons who don't respond to your faith but to the one who sent you. Jesus said, 'As the Father has sent me, so send I you.'

**A disconnected speed will result in a slowdown of your speed.** Your rightful and appropriate placement within the body of Christ has a great impact on how much of the supernatural you will enjoy. You should have a father. How do you know who your spiritual father or mentor is? Romans 8:14, "For as many as are led by the spirit of God, they are the sons of God."

41. Is more interested in your success than your affection. His focus is not the celebration of you, but the correction of you.

42. Is not necessarily your best friend. Your best friend loves you the way you are. Your mentor loves you too much to leave you the way you are. Jesus changed Peter's name from Simon [leafy] to Peter [rock].

    Your best friend is comfortable with your past
    Your mentor is comfortable with your future
    Your best friend ignores your weaknesses

Your mentor removes your weaknesses
Your best friend is your cheerleader
Your mentor is your coach
Your best friend sees what you do right
Your mentor sees what you do wrong
Your best friend settles for your present
Your mentor challenges you to recognize and use your potential to create your future

43. Sees things you cannot see.
    - He sees weaknesses in you before you experience the pain of them
    - He sees an enemy before you discern them
    - He has already experienced the pain of a problem you are about to create

44. Will become an enemy to the enemies of his protégé.
    Jesus proved this: Luke 22:31-32, 'And the Lord said, Simon, Simon, behold, Satan hath desired to have you, that he may sift you as wheat: But I have prayed for thee, that thy faith fail not: and when thou art converted, strengthen thy brethren.'
    He fights against any philosophy, pitfalls or prejudices that would rob the protégé of experiencing complete success in his life.

45. Can create an uncommon and extraordinary protégé.
    Jesus took Peter, a fisherman and turned him into a master preacher. Everything you know will come through mentorship, by experience or a person. Invest everything

to spend time and moments with your mentors and father God has chosen to sow into your life. A recognition, acknowledgement and appreciation of your mentor and father will prevent a thousand heartaches.

46. Exposes you to new orbits of ministry, accomplishments, new habits and new levels of expectations just like what a coach does to a sports star.

47. Raises the bar on you if you want to become the best. They ask for a little more effort and for better results teaching you to expect more from yourself.

48. In your desire and pursuit to become a winner, they may seem cruel and inconsiderate in their coaching and urging you to the top. Proverbs 27:6, 'Faithful are the wounds of a friend; but the kisses of an enemy are deceitful.' They love you enough to put you under a little pressure so you can be conformed to the image of Jesus Christ and reach your highest potential.

49. Grooms people for greatness from a spiritual, mental, psychological and physical standpoint by showing you what he did wrong which you shouldn't do or repeat.

50. Works alongside protégés to give them insight, wisdom and direction and prepare them for unexpected greatness and unlimited opportunities. Joshua had Moses, Elisha had Elijah, Esther had Mordecai, Ruth had Naomi, Mary had Elizabeth, Timothy had the faith of his mother and

grandmother - 2 Timothy 1:5, 'When I call to remembrance the unfeigned faith that is in thee, which dwelt first in thy grandmother Lois, and thy mother Eunice; and I am persuaded that in thee also.'

## SECTION TWO:

## The Crucial Role of MENTORS and SPIRITUAL FATHERS

Contrary to what many know-it-alls believe: YOU MUST FOLLOW SOMEONE TO BECOME SOMEONE! The wisest and richest man in his day had this to say to people who pretend or don't believe they must follow anyone or someone in particular to become someone in life as recorded in Ecclesiastes 1:7-11, 'All the rivers run into the sea; yet the sea is not full; unto the place from whence the rivers come, thither they return again. All things are full of labour; man cannot utter it: the eye is not satisfied with seeing, nor the ear filled with hearing. The thing that hath been, it is that which shall be; and that which is done is that which shall be done: and **there is no new thing under the sun**. Is there any thing whereof it may be said, See, this is new? it hath been already of old time, which was before us. There is no remembrance of former things; neither shall there be any remembrance of things that are to come with those that shall come after.'

There is no new thing under the sun; what you want to know, what you want to become, someone has been it before. Stop being proud and follow and learn. Acknowledge that someone knows what you don't know and they may either be older or younger than you but you need what they have. Find them, follow them and learn from them - that is the only way to become. Yes there are new inventions everyday like Microsoft but computers were here before Bill Gates showed up. He built and improved on what was before just like Isaac Newton said, 'If I have seen further, it has been by standing on the shoulders of those who went ahead of me.' The only person who created something and everything out of nothing is GOD. Everyone else has to use what God has created and learn from, work and cooperate with people he's put here on earth to create something and to empower them to fulfil their destiny.

## WISE SAYINGS:

1. SOURCE DETERMINES SIZE.
2. WHERE THE ELEPHANT EATS IS WHERE IT GATHERS ITS STRENGTH.
3. ELEPHANTS DON'T STRUGGLE TO BE BIG BECAUSE THEY CARRY THE GENES OF BIGNESS.
4. WHO FEEDS YOU AND WHAT YOU FEED ON DETERMINES YOUR SIZE, YOUR ACCOMPLISHMENTS AND YOUR PLACEMENT IN LIFE.
5. WITHOUT A ROLE MODEL YOU CAN HARDLY PLAY YOUR ROLE WELL.
6. YOU NEED A ROLE MODEL TO BECOME A ROLE MODEL.

7. WITHOUT A CREDIBLE REFERENCE YOU CAN HARDLY BECOME A REFERENCE POINT.
8. IF YOU DON'T REFER TO ANYONE NO ONE WILL REFER TO YOU.
9. YOU NEVER MEET A PILOT WHO TRAINED HIMSELF. EVERY PILOT IS TRAINED BY SOMEONE.
10. IT IS MEDICAL STUDENTS WHO GRADUATE INTO MEDICAL DOCTORS. THE ONLY WAY TO BECOME A DOCTOR WITHOUT GOING TO SCHOOL IS TO BECOME A WITCHDOCTOR.
11. WITHOUT FATHERS TO FATHER YOU, YOU HAVE NO FEATHERS TO FLY TO GO FURTHER IN LIFE THAN THEY WENT.
12. YOU NEED FATHERS TO FATHER YOU TO GROW FEATHERS TO FLY TO GO FURTHER IN LIFE. 'If I have seen further it has been by standing on the shoulders of those who have gone before me.' – Isaac Newton

John 1:12, 'But as many as received him, to them gave he power to become the sons of God, even to them that believe on his name:'

We are all called to become people of relevance and significance in life but not everyone becomes. That is because BECOMING INVOLVES A PROCESS.

**YOU NEED POWER TO BECOME!**

Genesis 26:12-13 says of Isaac, 'Then Isaac sowed in that land, and received in the same year an hundredfold: and the LORD blessed him. And the man waxed great, and went forward, and grew **until he became very great:**'

Another translation of verse 13 reads: '……and the LORD blessed him, and the man begun to prosper, continued to prosper **until he became very prosperous**.'

The message translation of verse 13 reads: '…..and the LORD blessed him, and the man got richer and richer by the day until **he was very wealthy**.'

FOLLOW THE TREND: He begun, continued to and became very I.e. synonymous with wealth and prosperity. There are factors that make people become great. THERE ARE THINGS YOU MUST BE AND DO TO BECOME SOMEONE AND EVEN AFTER YOU BECOME A SON OF GOD THERE IS WHAT TO DO TO BECOME WHAT YOU ARE CALLED TO BECOME. Jesus gave us the answer in Matthew 4:18-20, 'And Jesus, walking by the sea of Galilee, saw two brethren, Simon called Peter, and Andrew his brother, casting a net into the sea: for they were fishers. And he saith unto them, Follow me, and I will make you fishers of men. And they straightway left their nets, and followed him.'

Matthew 4:19 reads, 'And he saith unto them, Follow me, and I will make you fishers of men.'

Jesus said, FOLLOW ME and I WILL MAKE YOU… …..In other words, follow me and I will make you become.

**VITAL LESSONS on how to become:**

i. Until you follow, you cannot become.

ii. You don't become until you follow.

iii. You don't become someone until you follow someone.

iv. Who you follow determines who you become.

v. If you are not following someone you will never become someone.

vi. You can't become anyone if you don't follow anyone.

vii. You don't just follow anyone or else you will become just anyone.

viii. You must follow someone in particular in order to become someone in particular.

ix. Anyone not following anyone will remain just like anyone but anyone following someone in particular will become someone in particular.

x. You will never become someone until you follow someone.

xi. Someone has been who you want to become. Find them, learn from them, follow them very closely, sow into their lives, draw from them, serve them, guard such people and defend such people with your life. They carry what you need to become.

SADLY: Some people behave so 'spiritual' and all-knowing as if what they want to achieve or become no one has ever become it before so they act all sophisticated and proud and would only talk to God and seek no counsel from any man.

As you've read in my books, 'Leaders are ladders that others climb to get to the top.' JESUS said, 'You don't become until you follow.' He said, 'I only do what I see my Father do.' John 5:19 says, 'Then answered Jesus and said unto them, Verily, verily, I say unto you, The Son can do nothing of himself, but what he seeth the Father do: for what things soever he doeth, these also doeth the Son likewise.'

Jesus consulted with lawyers, teachers, doctors in Luke 2:46-49, 'And it came to pass, that after three days they found him in the temple, sitting in the midst of the doctors, both hearing them, and asking them questions. And all that heard him were astonished at his understanding and answers. And when they saw him, they were amazed: and his mother said unto him, Son, why hast thou thus dealt with us? behold, thy father and I have sought thee sorrowing. And he said unto them, How is it that ye sought me? wist ye not that I must be about my Father's business?'

In other words, in the pursuit and fulfilment of my destiny, my assignment, I had to ask men questions. So if even Jesus, who knew all things had to ask questions, consult in order to carry out his assignment here on earth, which he described as his father's business, where did you get the idea that in the pursuit of your part of the Father's business on earth he's assigned to you, you don't have to follow someone to become someone? It's unheard of!

i. Until you follow someone, you can never become someone.

ii. So it is until you follow someone that you are made to become someone.

iii. It is until you follow someone that you are made into someone.

iv. You don't just become - you are made to become.

v. You don't just become someone - you are made to become someone.

vi. If no one is making you become, you will never become.

vii. God is the Ultimate One who makes people become, but he uses people to make people become.

viii. When Jesus shows you who to follow, leave everything and follow the person immediately just as the disciples did.

**Paul speaking of when he got the call said in Galatians 1:15-19,** 'But when it pleased God, who separated me from my mother's womb, and called me by his grace, To reveal his Son in me, that I might preach him among the heathen; immediately I conferred not with flesh and blood: Neither went I up to Jerusalem to them which were apostles before me; but I went into Arabia, and returned again unto Damascus. Then after three years I went up to Jerusalem to see Peter, and abode with him fifteen days. But other of the apostles saw I none, save James the Lord's brother.'

After getting his assignment from God and going to Arabia, he returned after three years and stayed with Peter for fifteen days obviously consulting, explaining and asking questions and he also saw James, the brother of Jesus. He also learnt from a Pharisee, named Gamaliel, a doctor of the law, held in reputation among all the people. He testified in Acts 22:3, 'I am verily a man which am a Jew, born in Tarsus, a city in Cilicia, yet brought up in this city at the feet of Gamaliel, and taught according to the perfect manner of the law of the fathers, and was zealous toward God, as ye all are this day.'

His ministry was promoted and endorsed by Barnabas. Every one's becoming is traceable to someone else's help, assistance, mentoring, tuition, training, instruction, counsel, etc. through the grace of God.

**You are not made until you follow...** In 1 Kings 19, Elisha ran after Elijah immediately his mantle symbolizing a call, fell on him, but nearly got into trouble for asking to go and put things in order at home. Thank God, he sorted himself out just as quick or he would have lost out with Elijah's temper. 1 Kings 19:19-21, 'So he departed thence, and found Elisha the son of Shaphat, who was plowing with twelve yoke of oxen before him, and he with the twelfth: and Elijah passed by him, and cast his mantle upon him. And he left the oxen, and ran after Elijah, and said, Let me, I pray thee, kiss my father and my mother, and then I will follow thee. And he said unto him, Go back again: for what have I done to thee? And he returned back from him, and took a yoke of oxen, and slew them, and boiled their flesh with the instruments of the oxen, and gave unto the people, and they did eat. Then he arose, and went after Elijah, and ministered unto him.' **SO: You are not made until you serve or minister to the one you follow.**

i. Whenever you follow you are brought into the presence acquaintance of or to the one you are seeking after.

ii. When you follow, you are made……: Matthew 4:19, 'And he saith unto them, Follow me, and I will make you fishers of men.'

iii. When you follow, you leave the past behind you and the dead things are buried……Matthew 8:22, 'But Jesus said unto him, Follow me; and let the dead bury their dead.'

iv. After every call to follow, you arise……Matthew 9:9, 'And as Jesus passed forth from thence, he saw a man, named Matthew, sitting at the receipt of custom: and he saith unto him, Follow me. And he arose, and followed him.'

v. When you follow you, you are raised to where the one you are following is; **not erased** - John 12:26, 'If any man serve me, let him follow me; and where I am, there shall also my servant be: if any man serve me, him will my Father honour.'

vi. When you follow, you find what you are seeking for and even more - John 1:37-39, 'And the two disciples heard him speak, and they followed Jesus. Then Jesus turned, and saw them following, and saith unto them, What seek ye? They said unto him, Rabbi, (which is to say, being interpreted, Master,) where dwellest thou? He saith unto them, Come and see. They came and saw where he dwelt, and abode with him that day: for it was about the tenth hour.'

vii. When you follow, where the father is, the one you are following is, is where the follower will also be……… You eat what they eat, sleep where they sleep, enjoy what they enjoy, because you are exposed to their lifestyle and the higher they are and the higher they go, the higher you also go, e.g. 'They came and saw where he dwelt, and abode with him that day: for it was about the tenth hour.'

viii. When you follow the one you are assigned to follow, you are told who you really are which you were not aware of until you met the one you must follow - you receive a new identity – a change of name, a change of story, a change of status and a change of position. The one you are following has the anointing, enablement, empowerment and foresight to change your name, change your story through what they carry – so follow them and follow them well.

Serve from the heart, with all your heart, all your soul, all your might, all your strength including your substance. Don't serve them with just lip service. Pray for them always and go out of your way to see to their welfare and total wellbeing. John 1:40-42, 'One of the two which heard John speak, and followed him, was Andrew, Simon Peter's brother. He first findeth his own brother Simon, and saith unto him, We have found the Messias, which is, being interpreted, the Christ. And he brought him to Jesus. And when Jesus beheld him, he said, Thou art Simon the son of Jona: thou shalt be called Cephas, which is by interpretation, A stone.'

SERIOUSLY: from verse 40-45, you discover that Other people's destinies hang on your discovery of who you must follow and your dogged determination to follow them very closely without wavering or deviation, i.e. By your discovery of who you are to follow, and your following them unreservedly, others including your friends and entire family are exposed to them, what they carry for them and their own future benefit.

John 1:43-45, 'The day following **Jesus** would go forth into Galilee, and **findeth Philip, and saith unto him, Follow me.**

Now Philip was of Bethsaida, the city of Andrew and Peter. **Philip findeth Nathanael**, and saith unto him, **We have found him**, of whom Moses in the law, and the prophets, did write, Jesus of Nazareth, the son of Joseph.'

It takes someone to find who and what all of us have been looking for and waiting for, so when you find him who can teach, encourage, direct, pastor, promote, change people's destinies through the word, introduce them to others because their future and their entire family hangs on it. By being introduced to and following Jesus, Nathanael discovered that something good could come out of Nazareth, where Jesus, the one he was about to follow comes from – his opinion about the place changed – we are not the same, etc.

John 1:46, 'And Nathanael said unto him, Can there any good thing come out of Nazareth? **Philip saith unto him, Come and see.'**

He didn't say 'no' nothing good can come out of the one I am following so don't come. No, he said, 'come and see'; in other words I can vouch for this person I am following, you will never be disappointed. Come and see! And they came and saw and stayed.

HARD TRUTHS:
- You see, if you don't introduce someone well, you will never be introduced well.
- If you don't have a reference you can never become a

reference.

- If you don't give people good references, you will never have a good reference because what you sow is what you reap.

- If you don't tell people where you are getting your stuff they won't tell you where they get stuff either.

- If you don't follow someone wholeheartedly to point to them as a reference, you will never be referred to or used as a reference.

- Someone's opinion of pastors and churches can be changed by your words and defensive, heart-generated, sincere, meaningful, and enthusiastic introduction of your Pastor and your church which takes them from hell to heaven, defeat to victory, failure to success, poverty to prosperity, sickness to health, depression to confidence, doubt to faith because by a prophet Israel came out of Egypt, were delivered from Egypt, bondage, hardship, slavery and by that same prophet, not another, that same prophet, that same church, that same person, Israel was preserved (Hosea 12:13). You shall be preserved! When asked, 'Can anything good come out of Nazareth, your church, your family, your wife, your children?' You must reply enthusiastically, 'yes, come and see!' You tell them 'surely, come and see!' What you tell them, how you tell them, the way you tell them will determine whether they come or not and whether they stay and follow as well or not!

**The one you follow sees who you really are and what you are made of because they see you from afar.** John 1:47-48, 'Jesus saw Nathanael coming to him, and saith of him, Behold an Israelite indeed, in whom is no guile! Nathanael saith unto him, Whence knowest thou me? Jesus answered and said unto him, Before that Philip called thee, when thou wast under the fig tree, I saw thee.'

**When you follow, your eyes are open to see far beyond what you could see before – and even greater.** John 1:49-51, 'Nathanael answered and saith unto him, Rabbi, thou art the Son of God; thou art the King of Israel. Jesus answered and said unto him, Because I said unto thee, I saw thee under the fig tree, believest thou? thou shalt see greater things than these. And he saith unto him, Verily, verily, I say unto you, Hereafter ye shall see heaven open, and the angels of God ascending and descending upon the Son of man.'

The following biblical and contemporary leaders were mentors and had and those still alive have credible references who they acknowledge [d]:

i. Elisha was mentored by Elijah

ii. Joshua was mentored by Moses

iii. Disciples by Jesus

iv. Paul by Gamaliel, Barnabas

v. Timothy, Dr. Luke and Titus by Paul

vi. Dr. Creflo Dollar, Jerry Savelle by Kenneth Copeland

vii. Kenneth Copeland by Oral Roberts and Kenneth Hagin

viii. Kenneth Hagin by EW Kenyon, Smith Wigglesworth

ix. Bishop David Oyedepo by Kenneth Hagin, Enoch Adeboye, Archbishop Benson Idahosa, Kenneth Copeland, TL Osborn

x. TL Osborn - Branham

xi. Schambach - AA Allen

xii. Paula White - TD Jakes

## WHEN YOU...THEN YOU...

**When you follow you are made……..into what you need to become.**

John 8:31-32, 'Then said Jesus to those Jews which believed on him, If ye continue in my word, then are ye my disciples indeed; And ye shall know the truth, and the truth shall make you free.'

From Matthew 4:19, Jesus said, FOLLOW ME and I WILL MAKE YOU. In other words, follow me and I will make you become. (When you follow, then you become… i.e. when you, then you…)

Numbers 33:50-53, 'And the LORD spake unto Moses in the plains of Moab by Jordan near Jericho, saying, Speak unto the children of Israel, and say unto them, **When ye** are passed over Jordan into the land of Canaan; **Then ye** shall drive out all the inhabitants of the land from before you, and destroy all their pictures, and destroy all their molten images, and quite pluck down all their high places: And ye shall dispossess the inhabitants of the land, and dwell therein: for I have given you the land to possess it.'

Deuteronomy 2:3-5, 'Ye have compassed this mountain long enough: **turn you northward.** And command thou the people, saying, Ye are to **pass through** the coast of your brethren the children of Esau, which dwell in Seir; and **they shall be afraid of you:** take ye good heed unto yourselves therefore: Meddle not with them; for I will not give you of their land, no, not so much as a foot breadth; because **I have given mount Seir unto Esau for a possession.'**

**You have compassed about this mountain for too long - CROSS OVER! When you cross over the Jordan, then you will drive out the inhabitants of the land - Then you will inherit and possess your possessions.**

**Elisha asked Elijah for a double portion of what he had.** Elijah said to Elisha, 'If you keep following me i.e. if you see me go then you can have the double portion.'

At the end he said to him, I am crossing over to Bethel, Gilgal, Jericho, Jordan – stay here. The Double portion did not come on Elisha until he crossed the Jordan. He kept following till he saw him taken in the chariot. Crossing the Jordan means you have committed to a divine cause like David said, 'Is there not a cause?'

Matthew 3:13-15, 'Then cometh Jesus from Galilee to Jordan unto John, to be baptized of him. But John forbad him, saying, I have need to be baptized of thee, and comest thou to me? And Jesus answering said unto him, Suffer it to be so now: for thus it becometh us to fulfil all righteousness. Then he suffered him.'

Jesus arrives at the Jordan and says to John the Baptist, baptize me. Even though it was his will not for the Creator to be baptized, by him, he agreed, saying, 'I am committed - I am committed.' It must be done - to fulfill all righteousness. There is a point you get to in LIFE, your church and ministry where you know there is no going back. Because on the other side of Jordan there are giants and if God does not back you, it is over. But God said if you will cross the Jordan - we are marked. As we cross the Jordan, we will possess our possessions, the giants in our land will fall for our sakes - when we cross this Jordan we will possess our possessions. On the other side as Jesus said in Mark 5, 'let us go over unto the other side' there was a madman whose great destiny even though he did not know it, hanged on the arrival of Jesus and his men.

Michael Hutton-Wood

You must cross over in study, in knowledge, in understanding, in wisdom, change of thinking, mindset, before you can possess your possessions. Study, prepare for where you are going, get fully committed to your ministry's vision - tie it to your vision. The River Jordan is the place of baptism - we die - we take on the form of his resurrection - you go down one form and come out another form. He was told to erect 12 stones and leave them at the bottom of the Jordan meaning: Invest deeply in the place you get your nourishment. Let your roots in God, in your church and in the one you are following be deep. **Memorials make utterances for you when needed - they speak for you as they did for Cornelius. There is a memorial making utterances for me. My memorial is not in a plaque on a wall; it cannot be seen by men; it is covered but heavens can see my pain – my seeds, my investments in the kingdom and God's house and in the one I am following** - my crushing is provoking the anointing - something is working for me. The anointing oil came through a crushing of olives - your anointing for where you are going will come only through a crushing. There is a price to pay for greatness in ministry.

Don't let anybody point to the moments of your past or point to the moments of your death. The battle is not a man's battle; it is the Lord's. Congratulations on your new day - you are entering a new day - a new season. Now when you crossover you may have the same hair style, same clothes, same shoes, same amount of money in your bank account, but you are a different person, a different people, you have been re-invented - you are a different people. YOUR YEARS OF WONDERING AND STRUGGLING ARE FINALLY OVER! After we cross the Jordan, secrets for Jericho, Ai, strategies of movement, progress, growth, expansion, enlargement, influence, maximum impact are coming to us. It will be a new day; it will be a new season. The people we lead and pastor will look at us and notice something has happened; something has changed. The next time you meet your fellow ministers to compare notes, they will not recognize you. Your testimonies will be unbelievable, mind-blowing, mouth-opening, awesome and jaw-breaking. It will be said of us, what the Lord has done in us, with us, for us and through us – 'this is the finger of God; leave these guys alone' Your enemies will advise themselves; 'leave them alone because of what is working for them;' people will faint when they hear what the Lord is doing in your life and ministry. The thing God is about to do for you will be too much, your enemies will say, 'It is not them, it is God's hand on them. It is God's hand on them.' **Mark 1:17, 'And Jesus said unto them, Come ye after me, and I will make you to become fishers of men.'**

### HOW TO BECOME OR THE ART OF BECOMING:

i. Follow me and I will make you fishers of men.

ii. Therefore: Follow me and I will make you become.

iii. God uses people to make people become.

iv. You don't become without following someone.

v. You become who you follow; so the question is who are you following - God or the devil?

vi. As an associate, you must be in one church under one pastor not many churches and many pastors.

vii. If you are not ready to acknowledge or give anyone credit for helping you become, you cannot become.

viii. If you are not ready to acknowledge or give anyone credit for helping you become, you cannot help anyone become.

ix. If you are not ready to acknowledge or give anyone credit for helping you become, no one will ever give you credit for making them become.

x. If you don't become you can't make anyone become.

xi. You cannot become a reference without a reference.

xii. No one will refer to you if you don't refer to anyone.

xiii. Everyone is a product of someone's help - mentors.

xiv. If you don't acknowledge anyone in a book you write, or CD or DVD you release no one will ever acknowledge you in any book they write or CD they release

xv. Everyone's becoming is traceable to someone else's help, assistance, mentoring, tuition, training, instruction, counsel, etc. through the grace of God.

Despite what Paul the apostle carried, it was Barnabas who introduced Paul and recommended what Paul carried to the apostles in Jerusalem in Acts 9 & Galatians 2: He believed in Paul before anyone else did. He didn't wait until the apostles endorsed Paul before believing in him. In fact he believed in Paul, while Peter and the others feared him. Acts 9:26-30 reads, 'And when Saul was come to Jerusalem, he assayed to join himself to the disciples: but they were all afraid of him, and believed not that he was a disciple. But Barnabas took him, and brought him to the apostles, and declared unto them how he had seen the Lord in the way, and that he had spoken to him, and how he had preached boldly at Damascus in the name of Jesus. And he was with them coming in and going out at Jerusalem. And he spake boldly in the name of the Lord Jesus, and disputed against the Grecians: but they went about to slay him. Which when the brethren knew, they brought him down to Caesarea, and sent him forth to Tarsus.'

Galatians 2:1, 'Then fourteen years after I went up again to Jerusalem with Barnabas, and took Titus with me also.'

## BARNABAS AND THE LAW OF EMPOWERMENT
- Barnabas teaches us the Law of Empowerment:
- Secure leaders give power to others as we saw in Acts 9:27.
- Only empowered people can reach their potential.

i. Only secure leaders give power to others.

ii. Only empowered people can reach their potential

iii. Until you follow, you cannot be made.

iv. Until you follow, you cannot be made into or brought into.

v. Until you follow well, you cannot be made well.

vi. Until you follow well, you cannot turn out well.

Disraeli added, 'As a rule….he (or she) who has the most information will have the greatest success in life.'

You gather information from sources both human and from other avenues. When you follow, then I will make you. When you follow well, then I will make you.

## SPIRITUAL FATHERS:

**i.** Find by the leading of the Holy Spirit who is making you become. Wherever they are, find them and follow them very closely. Why?

**ii.** Your becoming is tied to what God has placed in them for you.

**iii.** Find the person God has ordained to make you.

**iv.** Be a son of a God-ordained father.

v. Find somebody you are following from the heart

vi. That is the only way you can become.

vii. If you cannot give up something from the heart and follow someone, nobody will follow you. Jesus said to the disciples, 'Leave your fishing and follow me.'

viii. Make sure you are following someone no matter how high God lifts you.

ix. Make sure you find somebody in the kingdom who is making you become - It is impartation and Principles!

x. There are principles that govern following a person, find them. Know them and do them - so you will know who will follow you. Finding, knowing and doing the principles that govern following a person gives you an indication of who i.e. - the kind of people who will follow you too.

xi. Following your God-appointed father gives you boldness to pray:

'Prove to me that you are the One who sent me; May your stamp of approval rest upon me, my assignment and over my ministry. I demand that the finger that parted the Red Sea into two, part every Red sea before me, my family and this ministry. May the God of my father answer me by terrible things in righteousness. As we minister your word, may the works of God which emanate from the supreme courts of the universe reign and the glory of

God cover our children both biological and spiritual. May it envelope the church members, may our books, tapes, CDS be covered with his glory and let the glory of God rest upon our offspring. Whatever I NEED FOR MY ASSIGNMENT AND MINISTRY, I command heaven and earth to release it to me; let the beauty of God be upon us for we shall be called by a new name - wonderful, beautiful. God establish the works of our hands.' Amen!

## PRINCIPLES FOR FOLLOWING:

**- The Principles which govern following to become: (Matthew 4:19)**

- There was something about that word 'Follow me….' from the lips of Jesus that made the disciples follow to become.

- If God breathes on you, your name will not matter; whether people can pronounce it or not.

- When God says it is your time and your season, your past is irrelevant - it does not matter.

- Follow me and I will make … … … (make, manufacture, I will create in you and what I create will cause a following) - passing the baton.

## FOUR CONNOTATIONS OF "FOLLOW ME AND I WILL MAKE YOU FISHERS OF MEN:"

i. I will in your following me transmit to you spiritual stuff for the future - your destiny - for your assignment

ii. As they followed him it came on them.

iii. When you follow to become, the blessing of the person you are following comes on you (Blessing - empowerment to prosper) e.g. the blessing on Jacob - when Esau arrived later, Isaac said, 'I have already given the blessing to Jacob. I cannot reverse or change it - I have no more to give you.'

iv. It's something that a man carries - it's like power to prosper, or power to heal and Isaac understood it and that is why he wanted to give it to his children before he passed on. He got it from his father Abraham hence enjoying a hundredfold harvest even in a time of famine.

## TWO DIMENSIONS BY WHICH BLESSING COMES ON YOU

1. Hands laid on you and
2. By serving and sowing: The most powerful way of receiving the blessing on a man's life is by serving him. Jacob served Isaac first. Isaac asked for his best food to be served him before he pronounced the blessing. You cannot really take a person's

blessing except you serve them. **The lesser is blessed by the greater. (Hebrews 7:7)**

BY DOING SO, YOU ATTRACT WHAT IS ON THEM:
i. It gives you favour for material blessings
ii. It gives you grace and blessing
iii. It makes an anointing available bearing in mind that it is the anointing that destroys yokes and removes burdens.
iv. It is the transmission of perpetuated covenants. When you serve to becoming (not just to get what you want and leave) whatever the covenants the fathers carry, you catch and carry too and pass on. The covenants Jesus had in becoming, the disciples were introduced to the same covenants. In John 8:58, 'Jesus said unto them, Verily, verily, I say unto you, Before Abraham was, I am.'

- Abraham had the Abrahamic covenant
- Isaac had the Isaac covenant plus the Abrahamic covenant
- Jacob had the Jacob (Israel) covenant plus the Isaac and Abrahamic covenants.

**SERIOUS CONSIDERATIONS IN MINISTRY:**

i. There are warfares and invisible battles you will encounter in life that your covenant alone cannot deal with - you will need something additional and higher than what you carry.

ii. They must confront not only yours but a transmission of covenants backdated. God never designed for us to go into battle or warfare with our covenant alone. God never designed for you to go into battle or warfare with your covenant alone.

**iii.** God often described Himself to His people as the God of Abraham, Isaac and Jacob; i.e. connected to generation after generation after generation.

When Israel cried out and her cry came unto God, Exodus 2:24-25 says, 'And God heard their groaning, and God remembered his covenant with Abraham, with Isaac, and with Jacob. And God looked upon the children of Israel, and God had respect unto them.'

So there are certain blessings, favours you enjoy because of your relationship with and God's covenant with the people you follow. For example: 1 Kings 15:4, 'Nevertheless for David's sake did the LORD his God give him a lamp in Jerusalem, to set up his son after him, and to establish Jerusalem:'

2 Kings 19:34, 'For I will defend this city, to save it, for mine own sake, and for my servant David's sake.'
2 Kings 20:6, 'And I will add unto thy days fifteen years; and I will deliver thee and this city out of the hand of the king of Assyria; and I will defend this city for mine own sake, and for my servant David's sake.'

These are ANOINTINGS that are condensed and with such heavenly backing, that miracles begin to happen beyond your prayer. Because when you speak, you are backed not only by the hosts of heaven but by the ones you follow whose prayer covering, prophetic declarations, pronouncements and blessings are following you because of your covenant with them. That was how the school of the prophets became convinced that Elijah's mantle was indeed resting on Elisha after Elijah was taken away in 2 Kings 2:13-15, 'He took up also the mantle of Elijah that fell from him, and went back, and stood by the bank of Jordan; And he took the mantle of Elijah that fell from him, and smote the waters, and said, Where is the LORD God of Elijah? and when he also had smitten the waters, they parted hither and thither: and Elisha went over. And **when the sons of the prophets** which were to view at Jericho **saw him, they said**, The spirit of Elijah doth rest on Elisha. And they came to meet him, and bowed themselves to the ground before him.'

When they see, they will know and they will say... ...

**WHAT DOES IT MEAN TO FOLLOW?**

# OUR RESPONSIBILITIES TO OUR SPIRITUAL FATHERS AND MENTORS

**HOW DO YOU FOLLOW i.e. how do you know you are following and following well?**

# 10 ACTIONS THAT SYMBOLIZE FOLLOWING

**I.e. what you do for the one you are following [your spiritual father/mentor] in order to become**

1 Timothy 5:17, 'Let the elders that rule well be counted worthy of double honour, especially they who labour in the word and doctrine.'

**Count them worthy of double honour, which will make you.**

**1. LIVE RIGHT (Live right and be an example of a believer)**

Luke 15:13, 'And not many days after the younger son gathered all together, and took his journey into a far country, and there wasted his substance with riotous living.'

Every time you do something you shouldn't do, it reflects on the person you are following. Don't cover your sin; if you fall, repent and forsake it. You are serving the person you are following. Your pastor / spiritual father or mentor shouldn't be hearing disturbing things about you – be accountable to someone and don't be freelance. What Gehazi failed to realize was that everywhere he went and whatever he did, it had a reflection on Elisha. That is why by not representing Elisha well through lying, saying he said what he hadn't said, he ended up inheriting Naaman's leprosy. When you are representing the one you follow both in your church and on your job [marketplace] represent them well.

## 2. TAKE HIS WORDS SERIOUSLY AND LEARN FROM THEM

2 Kings 5:26-27, 'And he said unto him, Went not mine heart with thee, when the man turned again from his chariot to meet thee? Is it a time to receive money, and to receive garments, and oliveyards, and vineyards, and sheep, and oxen, and menservants, and maidservants? The leprosy therefore of Naaman shall cleave unto thee, and unto thy seed for ever. And he went out from his presence a leper as white as snow.'

If you don't follow what those that you are following tell you, you inherit leprosies outside. Once you no longer take seriously the words of the person you are following, you are no longer following them. The man of God said, 'let the leprosy of Naaman stick on you because you did not follow what I told you.' The instruction was - let him take his money and gifts back with him - do not follow him to ask for money - Gehazi disregarded it and did it anyway - the independent spirit.

## 3. PRAY CONSISTENTLY FOR THE PERSON YOU ARE FOLLOWING

Do not criticize them privately or publicly, to insiders or outsiders. You cannot soil, poison or speak evil of the same fountain you are drinking from.

Matthew 26:31, 'Then saith Jesus unto them, All ye shall be offended because of me this night: for it is written, I will smite the shepherd, and the sheep of the flock shall be scattered abroad.'

When a follower/protégé starts criticizing the one he follows, he does irreparable damage. Miriam supervised the ark of Moses, when he was a baby put on the Nile with crocodiles and volunteered to go and look for a maid to look after Moses for Pharaoh's daughter; supervised worship services when they walked on the Red Sea but when she spoke against the one she was following, a spiritual figure, God was the one who heard it and God immediately struck her with leprosy. God initiated and personally supervised that leprosy. Note, the man of God never knew what Miriam had said about him or the church. God heard it from heaven and executed vengeance. There are a lot of followers with leprosy in the kingdom today. Financial leprosy, sickness leprosy, barrenness leprosy, etc. all because of wrong representation of those they claim they are following.

It is a very serious thing when spiritual stuff are being transmitted to you and you criticize or despise the source from which the spiritual stuff is coming. As justified as Miriam's complaint was, it was outside her jurisdiction. Never criticize the one you are following either in private or in public. You may notice certain things as you are close to them but defend them with your life.

## 4. ENDEAVOUR TO BEAR SOME OF THEIR BURDENS

You can't bear all but you can bear some. Jesus gave all the disciples different responsibilities. Carry some of the burdens - if he says he wants you to be with him, you go and serve. When they were looking for a man of God one day, someone said, 'there is Elisha, he was with Elijah' and they said 'find him'. Meaning the fact that he served Elijah means he can be a credible voice for God. Elisha, find him.

## 5. TREAT THE PERSON YOU ARE FOLLOWING WITH DOUBLE HONOUR - DOUBLE RESPECT like standing up when they walk in.

Every time you treat well the person you are following, their heart blesses you. Don't relate with them in the flesh. 2 Corinthians 5:16, 'Wherefore henceforth know we no man after the flesh: [Message: regard no one from a worldly point of view, like he's my relative or I've known him for years] yea, though we have known Christ after the flesh, yet now henceforth know we him no more.'

1 Timothy 5:17, 'Let the elders that rule well be counted worthy of double honour, especially they who labour in the word and doctrine.'

– The Message translation reads: 'Give a bonus to leaders who do a good job, especially the ones who work hard at preaching and teaching. Scripture tells us, "Don't muzzle a working ox" and a worker deserves his pay.'

2 Chronicles 20:20, '… …..Believe in the LORD your God, so shall ye be established; believe his prophets, so shall ye prosper.'

Hosea 12:13, 'And by a prophet **the LORD** brought Israel out of Egypt, and by a prophet was he preserved.'

The Lord through a prophet brought them out. He used a prophet, Moses. He could have but did not bring them out just on His own. He came down, but used a prophet. I prophesy: you will not be brought out without a prophet in your life – a pastor. Don't relate with them in the flesh or by the way they look or how they are dressed or their background or you will miss out on what they carry to make you. If you had met John the Baptist and you were told to follow him to point you to the Messiah, the Bible's description of his appearance and what he ate and where he lived would have put you off from following him:

## PROPHETS ARE AGENTS OF CHANGE!

Matthew 3:3-6 says, 'For this is he that was spoken of by the prophet Esaias, saying, The voice of one crying in the wilderness, Prepare ye the way of the Lord, make his paths straight. And the same John had his raiment of camel's hair, and a leathern girdle about his loins; and his meat [daily diet] was locusts and wild honey. [YET] Then went out to him Jerusalem, and all Judaea, and all the region round about Jordan, And were baptized of him in Jordan, confessing their sins.'

Even Jesus was baptized by this scruffy looking figure. Despite his appearance all Jerusalem, all Judaea and all the regions around Jordan went from the city to see him and be baptized of him in his church located in the wilderness.

SEE: When you follow well, serve well, defend well and catch what those that you follow carry, and your time comes, it does not matter where you are located, people will find you whether you are in Spintex Road or Abossey Okai in Ghana or OTA in Nigeria or Broken Arrow in Tulsa, or Mother Theresa with the poor and deprived in Calcutta, India, the Nobel peace prize will locate you, and people who matter and people who need what you have will locate you and come for what you have for them. John the Baptist lived a wild life, in the wilderness and ate wild stuff yet, he was the forerunner, the one who prepared the way for the Messiah; the one who baptized Jesus and pointed him out as the Messiah. Jesus the Saviour of the whole world was born in a manger, he was from Nazareth, a city that people thought nothing good could come out of, he was labeled a carpenter's son. So, find and stick to the church, the pastor who is definitely making you become - one who sees, speaks to and challenges the greatness in you and tells you what you need to hear in order for you to become all you need to become - not one who keeps telling you what you want to hear.

What you need to realize is that ministries are in stages and levels – and life is in stages and levels. God knows where he is taking you - seeing where he is taking you, he may do a shift. Only God knows who is capable and has the right combination of anointing to take you to your destination and make you become. King Saul indirectly brought out the best in David when he chased him around with a javelin; Barnabas brought out the best in Paul; Jesus brought out the best in Peter. The one you are following may not seem the right one for you or the treatment may seem harsh and that is why Paul said to the Christians in Hebrews 12:11, 'Now no chastening for the present seemeth to be joyous, but grievous: nevertheless afterward it yieldeth the peaceable fruit of righteousness unto them which are exercised thereby.'

The message translation reads, 'Discipline isn't much fun; it always seems like it's going against the grain. Later, however it produces a harvest of righteousness and peace for those who are trained by it.'

And to his son Timothy he said, 'Thou therefore endure hardness, as a good soldier of Jesus Christ.' - 2 Timothy 2:3

**ENDURE HARDNESS AS A GOOD SOLDIER!**

**6. COVER HIS/HER BACK/IMPERFECTIONS**

**Cover his back** - Genesis 9:23, 'And Shem and Japheth took a garment, and laid it upon both their shoulders, and went backward, and covered the nakedness of their father; and their faces were backward, and they saw not their father's nakedness.'

From the above passage, Noah's nakedness after his drunkenness was covered by Shem and Japheth after his mistake and uncovering by Ham. Don't say things like, 'I don't know that's how he behaves when he's annoyed; how dare he speak to me that way; doesn't he know who I am?' It's very unlikely you will meet any man or woman of God who will do anything you may not wander at or wonder about. But God says to leave them, and not touch them. The one you are following is your boss, don't touch them; rather cover them, defend them, protect them, learn from them, bless them, give them gifts occasionally.

Psalm 105:15, 'Saying, Touch not mine anointed, and do my prophets no harm.'

## 7. DEFEND HIM/HER and His/Her cause

Why? Because when you are following them, their vision and their assignment, you come under attack. What churches need now are Sons and protégés, not servants/hirelings or parasites: You see 'Nobody is really following a Pastor if his church/ministry is under attack and he can't find someone who will defend him.' TD Jakes said to one of his spiritual sons who is a pastor, 'Before I call you son and you call me dad, let us straighten some things. If something ever goes wrong and something bad happens to me in Potters House, the hirelings will try and come around to get what they will get but the sons will stand at the gate and say this place will not be plundered. I need to see in your eyes that when I run into trouble, you will first defend me and we talk behind closed doors later. i.e. look me in the eye and tell me; I NEED TO KNOW WHAT YOUR STAND WILL BE when I come under attack.'

When Peter denied Jesus thrice, the bible says Jesus looked back at Peter. Luke 22:60-62, 'And Peter said, Man, I know not what thou sayest. And immediately, while he yet spake, the cock crew. And the Lord turned, and looked upon Peter. And Peter remembered the word of the Lord, how he had said unto him, Before the cock crow, thou shalt deny me thrice. And Peter went out, and wept bitterly.'

That look was because of his failure to follow to the end what he said he would do and it was as if to say what happened to all the promises you made to stick with me and die for me? I need to see in your eyes that when I run into trouble you will first defend me. There are many defenceless pastors - they have hirelings but not sons who will say, 'I will fight to defend you and put my life on the line for you'.

**DEFEND YOUR PASTOR WITH YOUR LIFE!**

**Sons and real followers have a different attitude from all others**

**Real followers will defend the cause of their pastor/leader:** When King David came under attack, 2 Samuel 21:17 records the attitude of his mighty men, 'But Abishai the son of Zeruiah succoured him, and smote the Philistine, and killed him. Then the men of David sware unto him, saying, Thou shalt go no more out with us to battle, that thou quench not the light of Israel.'

**Real followers see their pastor/leader as their light:** 2 Samuel 18:2-4, '… And the king said unto the people, I will surely go forth with you myself also. But the people answered, Thou shalt not go forth: for if we flee away, they will not care for us; neither if half of us die, will they care for us: but now thou art worth ten thousand of us: therefore now it is better that thou succour us out of the city. And the king said unto them, What seemeth you best I will do. And the king stood by the gate side, and all the people came out by hundreds and by thousands.'

**Real followers see their pastor/leader as worth ten thousand of them:** 2 Samuel 20:2, 'So every man of Israel went up from after David, and followed Sheba the son of Bichri: but the men of Judah clave unto their king, from Jordan even to Jerusalem.'

**SONS ARE NOT FOR SALE AT ANY PRICE!**

**Real followers cleave to/remain loyal to their pastor/leader:** 1 Samuel 22:2, 'And every one that was in distress, and every one that was in debt, and every one that was discontented, gathered themselves unto him; and he became a captain over them: and there were with him about four hundred men.'

2 Samuel 23:8, 'These be the names of the mighty men whom David had: The Tachmonite that sat in the seat, chief among the captains; the same was Adino the Eznite: he lift up his spear against eight hundred, whom he slew at one time...'

**Real followers are transformed from people in debt, discontented and distressed into mighty men:** God Himself and the 21st Century churches don't just need members, we need sons who will say, 'If you need a son who loves you and has your back, count on me.'

## EXAMPLES OF FATHERS AND SONS
Oral Roberts - Kenneth Copeland – Benny Hinn
Fred Price – Dr. I. V. Hilliard, Joel Osteen
Kenneth Copeland - Creflo Dollar - Jerry Savelle - Keith Moore
Archbishop Benson Idahosa – Archbishop Duncan Williams - Bishop Oyedepo etc.
Pastor E. A. Adeboye - Bishop Oyedepo
Bishop Oyedepo - Bishop Abioye - David Ibiyeomie - Sam Adeyemi

**GREAT FATHERS BIRTH GREATER SONS!**

**YOU DON'T EMERGE A GIANT BY WALKING AMONG DWARFS!**

You always need a father to pastor you, speak into your life, correct you, impart into you, direct you for your assignment here on earth: till we all come... ...e.g. when your father passes away, you need another father chosen by God to continue to father you: Keith Moore had Kenneth Hagin and now, Kenneth Copeland; Bishop Oyedepo had Kenneth Hagin and Benson Idahosa now Pastor E. A. Adeboye and Kenneth Copeland, etc. What you must understand is that the higher up you go in life, and in ministry, and the more successful you become in life and ministry, the more enemies you have. There are many enemies out there; there are situations you will face that will only respond to the God and anointing of your father. Don't face loose cannons without your covering.

**THERE ARE NO BAD SOLDIERS UNDER A GOOD GENERAL!**

- NOTE:
- You are not following a person if you will not defend them.
- When your pastor walks into a room, stand up as a sign of respect and honour. When your boss walks in, get up from your seat and offer your seat - at least offer and let him say, 'no, sit'. I can't sit when my spiritual father or mentor is standing – no way! I can't have my pastor or mentor in a room and not acknowledge their presence or input in my life - these are principles that helps you live long on the earth – Ephesians 6:1-3, 'Children, obey your parents in the Lord: for this is right. Honour thy father and mother; which is the first commandment with promise; That it may be well with thee, and thou mayest live long on the earth.'

## 8. ENCOURAGE, MOTIVATE AND APPRECIATE HIM/HER

Followers should have an effect on those they follow and motivate them. If you are really following a person, you will motivate them. The leader takes the head butts. **What your son tells you means more to you than the 100's or 1000's. A real son!** When my spiritual father is in town, I am informed and I drop everything with my wife's approval and go down to meet him. When he or my mentors are holding programs I go down there and stand with him / them and for my own spiritual enrichment. That is what sons do.

## 9. GIVE OF YOUR SUBSTANCE – SOW INTO THEIR PERSONAL LIVES AND MINISTRY

It is unheard of and almost abominable for you to be desiring to become when what you have already become, you are not sowing it to become. You may not have a lot to give but those seeds matter. When Saul was looking for his father's sheep he said, 'how can I go and see the prophet without an offering in my hand?': 1 Samuel 9:6-8, 'And he said unto him, Behold now, there is in this city a man of God, and he is an honourable man; all that he saith cometh surely to pass: now let us go thither; **peradventure he can show us our way that we should go. [Men/women of God have been anointed with the ability to show people the way they should go]** Then said Saul to his servant, But, behold, if we go, what shall we bring the man? **[Occasionally go with a gift in your hand – don't go and**

**see them empty handed – One of my mentors said to me: 'You are always sowing seed.'**] for the bread is spent in our vessels, and there is not a present to bring to the man of God: what have we? And the servant answered Saul again, and said, Behold, I have here at hand the fourth part of a shekel of silver: **that will I give to the man of God, to tell us our way.'**

They didn't go and see the man of God empty-handed. Before Isaac blessed Jacob/Esau, he said go and [prepare me my best stew and my soul shall bless thee.]

What correlation is there between what a man of God likes and eternal blessing? A WHOLE LOT! Every month, I sow financially into the pastor who pastored me and ordained me into the ministry. Then I sow financially into my biological mother's life each month. Whenever my spiritual father is in town or I go down to the sons of the prophet meetings, I sow financially into his personal life. I book appointments just to go and see them to speak into my life and sow into their lives and listen to their messages every week. Then when I visit my mentors occasionally I sow as well. My spiritual father and mentors don't need my money or what I have to give them – it's the other way round and I do it out of love, honor, respect, appreciation, as the right thing to do (Ephesians 6:1-3) and to tap into their grace; what has made them and still keeps making them. They don't need it but l need what they have so out of love and appreciation I do it for my own making and those am called to. What they give me in their teaching, prayer, blessing and impartation into my life and ministry cannot be paid for with money.

**A WORD OF CAUTION TO MENTORS AND SPIRITUAL FATHERS** who abuse this principle and privilege. Don't apply for sons just so you can take tithes or offerings from them. **That should not be the motive.** True leaders don't raise offerings; they raise men! 2 Corinthians 12:14, 'Behold, the third time I am ready to come to you; and I will not be burdensome to you: for I seek not yours, but you: for the children ought not to lay up for the parents, but the parents for the children.'

WARNING - Before you make yourself a father to someone else, make sure you are also being fathered - make sure you have the spiritual capacity to father. To help father a person, make sure you also are being fathered because you will ultimately turn out to look like the fathers who have fathered you. Don't call yourself 'Papa' before your time.

The Law of Connection says: 'Leaders touch a heart before they ask for a hand.' So, you touch a heart before you ask for a hand. Once you touch them, you don't even have to ask them for anything. None of my mentors tell me to give to them – I know what is good for me so I do it willingly, cheerfully and of my own volition. They bless you, give to you and do all this of their own volition because they know it is their duty after their hearts have been touched to freely extend their hands to you as the apostle Paul confirmed in Romans 15:27: 'It hath pleased them verily; and their debtors they are. For if the Gentiles have been made partakers of their spiritual things, their duty is also to minister unto them in carnal things.'

TYPICAL EXAMPLE: Luke 8:1-3, 'And it came to pass afterward, that he went throughout every city and village, preaching and showing the glad tidings of the kingdom of God: and the twelve were with him, And certain women, which had been healed of evil spirits and infirmities, Mary called Magdalene, out of whom went seven devils, And Joanna the wife of Chuza Herod's steward, and Susanna, and many others, which ministered unto him of their substance.'

## 10. DON'T DISREGARD THEIR FAMILY

How can you say, 'I love the man but I can't stand his wife or his family?' How abnormal is that? Leaders watch the way their spouses and immediate family are treated. It tells them whether the protégés are following or not. REASON: Because, we and our spouses are one. If you love me, you love my family too; if they are ok, I am ok, if they are not, I am not. It encourages us to know somebody is thinking well of my family considering all the sacrifices and care we put into other people's lives. You can't be effective if your family is not well.

If God tells you follow, follow, if he tells you leave for another assignment for whatever reason, leave with a release and blessing from behind closed doors or as the leader may choose to do it but don't leave shouting, insulting, destroying, speaking evil of and harming where you've drunk and eaten from all this time or else you will be treading on dangerous grounds and incurring curses as you go along. Proverbs 20:20 warns us, 'Whoso curseth his father or his mother, his lamp shall be put out in obscure darkness.'

Who God says you should follow is the person you should follow to become. Now when you are introduced to your spiritual father, in the first few years you may not have access to him. Many may leave but, you shouldn't. It's all a test. The way you can tell your real sons are by those who don't leave.

Sons are put through the fire; sons don't go anywhere. Because of what you went through, you won't leave slightly or just suddenly. If you are really following someone, there are things they see which you cannot see. It's not every upset that makes you walk. THEY CAN BE HARSH ON YOU BUT RIGHT! **Nicodemus asked, 'What can I do? You tell me what I need to do.' Jesus said, 'Except a man be born again he cannot enter the kingdom of heaven.'**

**A Change of Fatherhood:**
**Sometimes the womb that has carried you so far cannot carry you to where you are going. Can a man change his father, and what are your responsibilities to your old father when you move on?**

**DON'T JUST REMAIN A SERVANT - BE A SON!**

Continue to do what you were doing before and heaven will honour what has been transmitted to you. E.g. Jesus was fathered by Joseph for a while; after 30 years there was a shift in where his fatherhood was in order to fulfill his destiny. You NEED: A Man of God - who knows God and a servant of God - who is given to serve God so the works of God will appear and the handiwork of God will manifest on our behalf. (Matthew 19:26) God makes a way where there seems to be no way. The works of God are not because of what we are but who we are. He confirms His word in your life because he says, 'I am the one who sent you.' – Luke 22:35

## THE LAW OF MENTORSHIP

Those who lead a mentor-less life never reach their fullest potentials because God has arranged men on your path to bring the best of you out of life. No man is an island in himself - Jeremiah 6:16, 'Thus saith the LORD, Stand ye in the ways, and see, and ask for the old paths, where is the good way, and walk therein, and ye shall find rest for your souls. But they said, we will not walk therein.'

**Show me any man without a mentor - you will never be able to trace leadership aura on his life. Every great leader is an offspring of another leader.** If you don't have any man that you are following, there may not be any man following you. **Hebrews 6:12 shows us how to identify a plausible positive mentor for your life. Paul said,** 'That ye be not slothful, but followers of them who through faith and patience inherit the promises.'

People have obtained what you are striving for or you want to obtain, look out for them, and try to uncover their secrets, follow them and engage those secrets in the pursuit of your own destiny.

My father in the Lord at the early stage of ministry, had a vision in which God appeared and spoke to him for eighteen hours in a row yet after that God pointed him to a human source, the General Overseer of Redeemed Christian Church of God for his ordination and mentorship. God connected him to a human source through which he could receive wisdom for the journey. Despite our divine connectivity, we still need God-appointed human connectivity to fulfil our destiny. God said to him, "I will not have you go as others have gone; I will have hands laid on you according to Deuteronomy 34:9, 'And Joshua the son of Nun was full of the spirit of wisdom; for Moses had laid his hands upon him: and the children of Israel hearkened unto him, and did as the LORD commanded Moses.' … …..and you shall be filled with the spirit of wisdom - don't lay hands on yourself - send for Adeboye; he will lay his hands on you and you shall be filled with the spirit of wisdom." **YOU NEVER EMERGE AS A GIANT BY WALKING AMONG DWARFS!**

Despite that 18 hour vision with God speaking, God still connected him to a human source through which he could receive those deposits. 20 years after he had been following Kenneth Hagin's ministry, God said to him in a vision, 'Pattern your ministry after this man - Kenneth Hagin.' He desired the serenity, calmness, the noiselessness of this man and ended up being told by the Spirit of God on the balcony of a Camp meeting in Tulsa, 'The baton has been passed over to you.'

**WHY?**
WHERE THE ELEPHANT EATS IS WHERE IT GENERATES ITS STRENGTH!
ELEPHANTS DON'T NEED ADVERTISEMENT: THEIR NAME CONNOTES SIZE! AND SOURCE DETERMINES SIZE!

YOU CANNOT BECOME A GIANT BY WALKING AMONG DWARFS!

LISTEN: There is no race you are running that someone else is not holding the baton for already. Where Kenneth Hagin stopped is where Bishop Oyedepo took over. Kenneth Hagin had the faith movement of the first order, faith movement of the second order passed to Bishop Oyedepo because he believed in Hagin's God and what they carry. Go after them, learn from them, believe in them; partake of it - their grace. The law of mentorship must be recaptured again. **If you don't have a mentor today, we cannot be sure of your future tomorrow.** Mentorship guarantees the future of everyone and prophetic declarations such as 'Fresh oil, fresh oil, Lord. Let not your head lack oil from now, my sword is your sword and my breastplate is your breastplate.' These are words pronounced by patriarchs that carry weight and changes people's levels.

**WHY WORK FOR SOMETHING YOU CAN GET IN A STATEMENT?**

Seeds into higher ministers and their ministries is what provokes such trans-generational prophetic declarations like what Jacob encountered after the blessing from the patriarch Isaac his father in Genesis 27:26-29, 'And his father Isaac said unto him, Come near now, and kiss me, my son. And he came near, and kissed him: and he smelled the smell of his raiment, and blessed him, and said, See, the smell of my son is as the smell of a field which the LORD hath blessed: Therefore God give thee of the dew of heaven, and the fatness of the earth, and plenty of corn and wine: Let people serve thee, and nations bow down to thee: be lord over thy brethren, and let thy mother's sons bow down to thee: cursed be every one that curseth thee, and blessed be he that blesseth thee.'

**Examples of mentoring through the law of empowerment:**

1. Abraham and Lot

2. Jacob and Joseph

3. Jethro and Moses

4. Moses and Joshua

5. Naomi and Ruth

6. Eli and Samuel

7. Jonathan and David

8. David and Mephibosheth

9. Nathan and David

10. Elijah and Elisha

11. Elijah and the prophets

12. Elizabeth and Mary

13. John the Baptist and the disciples

14. Barnabas and Saul

15. Barnabas and Mark

16. Paul and Silas

17. Paul and Timothy

18. Paul and Philemon

19. Paul and Aquila

20. Paul and Julius

21. Jesus and the twelve

Mentors / Leaders don't only shepherd and equip, they also develop. They focus not merely on meeting immediate needs but on producing a leader who could go on meeting needs without the mentor's help.

Let's examine the progression for growing beyond more shepherding to equipping and developing.

| SHEPHERDING | EQUIPPING | DEVELOPING |
|---|---|---|
| 1. Care | 1. Train for ministry | 1. Train for personal growth |
| 2. Immediate need-oriented | 2. Task focus | 2. Person focus |
| 3. Need-oriented | 3. Skill-oriented | 3. Character-oriented |
| 4. Masses | 4. Many | 4. Few |
| 5. Maintenance | 5. Addition | 5. Multiplication |
| 6. Feel better | 6. Unleashing | 6. Empowering |
| 7. Immediate | 7. Short-term | 7. Long-term |
| 8. Nurture | 8. Teaching | 8. Mentoring |
| 9. What is the problem? | 9. What do I need? | 9. What do they need? |
| 10. They begin to walk | 10. They walk the first mile | 10. They walk the second mile |

# CHAPTER TEN

# THE MINISTER AND HIS FAMILY

**21 KEYS TO NOTE:**

1. A successful ministry is highly dependent on a successful family life.

2. The minister and his ministry cannot be disassociated from his family.

3. A man who has strife and division in his family is most likely to have hot disagreements and factions within his ministry.

4. Behind every successful ministry is a successful family life.

5. The family as far as God is concerned is a single unit.

6. Marriage was ordained for one principal reason to make life better for the man God made.

7. An understanding of God's marriage institution will go a long way in helping you to build a successful life and ministry.

8. The man is the head of the woman and the head of the home. Adam represented God on the earth; he was to look after God's creation; Adam was the head of the government and God presented Eve to him to be under his government. He however did not tell Eve of the gravity of the instruction passed down by God. Instead he allowed her to do whatever she liked. No wonder she walked freely and carelessly about and got trapped in a conversation with the devil which eventually led to their downfall.

9. There is more to the responsibility of the husband as the head than is practiced today. Many problems in the home today are largely caused by the loose grip of the husbands over their wives. They allow their wives to buy whatever they like, dress anyhow and go all over the place as though they don't have a head. The husband should lead the wife in every aspect of life even to the type of friends she keeps and vice versa and none of them should see it as control. This is biblical and anything outside it is wrong. You cannot be pastoring a church in Taiwan and your wife be pastoring another permanently in Africa. That is out of order!

10. The wise grip of man on his home paves the way for wise decisions even when he is not there. (Ephesians 5:22-25) In God's family, the man is the head and the woman is the neck; the man should rule his house well. (1 Timothy 3:4-5)

11. The man is given a divine grace to rule his household. He is to love, instruct, correct, and rebuke with firmness. The man

who will play his role well has to be in constant communion with the throne of grace.

12. A man's rulership of a home should be done in love. Husbands are not meant to be taskmasters. They are to be examples of loving leaders. The home is governed in the fear of the Lord.

13. A Minister who wants a successful ministry must wake up to his responsibilities in the home. Rule your home in love and establish God's eternal purpose for the family in your life and home.

14. The woman is a helpmate. She is meant to help her husband in carrying out his God-given commission on earth. A woman who supposedly has a vision which is miles apart from that of her husband has not seen well. A wife's vision should complement her husband's, if not directly under her husband's.

15. God instituted the home to further his plans and purposes on the earth.

16. A woman who refuses to submit to her husband is disobeying God and the man who fails to cherish his wife in love is out of the will of God.

17. A successful home is dependent on total adherence to the biblical marriage principles. The Word of God does not grow

old; if it worked for them in bible days, then it will work now. When a wife is submissive she does not need to ask for anything before she gets it from her husband.

18. Husbands should give their wives all the love and honour due to them.

19. Your home is supposed to be run in accordance with God's biblical instructions. This is the only way to bring down God's glory in your life and ministry. It is a new era. The time for failure is past. God has given you a mission on earth. Take heed that thou fulfil it. (Colossians 4:17)

20. Do not destroy your destiny by disregarding His commandments as they relate to your home. If you are too smart to obey God, you will be too smart to enter into your covenant inheritance. Let us establish a Garden of Eden with a new order, where no one touches the forbidden fruit.

21. This is the secret of marital bliss in life. It is the secret of a successful ministry. Two are better than one, for they have a good reward for their labour. The good reward can only manifest when the two join hands together walking in the light of God's word.

[For more information and insight on fatherhood, read my books LEADERSHIP SECRETS, 101 TIPS FOR A GREAT MARRIAGE AND WHAT HUSBANDS WANT AND WHAT WIVES 'REALLY' WANT. You can order a copy from our bookshop or our website: www.houseofjudah.org.uk]

# CHAPTER ELEVEN

# KNOWING AND ENGAGING YOUR MINISTRY COVENANTS

Exodus 2:24-25, 'And God heard their groaning, and God remembered his covenant with Abraham, with Isaac, and with Jacob. And God looked upon the children of Israel, and God had respect unto them.'

GOD IS A COVENANT KEEPING GOD!

**What is the underlying covenant you have with God?**

Your covenant determines your confidence, courage, boldness and accomplishments in ministry. Demons respond to covenants, for e.g. in Acts 19:13-16, demons responded to Jesus and Paul because they had a covenant with God the Father unlike the sons of Sceva who were defied by demons because they did not have a covenant with the One whose name they were attempting to use to cast the demons out. Their reply to the demands of the sons of Sceva was, 'Jesus we know, Paul we know because we know they have a covenant with God, but who are you in covenant with? What do you have that we should respond to you?'

Demons don't respect or respond to commands from people who have no viable covenant. In 1 Samuel 17, David was able to face and defeat Goliath and was assured of victory even before the fight because he knew he had a covenant with God unlike the uncircumcised Philistine - in other words one without a covenant. So, authentic proof-producing ministry must originate with and be backed by known and applied covenants. Don't enter ministry without a specific personal and ministry covenant with God. **Ministry is what you are within you not what is on the outside. It is the transaction of covenant.**

Ministry begins with an assurance of your general, specific, personal and ministry covenant with God. When you understand the covenant you have, you have confidence and boldness to summon your covenant to deal with demons and hindrances that stand in the way of the fulfilment of your divine assignment. If you are sent, you must know the covenant that comes with your sending. Moses knew 'I am that I am' was with him to back up his words. So did David in 1 Samuel 17 – that's why he called Goliath an uncircumcised philistine. Daniel and the three Hebrew boys were fully persuaded of their covenant walk with God that they were not diplomatic or apologetic to threats in their response to the King Nebuchadnezzar, in the fire or in the lion's den neither was Elijah before the 400 prophets of Baal or Moses before Pharaoh or the Red Sea. The apostles knew He would confirm the words they preached with signs and wonders. Jesus knowing He was sent by God was bold enough to say, 'the works I see him do is what I do also', etc.

Ministry is sustained by an understanding of and operating in both your personal and ministry covenants [General, Specific, Personal and Ministry Covenants]. Those who operate a viable covenant in ministry say in response to those who say some nations are hard to reach or break through, 'If it is the word, it will work everywhere. It cannot be broken by climate or colour. The scriptures cannot be broken.' They are bold to say this on the premise of Deuteronomy 2:36 which says: 'From Aroer, which is by the brink of the river of Arnon, and from the city that is by the river, even unto Gilead, **there was not one city too strong for us: the LORD our God delivered all unto us:**'

**NO NATION IS TOO STRONG TO RESIST THE POWER OF THE GOSPEL** (Romans 1:16).

Our master responsibility is our commitment to the Word of God because it is the baseline for transformations and the baseline for manifestations. As we remain in covenant with God and with each other, our stories will get brighter and brighter by the day, Amen! Go and preach and show; the iron bars will not stop us. RESULT: GOD WILL COMMAND ANGELS, ANIMALS, FISHES, MEN, ORGANISATIONS, PEOPLE WHO KNOW OR DON'T KNOW YOU, people who love you, hate you or dislike you to give to you. God commanded a raven and widow to feed Elijah, Joseph of Arimathaea giving his tomb for Jesus' burial, willing partners to Jesus' ministry in Luke 8:1-3, Abimelech showing Abraham favour, Lydia offering Paul accommodation. All of this was in fulfilment of

1 Corinthians 9. God is responsible for His servants' upkeep and wellbeing. (Luke 22:35)

**COVENANT PRACTICE IS THE CURE FOR HARD TIMES! THE COVENANT WILL PREVAIL IN ANY CLIMATE! THE COVENANT IS FAR HIGHER THAN ANY CLIMATE! THE COVENANT IS SUPERIOR TO ANY CLIMATE! THE COVENANT WILL PREVAIL IRRESPECTIVE OF THE CLIMATE!**

There is something that separates those who have, are aware of, know and exercise their covenant from those who don't have one, or are [ignorant of] not aware of it or don't exercise it and so are defeated. When you understand the covenant you have, you have confidence and boldness to summon your covenant to deal with demons and hindrances that stand in the way of the fulfilment of your divine assignment. If you are sent, you must know the covenant that comes with your sending [in my case scriptures like Joshua 1:8,9; Isaiah 45, 54, 55 & 60-62; Jeremiah 1; Titus 1:5; Psalm 23 & 27; Malachi 3:8-12] were some of the few covenant scriptures I was assured of before I commenced my journey in ministry in 1995 and many more after that some learnt and caught from my spiritual father as he taught. As a result, being afraid or fearful of people or the future was not part of my package when I was called into ministry in May 1984 – God told me on one occasion in 1992, 'If you take care of my business, I will take care of your business' so my supplies were assured hence no begging, crawling, gimmicks to have my needs met. I have not prayed for money for years neither has my wife's wages been part of our budget at home since the Lord told me not to add hers to mine seven years ago or thereabout because I have been practising the covenant since 1989 till forever. (Order copies of my book: GENERATING FINANCES FOR MINISTRY [without sweating, begging toiling, gimmicks or resorting to tricks] from www.houseofjudah.org.uk)

**Go back to your root – your root will determine your fruit.**

Whenever you arrive on the scene, devils should know that someone who carries what the Most High carries just walked in.

## WHAT IS YOUR COVENANT WITH GOD?

**Covenants are the pillars behind the pillars!**
**Covenants are the invisible force and power that backs certain men and women of God up when they stand to speak and minister such as: Assuring statements from GOD like IT IS IMPOSSIBLE** for you to fail; for you to fail means I have failed. YOUR FAILURE MEANS HIS FAILURE on condition that **He called you and sent you.** Luke 22:35, 'And he said unto them, When I sent you without purse, and scrip, and shoes, lacked ye anything? And they said, Nothing.'

HOWEVER, if I called myself, I am alone. God said to Kenneth Copeland, 'It is impossible for you to fail because your mama's face is always in my face.'

## A MINISTER and MINISTRY COVENANTS

1. A minister without a covenant is like a soldier without a gun.
2. A minister without a covenant is like an officer without a rank.
3. What makes a minister is your covenant with God.
4. Your covenant with God is like your visa in your passport. What you have on your visa will determine what you can access. No visa, no access.
5. What you have on your visa will determine what you can do, where you can go, how long you can go for, the power you can wield, the authority you can exercise, etc.
6. The spirit realm functions by the transactions of covenant. Angelic beings, demonic spirits and even God Himself respond to covenants. With each of the great men of the Bible were specific covenants that were enacted with God such as: 'I am the God of Abraham, Isaac and Jacob' Moses and the burning bush experience, 'Moses is a friend I speak to face to face' David could say, 'I come to you in the Name of the Lord of hosts' because he had a covenant with God and he knew what God had said of him, 'David, a man after my own heart'.
7. When God's name is linked to a man, a covenant is enacted. You hear words like, 'I am the God that met with you at … ….' Or some say 'I am calling on the God who met with me at a certain place.' – There is a reference point.
8. Knowing the covenant is one thing; getting those covenants in motion to produce for you is another thing. How to get them in motion is what makes the difference.

9. **The authenticity of your calling is in the validity of your covenant.** To this end there is a crisis in the church in that ministers are identifying with their churches instead of identifying themselves with their covenant.

10. **You are not what people say you are; you are the summation of the covenant you have with God.** (Jeremiah 1:5-9) There are certain things which when certain pastors attempt to do, they cannot fail because of their covenant with God - one aspect being biblical insight – seeing things others cannot see because of your covenant; the heavens open on the spot.

11. The inability to accurately define the covenant you have with God means your ministry is undefined.

12. **Programmes and systems cannot make up for covenant. Systems work only when a covenant is in place.** The spirituality behind the principles is what makes the principles work. SPIRITUALITY!

13. Leading people but neglecting your covenant with Him is detrimental and leads to frustration, stagnation, struggles and failure. That is why you cannot copy what someone else is doing or envy anyone.

14. Find out and set up your own covenants with God through certain addictions to tithing, kingdom-promotion giving, uncommon seed-sowings, unusual promises, kingdom investments, sacrificial giving and sowing into covering ministers and ministries, etc. Certain men and women of God enjoy certain privileges from God that others don't enjoy due to certain promises they made to God such as Jacob: I will give you a tenth of all I have if you take me and bring me back;

an enactment of certain covenants such as 20% givings, 25% givings, 50% givings, 90% givings, like some of us giving our first salary of the year and financial year to God, some giving of their whole salaries or mortgage payments, monies, some taking no salaries, responding immediately to the Holy Spirit's biddings, certain scripture promises which became RHEMA to them, giving constantly to spiritual fathers and mentors and their ministries, etc.

**There are two Types of Ministerial Covenants:**
**1. GENERAL MINISTERIAL COVENANT**
**2. SPECIFIC COVENANT**

**1. THE GENERAL COVENANT OF A MINISTER**

There are 10 biblical facts about being a minister that changes our approach to life namely:

1. I AM BORN AGAIN – John 3:3; I am a citizen of God's heavenly kingdom with a responsibility to establish His kingdom on the earth. I am born of His seed. 1 Peter 1:23, "Being born again, not of corruptible seed, but of incorruptible, by the word of God, [which created all things – Hebrews 11:1-3] which liveth and abideth for ever."

2. I AM NOW A CHILD OF GOD – Romans 8:16; Galatians 3:26 with Jesus being the first born; the first begotten so, I am somewhere along the line among God's children – God who owns the cattle over a thousand hills – I am among His children. [Direct]

3. I AM A SON OF GOD – John 1:12; Romans 8:14; 1 John 3:1-2 - I am a son of the Most High God. The first covenant of a minister is to be called a son of God. If I am a son of God because I am born again, the ramifications are great. The religious folks in Jesus' day had a problem with him because he called himself the Son of God which they equated to his claiming to be equal with God as the following scriptures confirm:

John 19:7, "The Jews answered him, We have a law, and by our law he ought to die, **because he made himself the Son of God.**"

John 5:18, "Therefore the Jews sought the more to kill him, because he not only had broken the sabbath, **but said also that God was his Father, making himself equal with God.**"

**SONSHIP MEANS EQUALITY!** We want to stone you and kill you because you call yourself a son of God meaning YOU ARE EQUAL WITH GOD. So, being a son means I'm equal and I have no apologies in saying that I am not a human being [Oxford Dictionary] at all; I am a god. The moment you agree you are a human being, you cannot be a god at the same time. "I and the father are one" – John 10:30

Jesus spoke to winds, storms, rain, to be still; to demons to be quiet and come out of tormented people, rebuked infirmities, commanded sicknesses and diseases to be healed, the dead to be raised, deaf to hear, dumb to speak, blind to see, lame and crippled and paralysed to walk and they all obeyed; we are joint heirs with Him and when we speak to nature, and to all these conditions, they must obey because WE SPEAK AS COMMANDED AND DO WHAT WE SEE OUR FATHER DO.

John 14:9, "Jesus saith unto him, Have I been so long time with you, and yet hast thou not known me, Philip? he that hath seen me hath seen the Father; and how sayest thou then, Show us the Father?"

4. I HAVE BEEN SENT BY HIM AS HE WAS SENT BY THE FATHER e.g. JESUS Himself – I have been sent to bring many sons to the Father. Jesus said, 'As I was sent, so you are sent.' Whatever he had when He was sent, I have as I have been sent. (Luke 22:35)

5. I HAVE THE LIFE OF GOD IN ME [ZOE – Divine life; abundant life] E.g. Jesus said, 'As the Father hath life in Himself, so also has the Son.' You cannot speak negatively. By Him do all things consist and were made. He is the author of life – ZOE [GOD'S LIFE] both natural or spiritual comes from this life of the Father. 'I give that life to whoever I will.' In the same manner you are sent. That's the only way I can live – this is the measure by which I live; in Him I live and move and have my being; (Acts 17:28) his life flows through mine. The life I live, I live by the faith of the Son of God who died and gave himself for me. I have heard it, believed it and embraced it.

1 John 4:17, "Herein is our love made perfect, that we may have boldness in the day of judgment: because as he is, so are we in this world."

As Christ is, [not was], As He is in His exalted state, Magnificent in splendour, glorified, so are we. When I open my mouth and speak or say something, I am yet to see the demon who can stop it. James says in James 1:23, "For if any be a hearer of the word, and not a doer, he is like unto a man beholding his natural face in a glass:"

We behold his face as if in a glass transfigured to another level of glory. As I behold Him, if I can see God, then I can see as he sees. When we see him [His word as Him] we shall be like him. Believe in the oracles of God – the potential [of the word]. Romans 8:19, "For the earnest expectation of the creature waiteth for the manifestation of the sons of God."

1 John 3:8, "He that committeth sin is of the devil; for the devil sinneth from the beginning. For this purpose the Son of God was manifested, that he might destroy the works of the devil." DISCOVERIES: John 10:10 – The life of God is in me; the Son gives life to whom he chooses so I can give life to whom I choose and take life from whom I choose. So woe betide him that kicks against the pricks or the church as Saul of Tarsus found out in Acts 9:5, "And he said, Who art thou, Lord? And the Lord said, I am Jesus whom thou persecutest: it is hard for thee to kick against the pricks."

That is why Jesus was able to give life to those who were dead whom he chose to raise from the dead like Lazarus, the boy in Nain; healing to those he chose to give healing to, the man at the pool of Siloam, restoration to the man with the withered hand healing to Peter's mother-in-law, etc. When I walk into a building, demons must flee or submit.

James 4:7, "Submit yourselves therefore to God. Resist the devil, and he will flee from you."

For in Him dwells the fullness of the godhead bodily and we are in him so we are filled with the fullness of the godhead bodily. Colossians 2:9, "For in him dwelleth all the fulness of the Godhead bodily."

Colossians 3:3, "For ye are dead, and your life is hid with Christ in God."

The life of God is in me so I cannot share my body with viruses. 1 John 4:4, "Ye are of God, little children, and have overcome them: because greater is he that is in you, than he that is in the world."

He also said, whom the Son sets free is free indeed; whom I set free is free indeed; whosoever's sins I forgive it is forgiven and whosoever's sins I remit or hold on to, it is held on to or remitted.

MINISTRY is what you are within you not what is on the outside. It is the transaction of covenant. When He was sending me, He filled me with his divine life. Jesus walked into the city of Nain and stopped a whole funeral procession and commanded the dead man / a corpse to get up and did the same at Lazarus' tomb by calling him out of the grave. He said to Mary and Martha, 'I am the resurrection and the life;' he was not afraid of death because He was life - in him was divine life and this life was the light of [that lightened/lubricated/liberated] men. God did not call me/us to function by natural law. In Genesis 1, God stepped into darkness and said light in me be, so, despite the darkness, He steps in against the laws of nature and commands things to be – let there be dogs, cats, rhinos, etc. they just came out of mounds of sand at a command. You are my sons, do what I do – the works that I do greater shall ye do because I go to my Father.

## 6. YOU ARE 'gods'
Psalm 82:6-7 says, 'I have said, Ye are gods; and all of you are children of the most High. But ye shall die like men, and fall like one of the princes.'

Isaiah 41:23, 'Show the things that are to come hereafter, that we may know that ye are gods: yea, do good, or do evil, that we may be dismayed, and behold it together.'

John 10:34, 'Jesus answered them, Is it not written in your law, I said, Ye are gods?'

Ye are gods but you will die as ordinary men… WE ARE gods. When you walk into my office to see me, consider it as [assume] you are seeing God Himself because I am His representative – Genesis 1:28 says, "And God blessed them, and God said unto them, Be fruitful, and multiply, and replenish the earth, and subdue it: and have dominion over the fish of the sea, and over the fowl of the air, and over every living thing that moveth upon the earth."

7. AS HE IS, SO ARE WE…..
1 John 4:17, "Herein is our love made perfect, that we may have boldness in the day of judgment: because as he is, so are we in this world."

As Christ is, [not was], As He is in His exalted state, Magnificent in splendour, glorified, so are we. When I open my mouth and speak or say something, I am yet to see the demon who can stop it. James says in James 1:23, "For if any be a hearer of the word, and not a doer, he is like unto a man beholding his natural face in a glass:"

We behold his face as if in a glass transfigured to another level of glory. As I behold Him, if I can see God, then I can see as he sees. When we see him [His word as Him] we shall be like him. Believe in the oracles of God – the potential [of the word]. Romans 8:19, "For the earnest expectation of the creature waiteth for the manifestation of the sons of God."

1 John 3:8, "He that committeth sin is of the devil; for the devil sinneth from the beginning. For this purpose the Son of God was manifested, that he might destroy the works of the devil."

I decree there shall be mind-blowing, only-what-God-can-do testimonies in our lives and our churches; we are destiny-changers, miracle workers. The whole earth is waiting (chemical, biological, geographical, animate and inanimate objects) are waiting for the decrees of the sons of God here on earth representing the King of kings [kings – us] and Lord of lords [lords – us] – Revelation 1:6. Water is waiting for us to command it to be turned into wine; red seas are waiting for us to stretch forth our rod of God's word for it to open for us to walk on dry ground.

- It is an insult for us to succumb to problems on the grounds of natural parameters. There is nothing I cannot deal with. Jesus said, 'you can't kill me. The son of man has power to lay down his life and power to pick it up again.' So have we in Him [Christ]. I can't be in a plane for it to crash when I am on a divine assignment; I have supernatural body guards around me in the form of angels working for me. I don't need to bind Satan; all I have to say is thank you that I have arrived safely at my destination – It is a foregone conclusion. When Jesus needs something for kingdom business and I need anything for kingdom business it will be there for me. Jesus needed a brand new donkey for kingdom business and no one dared to dispute with him, because the master had need of it – what manner of man is this?

## 8. JESUS DID NOT JUST DIE FOR ME - I WAS CRUCIFIED WITH HIM – I DIED WITH HIM - I WAS BURIED WITH HIM AND I WAS RAISED/RESURRECTED

WITH HIM - I ASCENDED WITH HIM - I AM SEATED WITH HIM IN HEAVENLY PLACES IN CHRIST JESUS – on the right hand side of majesty God the Father Almighty far above all principalities and power, and might, and dominion, and every name that is named, not only in this world, but also in that which is to come: So when God made me a minister of the gospel, it was not just a title but an office. – Galatians 2:20; Ephesians 1:21; Colossians 3:1

9. I AM NOT JUST AN APOSTLE BUT A SAVIOUR AND A DELIVERER. They said to Jesus, 'show us the Father;' Jesus replied, 'Have I been long with you and still you don't know the Father. He that hath seen me hath seen the Father.' 'I and the Father are one.' To seek and save that which was lost or the lost. Sit with me here until the earth sees us and sees Christ Himself.

Psalm 110:1-2, 'The LORD said unto my Lord, Sit thou at my right hand, until I make thine enemies thy footstool. The LORD shall send the rod of thy strength out of Zion: rule thou in the midst of thine enemies.'

**RULE THOU IN THE MIDST OF YOUR ENEMIES; ENEMIES ARE NOT IN HEAVEN, THEY ARE HERE ON EARTH. WE RULE HERE.**

I beheld Satan fall as lightning from/out of heaven; how can you have deliverance sessions for sons of God, if Jesus was not taken through deliverance? The enemy has capitalised on our ignorance [of our identity in Christ] and so the servants are in the house while the princes are standing, walking or behaving as servants. We have an identity crisis among us ministers because we don't know where we sit in heavenly places; instead we are looking for titles here on earth. A CHURCH IS WEAK IF IT DOESN'T KNOW THIS BECAUSE OUR MEMBERS CANNOT SURPASS US IN STRENGTH.

I have the Spirit of God in me; I have the life of God in me; I am a son of God with equal rights with Jesus; I am equal with God; if I see Him do it, I can do it; Jesus said I do what I see my father do. I am a new creation – what does it mean? [**Study New Creation Realities by E.W. Kenyon**] Anything Jesus did, I can duplicate and go beyond. Whatever I see my Father do, I can do. [**Study the words of Jesus from Matthew – John and say believe and do the same**] Jesus laid a strong emphasis on who He is. The potential to do what Jesus did is within me; Have the God-kind-of-faith – Mark 11:20-24. You shall decree a thing and it shall be established unto you.

The dominion of Adam was lost after the fall; before then, he was never sick, never broke, never depressed. The first Adam never died, it was the second Adam that died; before then he named all the animals. Whatsoever you bind on earth is bound in heaven and whatsoever you loose on earth is loosed in heaven. Jesus came with and for a specific assignment and when he completed his assignment, he said, 'I have finished' and he gave up the ghost. When the time of my appearing comes, everything will fall flat on the ground. Habakkuk 2:14,

'For the earth shall be filled with the knowledge of the glory of the LORD, as the waters cover the sea.'

OPERATING ABOVE NATURAL LAW - Cocaine addicts and drug addicts respond to our covenant with God. The son of man is controlled by the Word and Spirit – I and the Father are one. Jesus operated above natural law. He commanded blind eyes to open, deaf ears to hear, cripples to walk, the dead to be raised. There was a boldness about Jesus that was difficult to explain. Same way: when I touch you assume that the Father has touched you. When I say, 'Be blessed', or 'I turn around that cascading of bad tidings in your life or ministry' all the agents of heaven are released to enforce what I declare. Elijah said, 'There shall be no rain according to or by my word.' So, behind all the systems you put in place in your church must come the unhindered life of God. Is it true that after you preach, virtue leaves because you are tired? No, it doesn't because it's not your virtue.

10. I AM IN THIS WORLD BUT I AM NOT OF THIS WORLD – my citizenship is of heaven. John 8:23, 'And he said unto them, Ye are from beneath; I am from above: ye are of this world; I am not of this world.'

John 18:36, 'Jesus answered, My kingdom is not of this world: if my kingdom were of this world, then would my servants fight, that I should not be delivered to the Jews: but now is my kingdom not from hence.'

John 15:19, 'If ye were of the world, the world would love his own: but because ye are not of the world, but I have chosen you out of the world, therefore the world hateth you.'

John 17:14, 'I have given them thy word; and the world hath hated them, because they are not of the world, even as I am not of the world.

John 17:16, 'They are not of the world, even as I am not of the world.'

The contemplation of ministry failure is not in my mind or in my vocabulary. When I am fasting, I am fasting to consecrate myself to God. What I see is guaranteed; all I need to do is see it, think it and I can have it – Jeremiah 29:11. Know your covenant – for they that know their God shall be strong and they shall do exploits. **Know your personal covenant with God about who you are in Christ – in His sight from Jesus' words, the epistles and the prophetic books.**

## 2. THE SPECIFIC COVENANT OF A MINISTER

This is a specific covenant that comes as RHEMA a revelation from God to you personally either when you read or study the scriptures it jumps at you or you hear it on your own and you know for certain this is a specific word for you. - Joshua 1:8,9; Jeremiah 1:1- fear not their faces; Isaiah 55 – I have made you a leader, a commander, a witness to the people; Isaiah 45 & 60 – arise & shine… …; Isaiah 62; If you take care of my business,

I will take care of yours.... Things will be alright from now; when you need it, it will be there; believe me for a continuous release of supernatural financial provision; house of Judah shall not experience a decline in numbers again from today, it shall rather experience increase, enlargement, expansion, growth on every side; I cannot fail; I cannot be poor; In Judah God is known, is revered, is renowned, His reputation is great. – Psalm 76:1. Come to a place in your belief system of full persuasion and unshakeable commitment where you can believe God for and expect to happen on a regular basis as a lifestyle, only what God can do in your life and ministry and for you, with you and through you in others' lives as well.

**I have given you the keys of the kingdom....**

Matthew 16:19, 'And I will give unto thee the keys of the kingdom of heaven: and whatsoever thou shalt bind on earth shall be bound in heaven: and whatsoever thou shalt loose on earth shall be loosed in heaven.'

**Every time God wants to move a man to another level, he cuts a covenant with the person (I CANNOT FAIL). For** example: Noah, altar sacrifice – no more flood; Abraham, - only son – Now I know... ... Isaac, Jacob, David, I will not give God anything that won't cost me something; Joseph, Moses, Solomon – 1000 burnt offerings – ask what I should do for you; even prostitutes like Rahab cut a covenant with the spies; Jesus, the Apostles, etc. So we must do things with covenant in mind.

**YOUR SPECIFIC COVENANT IS CRUCIALLY IMPORTANT AND REQUIRED IN ADVERSITY** e.g. when we went through turmoil in our ministry in the year 2000 and 2005, it was the covenant that brought us out and has brought us where we are. Elijah enacted a covenant with Elisha – 'If you see me go, you shall have a double portion of what I have.' So when Elijah took off, Elisha called on him, 'Father, Father' and the mantle was dropped on him which enabled him to do double what he saw his spiritual father do. **YOU CANNOT ACTIVATE CERTAIN ANOINTINGS IF YOU ARE NOT IN COVENANT! There are certain graces or 'anointings' I walk in by virtue of fulfilling my covenant obligations to my spiritual mentors and spiritual father with ease!** So the question is what is your specific covenant with God? You don't pick covenants with God from people's books. It is a conscious thing you do between you and God. I have covenanted with my eyes not to behold anything undesirable. I have covenanted with God to give my first salary in every year to Him and that makes Him covenant with me to do certain unusual things for me that others cannot partake of. For example my father in the Lord, Bishop Oyedepo responding to God to give his car and God saying to him, 'My son David, if even you did not want to be rich, it is too late.'

SPECIFIC COVENANT is what God said specifically to you directly or through a RHEMA WORD – his word. What God Said To ME!

## WHAT IS THE PROOF THAT YOU CALLED US?

- You must do warfare on the premise of the covenant.
- Covenant undergirds what you do.
- Covenant gives you unusual access.
- Covenant gives you uncommon confidence in the face of many odds to do that which others cannot do and say what others cannot say because your covenant is speaking for you.
- God, Angels, Satan, Demons understand covenant that is why they whipped and disgraced the sons of Sceva and yet responded to and obeyed Jesus and Paul and that was the same reason why Goliath, an uncircumcised, non-covenant person was defeated by David a covenant person backed by the man of war, the Lord of hosts, the commander in chief, who showed up in Joshua's day, the God of the armies of Israel.
- When you step out of your covenant, you are in unchartered waters. His covenant says, Paul planted, Apollos watered but it is HE that bringeth the increase. BRING US THE INCREASE LORD. (Acts 13; 12:24; Psalm 119:18; Ps. 1:1-3)
- If you will keep the grass green, I guarantee you, the sheep will find their way there. Why? Because it is covenant! He said, 'I am the Shepherd of the flock.' The Chief Shepherd knows where his appointed under-shepherds are and so will bring them where they will be fed with the right feed. (Psalm 23; Ezekiel 34)

LIFT UP THE TERMS OF THE COVENANT AND I WILL UPHOLD MY WORD TO YOU:

Psalm 37:18, 'The LORD knoweth the days of the upright: and their inheritance shall be for ever. They shall not be ashamed in the evil time: and in the days of famine they shall be satisfied.'

Psalm 37:23-27, 'The steps of a good man are ordered by the LORD: and he delighteth in his way. Though he fall, he shall not be utterly cast down: for the LORD upholdeth him with his hand. I have been young, and now am old; yet have I not seen the righteous forsaken, nor his seed begging bread. He is ever merciful, and lendeth; and his seed is blessed. Depart from evil, and do good; and dwell for evermore.'

Psalm 37:37, 'Mark the perfect man, and behold the upright: for the end of that man is peace.'

Judges 6:14, 'And the LORD looked upon him, and said, Go in this thy might, and thou shalt save Israel from the hand of the Midianites: have not I sent thee?'

Gideon was told 'Go in this your might. Have I not sent you?' The disciples were asked, 'When I sent you did you lack anything?' Their answer was 'Nothing.' (Luke 22:35) There are certain situations and places where you summon God on the premise of your covenant. Elijah did on Mt. Carmel with the prophets of Baal. To Moses, he said, 'Go with this rod and with this rod you will do signs and wonders.' [ROD symbolic of the Word of God (Covenant)] Joshua 3:15, 'Sanctify yourselves for tomorrow I will do wonders among you.' Your attitude must be: Despite my imperfections, I have a rod of covenant. When he sent me, he sent me with heavenly backing with a host of innumerable angels. People like Moses, Abraham, Isaac, David were not flawless yet they did remarkable and extraordinary things because of the covenant they had with God. Don't be surprised or envious about why some are enjoying certain privileges; find out what they are doing or have done that you haven't done, align yourself right by the leading of the Holy Spirit. As we break things in our city, we must replace them with God's covenant [word].

## CONFIDENCE IN AND PERSUASION OF YOUR COVENANT MAKES YOU:

- HEAR THE UNHEARABLE
- BELIEVE THE UNBELIEVABLE
- THINK THE UNTHINKABLE
- SAY THE UNSAYABLE
- SEE THE UNSEEABLE
- ACT THE UNACTABLE
- ACCESS THE INACCESSIBLE
- TALK THE UNTALKABLE
- HAVE THE UNHAVABLE
- DO THE UNDOABLE
- GO TO THE UNGOABLE
- SOW THE UNSOWABLE

Michael Hutton-Wood

- REAP THE UNREAPABLE
- TITHE THE UNTITHABLE
- GIVE THE UNGIVEABLE
- HARVEST THE UNHARVESTABLE
- REAP THE UNREAPABLE
- OPEN THE UNOPENABLE
- SOAR THE UNSOARABLE
- TOUCH THE UNTOUCHABLE
- FORGIVE THE UNFORGIVEABLE
- REACH THE UNREACHABLE
- SCALE THE UNSCALABLE
- VENTURE THE UNVENTURABLE
- WRITE THE UNWRITABLE
- LEAD THE UNLEADABLE
- TRANSFORM THE UNTRANSFORMABLE
- CLIMB THE UNCLIMBABLE
- DRIVE THE UNDRIVABLE
- EAT THE UNEATABLE
- SCALE HIGHER HEIGHTS
- ENJOY WHAT OTHERS CANNOT ENJOY
- GO WHERE OTHERS CANNOT GO

## PERSONAL/SPECIFIC COVENANTS

Making and commanding decrees – Elijah, Elisha, Jesus at the tomb of Lazarus, they spoke and turned and carried on their journey. God said in Jeremiah 9:23-24 and I believe it; whatever God says is a covenant/Law to me leaving me with a responsibility to do something for his covenant to come to pass for me. He is dependable and He will do it. I have delight in such – Psalm 37:4,6

1. Define Your Covenants and live them: When Isaac was in the wilderness and there was famine, he meditated on his covenant with God. His deliberation was not on the famine, it was on the covenant. How do we know? He did what you don't do during famine – He sowed! He did not keep his seed because there was no rain, he did not observe the wind or else he wouldn't have sown and because of sowing during famine he reaped a hundred fold when all others were still keeping their seed. Covenant works for you despite/even in famine. So, live the covenant. Meditate on the promise. Keep your covenant in front of you.

Keep it in the forefront of your mind otherwise your actions will not be based on your covenant. This is God's specific promise to you. You cannot act on a covenant you presume to have; once the covenant has been defined, live it just like living in your house – you live there. We are about to step into a new dimension of ministry. God is waiting for those who will act on the premise of covenant. I have placed my covenant

[word] above my name. Isaac's covenant with God was two-dimensional:

a. Passed on to him by his father, Abraham – contrary to what is around me, I shall be blessed. His confession and recitation was I am blessed, I am blessed, in multiplying I am multiplied and

b. God told him to sow – Move – Genesis 12. You are not living your covenant if your actions are not based on your covenant. If you cannot move on your covenant, your covenant won't benefit you. Until you move on that covenant, it won't benefit you. Abraham had to move on the covenant for the promise to manifest. The covenant is for adversity, famine and hard times.

2. The covenant comes from above (from God): it is not restricted or limited and it is given irrespective of and works irrespective of environment.

a. The covenant is from above and the earth must comply.

b. Within the covenant is the supernatural.

c. THE COVENANT IS THE BEDROCK, PILLARS, STONES OF OUR JOURNEY.

d. The covenant will speak for you in the house of Abimelech even if you are not there. Them that owe you, God will appear to them and instruct them to come to you; He will speak to people to come and feed you like the widow of Zarephath and Lydia, Mary Magdalene and cause people to perceive you are a man of God like the Shunemite woman. When you fly on the wings of covenant, even things you don't ask you will get. Abimelech had a dream because he was about to do something against what belonged to Abraham. The covenant must be lived. I LIVE IN MY HOUSE that is where I eat, sleep, cook, rest, bath, pray, think and go back to after each day – so it is with covenant.

e. RAISE YOUR FAMILY on the basis of your covenant – your covenant is where you eat, sleep, live, eat, drink; it is where you exist – live so you must know it by heart and live it. The devil is not allowed where your covenant is.

f. **IF YOUR COVENANT IS NOT POWERFUL ENOUGH FOR YOU TO LIVE, BE MOVED BY IT AND TO LIVE FOR** then there is a question mark. It was powerful enough to make Abraham leave his family home in Genesis 12. If it was powerful and reliable enough to make Abraham leave where he was to a land he hadn't seen and still believe after Lot had chosen the fertile land and left him with the dry land that he would still be the owner of the land; if it was powerful enough to make the disciples leave their respective businesses to follow Jesus, then your covenant must be big enough to move you. Your confession must be 'I don't see lack; all I see is covenant.' You can't appreciate someone totally sold out to the covenant - It cheapens my covenant for me to say to you, 'I am coming, pay me or appreciate me' when my supplies are from SOURCE (Philippians 4:19).

g. **It is the absence of the knowledge of covenant that makes us play games.** Abraham said in Genesis 14:21-23, 'It will never go on record that you/man made me rich!' It's beneath my covenant to 'charismatically' or 'pentecostally' take offering or beg or appeal to you or church members, leaders, deacons or elders for money for myself.

h. **REMEMBER: YOUR ANOINTING IS FOR YOUR JOB/KINGDOM WORK! YOUR COVENANT IS FOR YOUR DIVINE PROVISION! Don't mix the two!** Use your anointing to do your job and use covenant doings/principles to command and receive your divine provision.

**There Are Things You Must Do For God To Prosper You**

1. Practice the Covenant of Tithes and Offerings (Genesis 8:22)
2. Ministry is delivering to people the mind of God.
3. I cannot fail. I terminate the mindset of failure from me.
4. Live the covenant if you want to last in ministry; however if you don't want to last, then, play games and quickly leave.
5. Living the covenant means think it for as a man thinketh so is he; speak it for you shall have what you say.
6. Until your covenant has reached your heart, it hasn't reached you.
7. You must be soaked with the consciousness of your covenant. **IT MUST DRIP OFF YOU.**
8. **If you cannot boast about your covenant, it is no good to you.**
9. **It is below my dignity to ask you for money before or after I pray for you.**
10. **My covenant will prevail irrespective of the climate as I exercise my faith.**

[Order copies of my book: GENERATING FINANCES FOR MINISTRY [without sweating, begging toiling, gimmicks or resorting to tricks] from www.houseofjudah.org.uk]

## WHAT IS THE ANATOMY OF COVENANT?

If we can live this then we become an unstoppable force – Cross the line and live it. We must expect the unusual in the church such as people walking in and are healed without prayer or hands being laid on them.

How is a specific covenant enacted? How do I know it is a covenant and how do I use it? For example: Moses sees a bush on fire but not being consumed and turns aside.

1. Any time something happens in your life but it doesn't consume you, turn aside. Whenever you are frustrated about the church not growing, turn aside!

2. A covenant [terms of the covenant] is not something you take to God, God takes it to you or brings to you.

3. Covenant is for purpose and providence: The Order of Moses - Deuteronomy 18:15; [He was talking about Christ] Acts 3:22. So Jesus did not function in isolation, He functioned like Moses. How did Moses function? He turned aside and was given a covenant. God said to him, 'I have made thee a god to Pharaoh. With this rod go and perform signs and wonders.' This was said to a man with 80 years of frustration. We need to know how dependable our covenant is – Exodus 4:16.

God says to him:

1. SEE
2. I HAVE MADE YOU
3. A 'god'
4. TO PHARAOH

**1. SEE** [yourself in this thing - this new thing] **If you can get yourself to a place where you can see it, everything that intimidated you, you now intimidate it** - like Pharaoh who had intimidated Moses for 40 years. On his return to Egypt, him being a murderer was not an issue – he was above arrest, he was a god to Pharaoh; how can you arrest a god? Moses was arguing with God about his past flaws while God was trying to show Moses the possibilities, prophecies. **Your biggest struggle is not Pharaoh but your ability to see. Take time to mediate on what He says about our new position i.e. who we are in Him and how He sees us. <u>This is not about our holiness only; it's about what we see of who we are!</u>**

**Spiritual myopia is to be talking to God yet not see.**

**2. I HAVE MADE YOU** [cross-reference to the work of redemption - if any man be in Christ, he is a new creation; we are His workmanship created in Christ Jesus unto good works.] God says to us, 'I made you; it has nothing to do with you.' So, I am purely the workmanship of God. MY DUTY IS TO SEE AND KNOW THAT HIS DUTY IS TO MAKE (I have made you).

**3. A 'GOD'** – I am cutting a covenant with you; you are now a god unto Pharaoh. I have made you a god unto Pharaoh, not all kings but unto Pharaoh – the one thing that holds captive everything that pertains to your assignment. There is a principality/political - plotting, sitting down, scheming as in Psalm 2 and saying your assignment will not happen. To everything that will stand against your assignment, you are now a god.

## 4. TO PHARAOH:
## Definition of/Defining a god, Pharaoh and Moses
This Pharaoh is:
- The one that stands and opposes your purpose or assignment in life.
- The one who cannot be overcome by natural means.
- The one crowning himself over your assignment.
- This pharaoh has history, strength, natural advantage.
- He hates you with a passion and has decided you will not break out.
- He calls you and sees you as a failure and that can be very damaging.
- He hates and cannot stand Israel's growing in numbers / multitudes.
- He is a killer; he killed the firstborns of Israel to prevent the deliverer from manifesting.

UNTIL MOSES, The Pastor, i.e. the head steps in, nothing happens. Until the Pastor can confront Pharaoh, the people cannot go. Until the Pastor downloads the mind of God unto Pharaoh, the people will be bound. **The reason I am a minister is to bring them out like Moses did. The task at hand is beyond natural means. The instruction was 'go with this thy rod and do signs and wonders'. God visits the hand and the rod. We have to hold this rod [covenant in our hand]. The rod epitomizes the terms of the covenant [symbolic of**

**it]**. When Moses arrived, he said, 'Thus saith the Lord of the Hebrews, Let my people go that they may worship and serve him.' Pharaoh answers, 'who is this God?' So Moses became a god to prove who sent him. Pharaoh asked to see so he saw. A god determines what is law and what isn't; a god decrees, declares. Moses went to Pharaoh as God's mouthpiece here on earth. Every time Moses stepped into the palace, it was like God stepping into the palace.

**NOTE THE FOLLOWING:**
**1. Before the covenant, this man Moses was a man.**
**2. After the covenant this man Moses was a god.**
**3. It was after he became a god, that purpose and assignment was fulfilled.**
**4. BETWEEN A MAN AND THE FULFILMENT OF ASSIGNMENT WAS A COVENANT.** When Moses stepped into Pharaoh's presence, he literally became a god. God is not bound by space. When Pharaoh decided to prove difficult, he was looking at a man talking like a god. Pharaoh being an Egyptian all along knew what gods do. Moses did not say 'God in heaven'; he said to Pharaoh, I will show you Him. Moses takes Pharaoh and says to him 'at my word' then takes the rod [this covenant, the rod] and touches. As God he takes his word and commands natural things to perform resulting in blood, lies, flies, frogs, locusts, sun, darkness, boils, light separating of Goshen from Egypt. In the spirit, he draws a line between light and darkness. This is not a coincidence; it is a decree. Where are those people today?

We have pronouncement without the power to back it. Moses functioned completely as a god. Then in his retirement, he prophesies and passes it on to the next generation, Joshua and eventually passes the baton to Christ. So John the Baptist says, 'hear ye him.' The Father attests to it at His baptism and says, 'hear ye him'. And Jesus functioned making the same declarations. As he said when he was accused, 'Is it not written in your law that ye are gods so I say your sins are forgiven.' It is within our power to retain and forgive sins – **our decrees will change laws.**

MINISTERS: Do we know the platform/premise on which we are operating? Jesus operated in covenant; Peter and John in the same order – Three and half years in school with Christ. As I am sent, so are you. We and Christ are one – 1 John 4:17. They placed him in a pot of oil he refused to die and so they put him in Patmos. The order of Moses passes to Jesus and then to his disciples including us. They said to them heal but don't preach in the name of Jesus and they refused because that is where the power is. Examples of great men who made and had covenants with God through the power of ALTARS: Noah, Abraham, Isaac, Jacob, Gideon, David, Solomon, etc.

## ENACTING PERSONAL COVENANTS

How? We have a choice either to live or die. We either, live and do what we must do or die. See! What do I see? The hardest part is seeing yourself in it. It is easy to see others in it but not you but one must start to see. Not many people who know this truth about covenants tell other ministers. You and I have an obligation to go and tell others about these discoveries as we were taught by our mentors and fathers hence it being recorded in this book to help take the struggle out of your assignment. The kingdom of God is suffering untold damage because some want only their ministries to grow. **Vow that if God teaches you something and it is working for you that you will help, tell, preach, teach and train others who will be willing to listen and do it. That is the way your generation will be impacted.**

## HOW IS A PERSONAL COVENANT ENACTED?

i. When He appears to you when you are driving and says something. Those little nuggets of truth God drops in your spirit and it is God who decides the time of the meeting, not you. For example: Gideon was hiding away; Abraham was busy in Ur of the Chaldees; Peter was fishing; Saul of Tarsus was on his way to Damascus; Daniel was a slave, captive in Babylon; Jacob was asleep on a stone he was using for a pillow; Matthew was collecting taxes.

ii. **It is not the location that consecrates the covenant. It is the covenant that consecrates the location.**

iii. God will not shout when he is enacting a covenant with you. There will be no fire, light sparks. Expecting that will deny you the ability to hear. The next phase of Elijah's covenant and assignment came from a still small voice. (1 Kings 19:12)

iv. When the storm was raging, Jesus was asleep on a pillow in a boat and He arose and said, "Peace, be still." (Mark 4:37-39) First address the internal before the external, i.e. speak peace to your soul then deal with the external. Never allow the external [without] to be within. Isaac never allowed the famine around him to enter within. (Genesis 26)

v. Fasting and prayer are not effective when principles are left behind or abandoned. To really consistently hear and enact covenants, guard your heart with all diligence for out of it are the issues of life. (Proverbs 4:20-24) As long as you continue to see Pharaoh as big, you cannot activate covenant. You cannot hear Him.

vi. **People coming to church is not a function of your preaching. Example of how the covenant is cut, the Holy Spirit says, 'I bring them; I will bring them and you teach them.'** – In Acts 13, they taught them, the city heard the testimony and the whole city turned out to them. 1 Corinthians 3:6, 'I have planted, Apollos watered; but God gave the increase.' Covenants: Marriage, children, ministry, home, finances, stay with them. God is always cutting covenant; adding more so live them.

vii. Relate right with your man of God. There is a way you relate to your man of God that you can't receive from him. Matthew 10:41, 'He that receiveth a prophet in the name of a prophet shall receive a prophet's reward; and he that receiveth a righteous man in the name of a righteous man shall receive a righteous man's reward.'

Other related scriptures are: Ephesians 6:1-3; 2 Chronicles 20:20; Hosea 12:13; Jeremiah 3:15) Non-tithers are under a closed heaven and so certain pronouncements cannot hold for them. (Malachi 3:8-12) [Order copies of my book: WHY YOU MUST AND HOW YOU SHOULD PRAY FOR YOUR CHURCH AND PASTOR DAILY from www.houseofjudah.org.uk]

viii. RHEMA words are covenants. If you have a problem receiving specific covenants, take God's promises and they will work for you. You don't say I will do this and you do this because it is God who cuts and initiates the covenant. Vows are different from covenants.

ix. Fasting subdues the natural [mind/flesh] and enables the spirit man to take the upper place. Turn aside and ask what are you saying?

x. ABOUT SPIRITUAL FATHERS: Spiritual fathers are chosen by God, both son and father: Hebrews 7:7 says, 'the lesser is blessed by the greater.' As people bless you, pass on graces and pray for them; bless them and tell them to go and enjoy what you enjoy. It is at the latter stage that children give and not before. Fathers provide. A real daddy will do everything to ensure his son prospers. 2 Corinthians 12:14, 'Behold, the third time I am ready to come to you; and I will not be burdensome to you: for I seek not yours, but you: for the children ought not to lay up for the parents, but the parents for the children.' Always remember who made you and is making you. It's a law!

xi. What to pray for: Show me Thy will, give me insight, revelation, understanding, wisdom. Pray HEAVEN'S SYLLABUS OF PRAYER, known as the Lord's Prayer in Luke 11:1-4 and for revival (Psalm 2:8; Matthew 9:37-38; Isaiah 66) Bring the flock into maturity and their destiny (Galatians 4:19). Pray Ephesians 1; 3; Colossians 1. For Sunday service don't pray for the anointing. We cannot insult the integrity of your word to pray for you to be here when your word says where two or more people are gathered, you are there in our midst and the Holy Spirit lives in us so we welcome you. When travelling, thank God for angels who bear you up (Psalm 91, 92, 103 and Hebrews 1:14).

Michael Hutton-Wood

# THE GREATEST GIFT

If you want to take advantage of the contents of this message by asking God to give you power to lead, from which Adam fell, you need to give your life to Jesus Christ. If you have never met or experienced a definite encounter with Jesus Christ, you can know Him today. You can make your life right with Him by accepting Him as your personal Lord and Saviour by praying the following prayer out loud where you are. Pray this prayer with me now:

PRAYER FOR SALVATION: 'O God, I ask you to forgive me for my sins. I believe You sent Jesus to die on the cross for me and confess it with my mouth. I receive Jesus Christ as my personal Lord and Saviour and confess Him as Lord of my life and I give my life willingly to Him now. Thank you Lord for saving me and for making me a new person in Jesus' Name, (2 Corinthians 5:17) Amen.'

If you prayed this prayer, you have now become a child of God (John 1:12) and I welcome you to the family of God. Please let me know about your decision for Jesus by writing to me. I would like to send you some free literature to help you in your new walk with the Lord. So please write to me at the following address:

**Correspondence address:**
Michael Hutton-Wood,
House of Judah (Praise) Ministries

P. O. Box 1226,
Croydon. CR9 6DG. UK.

Or call:
Within the UK:
0208 689 6010, 07956 815 714
Outside the UK:
+44 208 689 6010, +44 7956 815 714

Alternatively Email us at:
Email: info@houseofjudah.org.uk
michaelhutton-wood@fsmail.net
Or visit us at: Website: www.houseofjudah.org.uk

Watch our 24hour internet TV experience on
www.judahtv.org

# OTHER BOOKS AND LEADERSHIP MANUALS BY AUTHOR

1. A Must For Every New Convert
2. You Need To Do The Ridiculous In Order To Experience The Miraculous
3. 175 Reasons Why You Cannot And Will Not Fail In Life
4. What To Do In The Darkest Hour Of Your Trial [125 Bible Truths You Must Know, BELIEVE, REMEMBER, CONFESS AND DO]
5. Why You should Pray And How You should Pray For Your Pastor and Your Church Daily
6. 200 Questions You Must Ask, Investigate And Know Before You Say 'I Do'
7. I Shall Rise Again
8. How to negotiate your desired future with today's currency
9. Leadership Secrets
10. Leadership Nuggets
11. Leadership Capsules
12. What is Ministry
13. Generating Finances For Ministry
14. 101 Tips For a Great Marriage
15. What Husbands Want And What Wives 'REALLY' Want
16. My Daily Bible Reading Guide.

Michael Hutton-Wood

# TRAINING MANUALS FOR IMPACTFUL LEADERSHIP & EFFECTIVE MINISTRY

Academy 101 [House Of Judah Academy Curriculum]
Ministry 101
Leadership 101
Kingdom Prosperity 101 From School Of Kingdom Prosperity & Financial Management
Pastoral Leadership 101 From School Of Impactful Pastoral Leadership
Prescriptions For Fulfilling Your Ministry

*To order copies of any of these books, ministry or leadership manuals or for a product catalog of other literature, audiotapes and CDs, DVDs, write to:* **Michael Hutton-Wood Ministries, P. O. Box 1226, Croydon. CR9 6DG. UK. or [in the UK call] - 0208 689 6010; [outside UK call] + 442086896010**

You can also place your order online as you visit our website: **www.houseofjudah.org.uk**
You can also email us at: Email: **info@houseofjudah.org.uk;** or **michaelhutton-wood@fsmail.net**

# GLOBAL INITIATIVES AND MINISTRIES WITHIN THE MINISTRY

**TV MINISTRY IN THE UK**
Watch Leadership Secrets on KICC TV
SKY Channel 594

Tuesday & Thursday – 3pm & Saturday 5.30pm

Monday-Friday 2pm on FAITH TV
Sky channel 593 & Saturday 3.30pm

**LOG ON AND WATCH OUR INTERNET TV**

**PROGRAM on WWW.JUDAHTV.ORG**

Anytime - anywhere.

**Featuring the:**
Teaching Channel
Motivation Channel
Leadership Channel
Family/ Relationships Channel
Upcoming Events/ Products

WATCH US ON YouTube and AUDIO STREAMING
EVERY WEEK
@ www.houseofjudah.org.uk

# PARTNERING WITH A GLOBAL MINISTRY WITHIN A MINISTRY

Michael Hutton-Wood Ministries (The HUTTON-WOOD WORLD OUTREACH MINISTRY) is the apostolic, missions, world outreach, and evangelistic wing of the House of Judah (Praise) Ministries with a mission to God's end time church and the nations of the earth. This ministry was born out of a strong God-given mandate to reach, touch and impact the nations of the earth with the gospel of Christ and bring back divine order, discipline, integrity, godly character, excellence and stability to God's people and God's house. It has a strong apostolic mandate to set in order the things that are out of order and lacking in the church [The Body of Christ] – (Titus 1:5).

Its mission is to save the lost at any cost, depopulate hell and populate heaven with souls that have experienced in full, the new birth, renewal of mind, to produce believers walking in the fullness of their Godly inheritance, divine health, prosperity and authority to take their homes, communities, cities and nations for Christ and occupy till Christ returns. It is to raise a people without spot, wrinkle or blemish. The man of God's passion and drive is that as truly as he lives, this earth shall be filled with the knowledge of the glory of the Lord as the waters cover the sea. His determination is not to rest, hold back or keep silent until he sees the body of Christ established as a praise in the earth. (Numbers 14:21; Habakkuk 2:14; Isaiah 62:6-7)

If you would like to join the faithful brethren and partners of this great ministry by becoming a partner as we believe God for ten thousand partners to partner with this vision prayerfully and financially, ask for a copy of the partners' club commitment card by writing to:

**Michael Hutton-Wood Ministries**
**[Hutton-Wood World Outreach]**
**P. O. Box 1226, Croydon. Surrey.**
**CR9 6DG. UK.**

Alternatively, you can send a monthly contribution by cheque payable to our ministry or donate online at www.houseofjudah.org.uk or request a direct debit mandate or standing order form from your bankers or us made payable to Michael Hutton-Wood Ministries. Call +44 [0] 208 689 6010 for more details. Philippians 4:19 be your portion and experience as you partner with this work and global mandate. Shalom!

# GENERATIONAL LEADERSHIP TRAINING INSTITUTE
## *(The Leaders' Factory)*

The Mandate: Raising Generational Leaders, Impacting Nations.

The Generational Leadership Training Institute (GLTI) is the Leadership training and mentoring wing of our ministry with a global mandate to raise leaders with a generational thinking mindset, not a now mentality and to fulfil the Law of Explosive Growth – To add growth, lead followers – To multiply, lead leaders.

This is a Bible College, Leadership Training Institute fulfilling the Matthew 9:37-38 mandate of developing and releasing labourers for the end time harvest. We offer fulltime and part time certificate, diploma, degree and short twelve-week courses in biblical studies, counselling, leadership, practical ministry and schools of prosperity. Its aim is to raise leaders who know and live not just by the anointing but by ministerial ethics, leaders who build with a long term mentality, who live today with tomorrow in mind. The mission of this unique educational and impartation institution is to transform followers into generational leaders and its motto is to raise leaders of discipline, integrity, godly character and excellence

- D.I.C.E.

For correspondence, full time, part time, online courses, prospectus, fees and registration forms for the next course, call 0208 689 6010 or write to the Registrar, **GLTI, P. O. Box 1226, Croydon. CR9 6DG. UK or from outside UK call +44 208 689 6010.**

Additional information can be obtained from visiting our website www.houseofjudah.org.uk looking for THE LEADERS FACTORY.

Log on to www.judahtv.org for Leadership Secrets and other teaching.

This is a hutton-wood publication

# LEADERS FACTORY INTERNATIONAL

**MANDATE:** 'In the business of training, developing and raising and releasing more leaders and leaders of leaders.'

'Leaders must be close enough to relate to others, but far enough ahead to motivate them.' – John Maxwell

'You must live with people to know their problems, and live with God in order to solve them.' – P. T. Forsyth

If you, your organisation, college, university, business or church would like to invite Dr. Michael Hutton-Wood for a Motivational-speaking, mentoring or leadership coaching engagement or to organize or hold a Leaders Factory seminar or conference, Leadership Development or Human Capital building seminar, Emerging leaders seminar, Management seminar, Business seminar, Effective people-management, Wealth-creation seminar or training for your workers, leaders, staff, ministers, employers, employees, congregation, youth, etc. you can contact us on 0208 689 6010 [UK]
+44208 689 6010 [OUTSIDE UK].

**Alternatively by email at:**
- info@houseofjudah.org.uk
- michaelhutton-wood@fsmail.net
or leadersfactoryinternational@yahoo.com
VISIT our website: www.houseofjudah.org.uk
You can watch our internet TV experience www.judahtv.org [Maximizing Destiny and Leadership Secrets].
This is a Hutton-Wood publication

# MANDATE:
Releasing Potential - Maximizing Destiny

Raising Generational Leaders - Impacting Nations

# SIMPA
## SCEPTRE INTERNATIONAL MINISTERS & PASTORS ASSOCIATION

This covenant mandate comes from Genesis 49:10: 'The sceptre [of Leadership] shall not depart from JUDAH, nor a lawgiver from between his feet, until Shiloh come and unto Him shall the gathering of the people be'

Other covenant scriptures backing this mandate are: Isaiah 55:4 & Titus 1:5. We have a leadership assignment to RAISE GENERATIONAL LEADERS TO IMPACT NATIONS BY DISCOVERING MEN/WOMEN AND EMPOWERING THEM TO RELEASE THEIR POTENTIAL TO MAXIMIZE THEIR DESTINY.

SIMPA is a multi-cultural fellowship/network of diverse Christian leaders, pastors and ministers that recognize the need for fathering, covering and mentoring. The heartbeat of the man of God is to pour into the willing and obedient what has made him and keeps making him from what he's learnt from his father in the Lord, his teachers and mentors which is working for him and producing maximally. He said: 'I discovered this secret early: Not to learn from or follow those who make promises but from those who have obtained the promises, proofs and results. REMEMBER: YOU DON'T NEED TO MAKE NOISE TO MAKE NEWS. SO: FOLLOW NEWS-MAKERS NOT NOISE-MAKERS!'

These are a few of the mindsets of the man of God:

When the students are ready, the teacher will teach.

'YOU NEED FATHERS TO FATHER YOU TO GROW FEATHERS TO FLY.' – Bishop Oyedepo

'Without a father to father you, you can never grow feathers to fly and go further in life, than they went and accomplish more than they did.' – Michael Hutton-Wood

Don't raise money; raise men and you'll have all the money you need to accomplish your assignment.

There is no new thing under the sun – King Solomon

What you desire to attain, become and accomplish in life, someone has accomplished it – find them, follow them, learn from them, sow into them and their resource materials and you will do more than they did and get there faster.

Teachers, Trainers, Mentors and Fathers give you speed/acceleration in every field of endeavour.

Isaac Newton is known to have said the following:

'If I have seen further it has been by standing on the shoulders of those who have gone ahead of me.'

Variant translations: 'Plato is my friend, Aristotle is my friend, but my best friend is truth.'

'Plato is my friend — Aristotle is my friend — truth is a greater friend.'

'If I have seen further it is only by standing on the shoulders of giants.'

Without a reference you can never become a reference.

If you don't refer to anyone no one will refer to you.

Who laid / lays hands on you and what did / do they leave behind?

This is not a money-making venture but rather about covering and empowerment for fulfilment of destiny and assignment within time allocated.

The goal of SIMPA is to spiritually cover, strengthen, equip, empower, train, mentor and encourage and lift up the arms/hands of both emerging and active [full and part time] pastors, ministers and leaders and by so doing release them to fulfil their respective assignments both in ministry and the market place.

IF YOU WOULD LIKE TO BE A PART OF SIMPA, ASK FOR A REGISTRATION FORM & PAMPHLET FROM OUR INFORMATION DESK in House of Judah or email info@houseofjudah.org.uk or call [in the UK] 0208 689 6010 [outside UK call] + 44 208 689 6010 requesting for SIMPA registration form and pamphlet.

– SEE YOU ON TOP!

Shalom! – Bishop

**PARTNERSHIP:**

In the UK write or send cheque donations to:
Michael Hutton-Wood Ministries
P. O. Box 1226
Croydon. CR9 6DG. UK.

In the UK Call: 0208 689 6010; 07956 815 714
Outside the UK call: +44 208 689 6010;
+ 44 7956 815 714
Fax: +44 20 8689 3301

Email:
info@houseofjudah.org.uk
michaelhutton-wood@fsmail.net
leadersfactoryinternational@yahoo.com
judah@houseofjudah.freeserve.co.uk

Or visit or donate online at our secure
WEBSITE: www.houseofjudah.org.uk

Watch our 24 hour internet TV experience by logging on anywhere - anytime @ www.judahtv.org

Michael Hutton-Wood

# BOOKS AND LEADERSHIP MANUALS
## BY BISHOP MICHAEL HUTTON-WOOD

- What is Ministry
- My Daily Bible Reading Guide 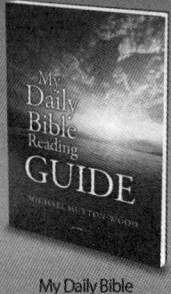
- Leadership Nuggets 
- 175 Reasons Why You Cannot And Will Not Fail In Life 
- I Shall Rise Agian 
- Leadership Capsules 
- What To Do In The Darkest Hour of Your Trial 
- Generating Finances For Ministry 

**TRAINING MANUALS FOR IMPACTFUL LEADERSHIP & EFFECTIVE MINISTRY**

Please log on to **www.houseofjudah.org.uk** for more information

# OTHER BOOKS BY THE AUTHOR
## - BISHOP MICHAEL HUTTON-WOOD -

Why You Should Pray for your Pastor And For Your Church Daily

200 Questions You Must Ask, Investigate And Know Before You Say I Do

A Must For Every New Convert

How To Negotiate Your Desired Future With Today's Currency

Leadership Secrets

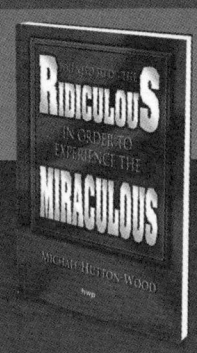

You Need To Do The Ridiculous In Order To Experience The Miraculous

101 Tips For A Great Marriage

Taking The Struggle Out Of Ministry

What Husbands Want And What Wives **'REALLY'** Want

Please log on to **www.houseofjudah.org.uk** for more information